THE GRAPHIC ARTS SERIES

ETCHING

THE GRAPHIC ARTS SERIES FOR ART
ISTS, STUDENTS, AMATEURS AND COL
LECTORS. EDITED BY IOSEPH PENNELL
VOL   I LITHOGRAPHY SECOND EDITION
VOL II ETCHING   FOURTH EDITION
VOL III PEN DRAWING FOURTH EDITION

ETCHERS AND ETCHING

CHAPTERS IN THE HISTORY
OF THE ART TOGETHER WITH
TECHNICAL EXPLANATIONS OF
MODERN ARTISTIC METHODS

BY

IOSEPH PENNELL

N.A.

MEMBER AMERICAN ACADEMY
OF ARTS AND LETTERS DIRE
CTOR GRAPHIC ART SCHOOL
ART STUDENTS LEAGUE NEW
YORK CITY FORMERLY LEC
TURER ON THE GRAPHIC
ARTS SLADE SCHOOL UNI
VERSITY COLLEGE LONDON
AND AT THE NATIONAL ACA
DEMY OF DESIGN NEW YORK

FOURTH EDITION

THE MACMILLAN COMPANY
NEW YORK   MCMXXXVI

TO
THE KEPPELS
AND THOSE OTHER PRINTSELLERS
AND PUBLISHERS WHO HAVE BEEN
MY LIFELONG FRIENDS AND PATRONS
I
DEDICATE THIS
BOOK

GENERAL PREFACE TO THE GRAPHIC ART SERIES

THERE are endless series of art books—and endless schools of art, endless lecturers on art and art criticism. But so far as I know there are no series of books on the Graphic Arts, written or edited, by graphic artists. This series is intended to be a survey of the best work in the past—the work that is admitted to be worth studying—and a definite statement as to the best methods of making drawings, prints, and engravings, written in every case by those who have passed their lives in making them. J. P.

PREFACE INTRODUCTORY AND EXPLANATORY

I AM not, in the technical part of this book, going into the history of the methods of work, or the chemical problems involved in etching, unless they are in general use, or of value to etchers. I propose to describe and explain as fully and as clearly as possible, the best manners of making etchings, especially those not yet described, but employed to-day; and supplement these descriptions and explanations by examples gathered from my own practice and that of other etchers in America, France, Germany, Italy, and England.

There are two technical books by Etchers, on Etching, which may be read with profit: Lalanne's *Treatise on Etching* (*Traité de la Gravure à l'Eau Forte*, in the original French), and Short's *On the Making of Etchings*, re-issued as *Etchings and Engravings*. Singer and Strang's *Etching and Engraving* should have been perfect—one of the authors is an acknowledged authority on the history of the art, the other a recognised etcher, but the combination was not altogether a success. Hamerton's *Etcher's Handbook* was written by an amateur for amateurs. And there are endless others in endless languages, but all alike are of little importance. Hamerton's *Etching and Etchers*, while it certainly did turn the attention of the artless to etching, and gave it a financial standing in modern times, had nothing to do with encouraging etchers, as the two or three then living, whose art is discussed, had already encouraged Hamerton, by their work, before Hamerton began to encourage them, by writing of what they had done. His chapters on processes and methods are of small value, mostly disused, while others never were used, unless by himself. His *Etcher's Handbook* too is completely out of date, and even Lalanne and Short have no knowledge of many of the present methods or do not refer to them, while some later writers are too conservative, or stupid, or hide-bound to have anything to do with the newer ways of working. Other writers are authors, not artists, and what they say is of no importance technically, unless some artist told them to say it, and then they frequently flounder into technical traps. Far away the best recent historical work is Prof. Dr. Singer's *Die Moderne Graphik*, Leipsic, 1914. Haden's *About Etching* contains many interesting comments but few practical instructions.

Everything about making an etching can be learned from an etcher in a morning: but it will take the student all his life to put his learning into practice: and even then he will almost certainly fail to become an etcher; though he can easily become a successful manufacturer of commercial copper plates, commercial states, commercial catalogues, and, the end of all, a commercial success.

As for the historical, or rather critical, section of this book, the trouble about all historical works on etching, or any of the arts, is that the authors without any discrimination, have included all those who have made a name, a notoriety, a plate, with the result in my case, when reading years ago Hamerton's *Etching and Etchers*, that I thought in my ignorance all the work of all the artists discussed in it should be studied, though for the life of me I could not see why, and it was not till years after that I learned it was to be mostly avoided, and only Hamerton's ignorance, or plates he had got hold of, gained such etchers a place in his big volume. This sort of writing is not only harmful—it is disgraceful, as it is founded either on ignorance or a wish to pad out a volume. Then there are other sorts of art writers : parrots—a whole aviary of them,—but they need not be listened to. The real history is usually as pompous as ponderous, and as incomplete as unreliable, useless as a book of reference, unreadable as literature. Such books, however, are taken deadly seriously—and they are deadly—even if mostly made by "authorities", or maybe because of it. Another sort is the snippety, chirpy, chatty kind; and then there is the gaudy volume with specially prepared plates, sometimes a method of selling a collection, or gratifying the collector's vanity, or exposing his ostrich-like ignorance; sometimes the work of an amateur with a mission.

Now this book is intended for the student and collector, and I propose in the historical part, which will be as short as possible, only to discuss the work of etchers of universally admitted position, and that without any reference to their lives, or their gains, or their scandals, or their period. I cannot be responsible if by so doing the student should go wrong. If he, or any other reader, thinks I have left out a great etcher, I should like to know of him. I do not think I have—that is among the masters who have gone from us—and this book is not an advertisement of living etchers. The trouble is that in all art books, not only art histories, all art teaching, there is no discrimination. It is not what the student learns from books or teachers, but what he has to unlearn for himself that is so difficult. But, if he starts by looking at good art intelligently, and working scientifically, he has—if he has anything in him—only to go ahead.

One big modern artist has confessed that it was just because he did not have to unlearn things that he had time—and the ability—to learn and then to practise them. Another big modern teacher has said that he could teach any student to paint, draw, etch, but God alone could make him an artist.

And it is with the idea of keeping such rules and laws before the student, that this book has been written, and by writing it, I hope I have done the weakest brother no harm, even though I should persuade him not to try to become an etcher.

> "We are apt to assume that there was little or no bad work done
> " in the old times. For my own part I believe on the contrary there
> " were mountains of it, but that it has mostly, mercifully for us, passed
> " out of existence,"

has been written recently. This is true, and if by the things I have said, the methods I have explained, and the examples I have shown in this book, I have not said, explained, or shown anything that might tend to preserve, even a mole-hill, or waste paper basket full, of bad prints to be trampled on in the future, I shall be glad.

I have scarce referred to metal engraving for the simple reason that to-day it is scarce practised. In the past Dürer, Marc Antonio and Mantegna carried it to perfection succeeded by original engravers, like Nanteuil later, but copyists like Reynolds and Lucas still later, were not really creative artists, only astonishing plodders. Engraving and mezzotint are for the methodical, the mechanical. Etching is for the creator, the personal, passionate artist. The reproductive engraver has for the time disappeared,

PREFACE

the commercial etcher has ousted him, but there are no reproductive etchers who have surpassed him.

As a record of fact, the photograph—the unfaked, untouched, photograph—surpasses both sorts of copyists.

But this book is about Etching, not about Engraving. Haden puts the matter very well in his pamphlet *About Etching*, when he says "the moment the possibility of acting upon the plate by an implement used like a pencil was shown to them (the Engravers) the burin fell from their hands and they became Etchers. While the graver descended at once to a class of men who thenceforth undertook by a slow and laborious process, to which the instrument was not ill adapted, to reproduce the works of others."

And he further says after at length pointing out the degeneracy of the modern steel engraver—despite his mechanical dexterity,— "The comparison of the etching needle with the burin is the comparison of the pen with the plow."

I have used as illustrations examples of my work in the different methods of etching. These are published as examples, not models, though they are considerably better, I know, than most prints which are being made to-day; but, apart from this fact, as I made them, I can explain how they were made, for most of the authorities never made an etching and many others can't or won't describe the process.

Finally, Etching is the art of making sunken lines in, and printing from, metal plates: this and the great etchers and their methods are the subject of this book.

LONDON, JANUARY, 1916.   JOSEPH PENNELL.

POSTSCRIPT TO PREFACE

THE publication of this book was stopped for four years owing to the war, and instead of being issued in London by Mr. Fisher Unwin first, it has been made by Messrs. Macmillan in New York. This however is but a small matter in comparison to what art in a big way has suffered. Many artists have given their lives; more have been ruined; and a few have found opportunities—subjects—in the horrors and miseries of the war. Galleries in Europe ceased to acquire the few contemporary works that were made, unless these were commanded by the state. Some of the galleries are reported even to be destroyed. Exhibitions, save for the raising of war funds, mostly ceased, especially in Europe. And even as peace dawns, art still flies away. The belief in some quarters that a new art, or a new inspiration, would come from the war has not been realized. No one who knew anything ever thought it would, save in the case of those who recorded the war.

But art will never die, it is everlasting, eternal; and though artists have suffered more than the members of any other profession, they will come into their own again.

Precious records have vanished. For a while in Europe even those etchers who had the opportunity to work, unless in the government service, could obtain neither copper nor tools nor acids to carry on with. Paper mills in Italy have been burned and bombed. Old paper has disappeared. Technical schools have closed. Dealers

PREFACE

were unable to obtain prints. Collectors had no time to collect. That such a state of things should come to pass was incredible. Yet it happened in our day and generation.

Tradition in art, too, was in danger of being forgotten. It is with a view, then, of recording what I have seen and studied and experienced and practised, with a view of trying to carry on tradition and recording facts, I am glad to have had the volume written and ready to issue in the first year of the war—published now that I hope it is ended, now that I hope there may be no more war. And if the world really cared for art and literature and the arts of peace, there would be no more war or rumours of war. We have relapsed into vandalism and vulgarity. The world is now made up mostly of prigs and prohibitionists; they will venture on the suppression of art as they have ventured on the suppression of wine and song and brought about the unsexing of women. But art will arise again, and laziness, hypocrisy, and sentiment, which crush and cumber the earth, again will be swept away. I shall not see the new earth, but it will come forth.

FINALLY FINISHED PHILADELPHIA, JANUARY 1, 1919.   J. P.

NOTE. I wish to thank the Fine Art Society, and Messrs. Dowdeswell and Dowdeswell for permission to reproduce Whistler's Venice Etchings, Messrs. F. Keppel and Co. for much help in the preparation of the illustrations, Mr. H. V. Allison, M. J. H. Guest of the Cincinnati Art Museum and Mr. Weitenkampf of the New York Public Library for the Duveneck plate and Miss Koehler of the Library of Congress for looking up her father's works, and last but not least Mrs. Pennell for reading the proof.

PREFACE TO THE SECOND EDITION

SINCE the First Edition of this book was issued etching has again come upon the world and etchers are as the sands on the shore. I do not flatter myself, as Hamerton—or his friends did,—that the present fury in etching and flurry among etchers was caused by it—nor have any great etchers been made by my book, because the great etchers were already here as when Hamerton wrote. As for my book: I only am aware, but I even may be mistaken in this, of the presence among us, and the appearance, I think, since it was issued of one solitary etcher of merit, and he may not have seen it, and I do not know if he will maintain his position— or even continue to etch—though he does not seem to be a manufacturer of prints for publishers. But I do know that the book sold out, despite the fact that it was reviewed at length mostly unfavorably by American reporters and professors, and English hacks and dealers, but what most of them said I forget. I only remember there was not one practical suggestion or correction made by them of anything in it. They mainly repeated that an artist should not write of his craft—they can not write even,—their craft is money making or making copy, but the book, I know, has found a place in many libraries and collections and I am glad to say has been bought for art schools and by many artists. Of this I am proud. On the other hand a mass of cheap books from manuals to histories, have been ground out by crowds of collectors, amateurs, curators, dealers, lawyers, every one but artists of reputation, etchers who cant etch, dealers who can sell, collectors who cant collect and professors who can preach what they cant practise or teach. They have not only written books, but brought forth schools, clubs, societies of etching, but not one single etcher have I been able to find as the result of their advising, tea drinking, suggesting, exhibiting, dealing—and the last covers the whole. And all this excitement is because etching has paid a few etchers. But these authorities have done harm. "Even a fool can do harm," Whistler said. The Slade Professor too of the University of Oxford—incidentally an official in the Print Room of the British Museum,— and quite a number of these authorities occupy similar positions, knowing as much practically of art as the guard at the door of their departments—this official, Professor A. M. Hind, has written a book, *A History of Engraving & Etching*—it is so popular among the serious, that it has gone into several editions—and in it he describes the methods of making etchings.

The Professor in his introductory chapter on the technique of Engraving and Etching, "Introduction Processes and Materials" records, I think, every antiquated and obsolete method of working—all of which he got out of books that have been discarded for years by intelligent craftsmen, (page 6) he explains a manner of Laying Grounds which was given up long ago in this country—and also by intelligent etchers in Europe. The roller ages ago replaced the dabber. On the same page his method of transferring drawings to the plate has been discarded, by those who know anything of modern methods, and when he talks, still on the same page, of "opening up the lines" with the etching needle—he means drawing on the plate—one is inclined to suggest that the head of the etcher who accepted his statements should be opened up—and a little modern information injected.

He apparently knows nothing (page 7) of the modern methods of biting invented near half a century ago by Whistler and, I thought, practised by all etchers to-day, and he is no more helpful when he prattles (page 11) of aquatint or (page 14) quotes "Goulding and his pot of treacle" in his description of printing. But concerning the best methods, which happen to be new ones and also worked out in this country—maybe that is the reason—the Professor is silent, ignoring them completely. This is the kind of serious, solemn writing that is given the collector and dealer and from professorial platforms and in ponderous publications, so creating print clubs and an interest in etching—occupations mostly for the indolent. I hope students even in England know more than to follow this authority, even though here anything English is still taken seriously by the solemn ones. His remarks on modern men are as quaint as his knowledge of present day etchers is limited. This is the sort of information given the collector and the dealer. But in what other profession would an outsider and amateur be allowed to lay down the law, and in what craft or trade would a man devoid of technical training pretend to discuss technical facts?

I would not therefore trust a word he says, unless I know it to be true, in his historical chapters, though I presume he "got it all out of books," as another of his colleagues advised, but I do know that his modern historical chapters are but the record of his own opinions, and that it is on a basis of this sort that collections are sometimes formed and collectors sometimes created to their discomfiture and disgust when they unload their collections, and etchers sometimes mislead when they try to etch. This is the most pretentious but not the most misleading volume that has—or a new edition of it has—appeared since my book was written. Most of the other authorities are as popular as pathetic, while a new class of writers—touts for dealers—have come to the surface who grind out gift books, for provincial consumption. Or special numbers for the use of old blocks or the intriguing of artists for new ones. On the other hand, Dr. Singer has issued new editions of his books, intelligent and straightforward, and in consequence has been imitated and pilloried in Germany—even side tracked in his own gallery, which he does so much to maintain and improve. In England Mr. Campbell Dodgson, Keeper of the Print Room at the British Museum, has stated in a monograph on Whistler that the American is the greatest of modern etchers and the equal of Rembrandt—as I have been saying for years but never expected to hear an Englishman admit—but the war brought strange things about, even to Mr. Dodgson's taking over an American magazine of etching, *The Print Collector's Quarterly*, which is always searching for new etchers and finding none though it does contain most interesting articles. Endless series of booklets and tomes have been published, but no new etchers to make new books out of have dawned or, at any rate, arrived, while most of the artists who really etch are not written about, the reason being that they will not give their plates for nothing to advertise authors and publishers.

Though no new etchers have made a name or fame in the last four years, several well-known men have died, among them Auguste Lepère, a brilliant artist and craftsman, thoroughly trained, who could express himself by any of the Graphic Arts, but I can not help thinking he was more successful as a wood engraver of his own designs than in any other medium, and to compare his brilliant wood engravings and wood cuts with the clumsy bungling of many of his more notorious and financially, probably, more successful contemporaries, is to understand that the public, some collectors and some dealers do not know good from bad, certainly do not know a good thing when they see it and take the bad one. A second French artist, not so well-known for his etchings as Lepère, but far better known as an illustrator, was Paul Renouard whose aquatints and dry points of the ballet and other theatrical subjects have great merit. I saw Renouard for the last time at Verdun in 1917 where he and I were trying to work at the French Front. I failed completely. I do not know what—if anything—he did there, but later I saw an announcement of war etchings to be issued by him, and a reproduction of a dry point of the ruins of Rheims which was very fine. Renouard's great reputation was, however, gained as an illustrator.

Another death to be lamented was that of Zorn, though I can not say I much regret the end of the output of his prints for they had become feeble and photographic beyond words—though the last had none of the photographic look about them. Zorn was the sky rocket of etching—and the stick is on the way down.[1] A most brilliant painter utterly devoid of a sense of line, he made, however, an enormous financial success practising a craft which he had not the most elementary real knowledge of. His success was like that of his fellow countryman Axcl H. Haig, from whom he learned etching, and I fear his end will be the same. Zorn was the collector's etcher, the painter's etcher—not the etcher's etcher, but his anathema.

It would be best to explain why Zorn is not among the great etchers. Everything he did looks like a sketch in oil paint—no separate line counts—his work is all tone—or a suggestion of tone. Compare Zorn's best plate, said to be one of his first, *Le Toast*, with Whistler's *Riault The Engraver*, and you will, or should, see—that one artist's line is meaningless—all the coat, for example, could bc left out—the color of it; with the other, every line is full of, alive with meaning and color yet all is suggested by vital expressive line. It may be asked which artist I am praising and which I am condemning—it is just such ignorance of line in art that has evolved so many bad etchers and print societies which they produce and collectors who flock to them. Lately I was talking before one—I do it to educate them—or attempt to—and when I had finished, a lady sailed in, (she had just come in. She had not heard a word I said—she did not look at a thing on the walls)— but she sailed up to me furry and smelly and said "Oh Mr. Pennell, your exhibition is so beautiful, and it was so sweet of you to come and tell us all about it." "Yes madame, I can say it is beautiful because it is by the greatest artist of modern times." She rather stared. Possibly I reminded her of her husband's methods in his business. "Why," said she, "I thought it was yours." "I regret madame it is not, you are looking at the work of Whistler,"—and she is an official of this print club! Great is American education, and the effect of etching on the classes.

Steinlen has also gone but his etchings were few and unimportant. Two Americans, J. Alden Weir and C. Harry White, have died. Weir will be remembered for his experiments specially in engraving, and White for his early work and what he might have done had he lived: Klinger and Greiner died in Germany. The best known etcher, however, who passed away was William Strang, a remarkable craftsman, and an interesting artist, if Strang had only tried to be himself, instead of imitating, even if successfully, every celebrity or notoriety of the moment he would have been a bigger man. It is in his portraits that he shows best what he could do, in his other work he jumped, but most skillfully, from Rembrandt to Legros, with whom he studied, and he ended by imitating the utterly weak and meaningless scrawling of Forain. Though he could not help getting more feeling in his line than Forain, Strang was a great worker as well as a great craftsman, and he has made a place for himself among etchers.

The New Art has invaded etching, and the same old stenciled tricks have been played with it as with paint. I suppose it amuses the people who perpetrate it and the fools who are fooled by it. American up to date students practise it, it is so easy and artless.

Another matter which may call for comment is the price of prints. For some time—

[1] At a recent sale in New York, Zorn's prints realized at public auction about ten cents on the dollar a collector had paid for them.

ANDERS ZORN: THE TOAST AND WHISTLER: THE ENGRAVER

No plate by Zorn—the overrated—shows his weakness as an etcher better than this—The composition is interesting and the drawing is good—there is little of that photographic snap shot feeling in it which eventually overpowered him and his fellow countryman Thaulow. There is much color too—but the lines with which the drawing is done are worthless, meaningless, half of them could be omitted and there would be as much color, more if he had known how to bite—and the other half are merely an attempt to paint with a point—Zorn was a painter and a brilliant one—but he was not in the right sense an etcher at all for he had no sense of line at all, the face—though filled with the look of hot flesh —is simply stupidly rendered—without the least idea of quality of line—the hands are like paint—and the coat is like nothing at all—the man who cannot etch a black coat without covering it with black monotonous lines—to show it is black cannot etch at all. Compare Zorn's work with Rembrandt's and Whistler's they were etchers he was not. The proof of this, is in the portrait of Riault the engraver by Whistler, Riault wears—any one with sense can see—a dark coat yet it is left white without any

work in it—save just where—in the shadows—to those who can understand suggestion—it is shown to be black—and then not with meaningless cheap, endless lines but by a few which tell. Compare the hair of one with the other and as to the face—poor Zorn's stupid, stodgy, flat lines all of the same force with Whistler's vibrating expressive vital work—anyone who cannot see this can never see or feel an etching. Most can't and so get entangled with a collection. The Zorn is bitten the Whistler is dry point but the Whistler is a work of art while the Zorn is a worthless, an artless machine, as an etching.

in fact since the time of Rembrandt,—as is proved by the name of his *Hundred Guilder* print—the sum he or his dealer got for it—there was a slump or slackening until our day in the print business, but lately prints have been boomed financially and corners in certain men's work made. Formerly it was not till an artist was dead and no more of his prints could be had, though to the supply of some deceased masters' works there seems to be no end, that his prices rose. Now, however, arrangements are made for the artist's prices once the prints have left his hands to rise. To such an extent has this been prac-tised that prints bring at times more in an auction than their price at a dealer's, while the dealer's price may be higher than the artist's. I have every respect for honest, capable and intelligent dealers and do not know any others, and they must make a living, and if they do, they also make a living for the artist. But this inflation is nothing more than applying the methods of the stock exchange to prints and the same thing will happen to them as to inflated stocks, it is happening. Of course the owner always has his print, when the genius of the moment collapses, the purchaser of a share may only have a very in-artistic piece of paper left on his hands. But this booming can only have one end, a slump in etching and for these boomed prints, it is here. This has already happened once or twice in the past and it will happen again. Still the saving remnant which has carried on since the first artist scratched his etching on the wall of his cave, will carry on, and we may some day have a greater etcher than James M. N. Whistler.

There is another financial matter that should be alluded to. It is the fashion to-day for small galleries and museums outside the large cities of America to take over exhibi-tions arranged by the directors of the large galleries or by societies, and even international exhibitions arranged by young ladies and politicians,—artists are not wanted to manage their own affairs,—which exhibit prints unframed and unglazed—and, if possible, unin-sured. As to selling the prints or endeavouring to appeal to visitors, that is about the last occupation in the thought of the gallery director—and as to the museum purchasing any-thing in many of these provincial places that is unknown—what they do is to get some sweet girl graduate or benevolent business man to lecture on the prints, or the artists. That any etcher should be trying to make a living by selling his prints is unheard of—or unthought of. What should be done is, for the artist who is invited to show a collection of his prints in such a public gallery, to demand that some should be purchased in return—otherwise he is likely to get them all back but in a sadly damaged condition.

A strange thing is the American painter's inability to appreciate any form of art but oil paint and his hoggish promotion of that was manifested this year when the National Academy of Design refused to exhibit etchings and engravings, maintaining that because there were so many painter members there was no room in the annual exhibition for the engravers, utterly failing, or pretending, to see, that it was not their members who were being excluded, they could not prevent their showing, but the etchers and engravers of the country, whom they were depriving of an exhibition place, a pretty way of "encouraging the Arts"—the function of the Academy.

I, also, since the book appeared, thought I could found a great Graphic Art School, uniting all the crafts of book making and the printing arts. I did get the backing of a few professional lithographers, notably Mr. P. R. Heywood of Heywood Strasser & Voigt, and the enthusiasm of the Art Students' League of New York, but as to the craftsmen teachers, one left in a huff because, though he was king in his alley, when he got to the school he was nobody. His conceit of himself was as great as the pupils' ignorance of him. Another, a professor, has never been inside the class room, and never done anything but talk in the school. The illustration class poses the models, but has no technical or practical instruction and learns nothing of the crafts, knows nothing and is happy. My class is doing things and getting things—has even become known to the English. Prof. Morley Fletcher has visited it for a morning, and Germans have come to it, from Prof. Orlik to pupils from Munich, who remained to study, and are interested and really work, harder than any Americans except my Hebrew pupils who work more steadily than any, though Orlik called the place a "*schweinerei*." Foreigners are now coming here to learn technique which they cannot learn at home. Americans hide at home, proud and cocksure in the valour of their ignorance, or, when they go abroad, herd in schools by themselves and wonder what the foreigners do as they hang around their protected boarding-houses. No American educators, teachers, professors, have condescended to visit my school which succeeds without them. Still, there is a saving remnant in my class, which I have described in the book.

There are several interesting facts which I have discovered in my two years of teaching in the United States. First, the appalling ignorance of and indifference to the Graphic Arts in the country, which is proven by the fact that with a population of one hundred and ten millions it is with the greatest difficulty that an artist of the greatest reputation can sell one hundred prints from a plate—usually he cant sell fifty—and even when he does, it is mostly because of some extraneous circumstance, or because it is considered a "good buy," the merit of a work even counting against it. Though the artist often asks a prohibitive price for his work, Americans of to-day will, however, purchase a million nasty rotogravure copies of a poor photograph of some poor nonentity and each hang one on his walls and be proud of the fact and be sure he has got a good thing because he finds it in the parlours of all his friends on Main Street. Artistically these United States are in the Main Street, mid-Victorian age, and like England at that epoch, we are blindly proud of it.

Quantity production is the thing, that is the reason for the success of the cheap and nasty publications which flood the country, everyone takes them, so they are right— no matter what rotten rubbish they are loaded with. The rich American does buy art, but old art and dealer-boomed art, either as an investment or because he must have what his rich neighbour has. In the past such people had their portraits etched and lithographed, now they go to a fashionable photographer. The public—there never was, I know, an artistic nation—but there never was such an artless one that prated so much of art as this. Remember the scheme for an Art Centre in New York. The heavens of mediocrity were opened to protect the Park—that they gave themselves away as artless oafs was nothing—but it proved a hate of art in that they refused to have an art gallery in it. Again in the school I have found that the pupils begin by loathing to work with their hands, to get dirty. I have a cowboy who prints in gloves to save his fingers. Yet the mess he makes around him is unspeakable. Still, somehow, sometimes he does excellent work and makes interesting experiments. Many of the other students in the other classes in the school have no interest whatever in the crafts. They will starve sooner than learn one—and scarce a pupil becomes even an oil painter; most take to other jobs if they cant succeed immediately with oil paint, which they never can succeed at—but they can muck around at it, which they can not at etching. To paint you do not have to learn to draw—to etch you do, though I find there are students, not mine, who do their best to prove they can not.

The average American student has no stick-at-it-ness. He and she are mostly expecting success to fall upon them at once, by which they mean cash, without waiting years and working hard for it. Most of their time they loaf, smoke and admire each other. Scarce a collector or teacher or dealer has visited my class; art critics avoid it. It is not yet catalogued and to have an opinion of your own is fatal in this standardized land. The students have no interest in crafts either, but they will study a cracker factory, a packing house or an uplift journal office, conducted around personally by guides to see quantity production, visiting it in a rubberneck wagon. Individual effort is beyond them. The teachers too in many schools know it all, all the theory, and are incapable of doing anything themselves and not a few American teachers of Art take money for teaching what they can not practice. I know this because students, or would-be students, write me from all over the country and tell me of their experiences and hopes and fears—and failures.

As for the critics of art in this country, but two members of that profession—or oc-cupation—have visited the school in two years. Not an adequate or intelligent notice of it—save those I have written myself—has appeared. But then there are no authorita-tive critics of art in America writing for the press—and scarce any, if any, in England. On the continent there are a few, but art criticism here means mostly writing up shows that advertise in the critics' papers. Some papers even demand to be paid for inserting illustrations. In any other country this would be called by another name, here it is publicity—and efficiency—encouraging art, advertising artists.

I have no idea what my school may produce—if anything—but I have a definite proof that because art means individuality, and independence and character it has no future in this standardized, stabilized, hypnotized land, in which every attempt at individual creation is stifled by mass production. Still I am staying on and going on— though doubtless before long, if I succeed at all, some squirming, intriguing worm will drive me out and try to steal my ideas, but only undo all I have done. Still, certain things have been done in the school and certain pupils have got certain things out of it. But they are all in too much of a hurry to have time to learn that art is long—they are too fleeting—and most of them give up as soon as they encounter difficulties or else they are content with the merest smattering of methods of work and knowledge. Still, there is a saving remnant of workers.

I started some years ago the idea of giving demonstrations of etching and lithography in this country. I was not the inventor of it. It was invented at the Art Workers' Guild in England, but now every little museum in every little town wants me to come and show them how to make prints—but when I do not go, they are far better satisfied to have their own local genius do it instead and they usually expect me to perform freely, for the good of art and to keep them from sleeping of an evening when their radio has gone wrong —they read no more, they see no more, they understand nothing. Such are the things which infest what used to be my country, but is now theirs.

I wish to thank Mr. Frank Weitenkampf, his staff and the officials of the New York Public Library for granting me permission to reproduce prints in their possession, and I would also like to call attention to their photo-stat department by means of which most excellent reproductions of prints can be had, very valuable in teaching, lecturing and for exhibition purposes, and, even more remarkable, very cheap.

In revising the book I find it much better than I thought—therefore, and because the book has been a success and the Graphic Art School a success, the critics rave.

BROOKLYN, SEPTEMBER, 1924.   JOSEPH PENNELL.

NOTE. I wish also to thank Mr. Ernest Haskell and Mr. H. Devitt Welsh for valuable information with which they are credited in the book. And my pupils Messrs. Fagg and Ziegler for methods they have invented and allowed me to make use of. Miss Reinthaler for writing of my class at the Art Students League. There are other students whose work in the class has been suggestive and useful.

PREFACE TO THE THIRD EDITION

I WAS surprised to learn from the Publishers, a few days ago, that the Second Edition of this book, issued last October, had been exhausted, that they proposed to reissue it, and that, if I wished, I might write a new Preface.

This gives me a chance to do two things; first, to acknowledge, after seeing several collections of Alphonse Legros' prints, in which he forgot himself, or rather his slavish imitation of the technique of the backgrounds of the Old Masters and his mawkish sentiment, for most of his plates reek of the mannerisms of the past and the pathos of the present, that there was something in the man as an etcher to inspire the devotion of artists like William Strang and Charles Holroyd—I have placed their names in the proper artistic order—as well as many other of his Slade School pupils. I had not understood why, but had wondered why, they should so greatly admire a man to whom they were, I thought, so superior as etchers or, at any rate, Strang was. And I believed the painters of England right in electing Strang for his etchings to the Academy and the Government in knighting Holroyd, though that was because he was appointed Director of the National Gallery, not on account of his art. They were acknowledged, Legros was ignored. But lately there have appeared in certain exhibitions certain prints by Legros which prove that he was not only an artist, but a far bigger artist than these followers and imitators of his best work, the best of which I had never seen. Why did they never refer to it? Why, though I knew them, never talk about it or show it to me or to any one else I ever met? It was here in America, in the last year, that I saw it and learned

A. LEGROS: PORTRAIT OF DALOU. PROMENADE DU CONVALESCENT

The portrait of Dalou, the French Sculptor, though far more influenced by Van Dyke, might well be compared with the Whistler dry point of Riault, and Zorn's Toast, it has far more lines in the face than the Whistler but they are far more expressive than the Zorn. The Promenade du Convalescent is a remarkably fine and right dry point. Every line has a meaning and weight which tells, from

the extreme refinement and delicacy of the lines in the face of the woman to the rugged rich strength of those in the trees. Color too is rightly suggested both in the man's and the woman's clothes, and the trees behind them are drawn with the greatest character, put down with the most expressive lines. How much of all this color is due to Delâtre, the printer, who instead of Legros, the artist, pulled and signed the proof I do not know—Goulding once told me Legros used to bring him batches of unproved plates to print, those he liked when he saw the proofs he told Goulding to print, the rest he destroyed.

that Legros was an etcher worthy of a place in this book—I learned it last winter in an exhibition at the Brooklyn Museum. This being so, why did Poynter whom he etched, and the other Academicians who knew his paintings keep him out of the Academy and elect his pupil Strang, and why was he kept out of a knighthood bestowed on his other pupil Holroyd, when he had not only done this interesting work but given up his French citizenship to become a British subject and meet the sneers of his former compatriots, the French artists, who always asked "What have you gained?" and he always answered *"What—Comment? moi, j'ai gagné la bataille de Waterloo."* But in the last few months, as I have said, I have come across some most interesting plates by him and, though I make no apology for what I have written about the works I had seen before, for they had little character, the works I have just seen have much and I am glad to include them and him among my great etchers. Hamerton too made the same mistake.

This Third Edition permits me to point out that my book has had no criticism by critics of any authority, scarce any at all. But, as I wrote at the end of the Preface to the Second Edition, "the critics rave"—or rather screech—and this Third Edition is my answer to them. The book has chiefly been used as a mine by art editors to extract illustrations from, either without any criticism of it or to illustrate notices of other books with them, owing to the utter rottenness of the American law of copyright and the almost complete corruption of the American art editor and art critic so called, who are mostly only advertising agents for their taskmasters, publishers and proprietors who run the papers they write for. One critic has, however, remarked in what he would call a notice, but which is only a bid for acceptance among his class in England, that I do not know whether Dürer's *Cannon* is an engraving or an etching. I do not and could not tell unless I saw the plate, and maybe not then, but I believe it was drawn with a graver on a grounded plate and bitten in, and any one can see I am right by comparing it with the Rembrandt reproduced on the same page—I mean any one save a critic. This authority too states that I cannot tell the difference between an etching and a lithograph by Goya. As to those I was referring to, some prints catalogued in the British Museum as etchings, in other collections as lithographs, I can no more tell what they are than the cataloguers who confuse them, though I know that as Goya was a great experimenter in etching and lithography, no one, unless he had positive evidence in writing of the way the work was done, and there is none, would be sure. But then the average expert, critic, authority— I am only an artist—is always sure and is never weary of proving he is wrong, fooling others by his ignorance of everything he does not get out of books, which are as incorrect in their facts, as he usually is in his. But is there any one, save a few artists, now left in the world who knows anything about art though everyone now cackles about everything? I am further told by this same authority that I do not know the difference between an etching and a lithograph anyway. In some cases I do not—It is only such authorities who always know, only they don't know they are always wrong, for in our country we know everything, save that most critics, frequent professors and many curators do not know enough to keep their mouths shut, and not only make themselves ridiculous, but do harm to those more ignorant than themselves every time they open them, for there are still more ignorant people, strangely, than themselves to humbug—else the authorities would not exist.

And, though for them Whistler may be dead, it is because they did not buy his work for the Museums they mismanage and the colleges they misdirect when they could and will not spend enough now to get it if they can. Business is as rank in art as in stock-broking, both are run from the same standpoint, yet they might remember what Whistler, the greatest American artist, said of the authorities who boast of the knowledge gained by passing a lifetime in their galleries—that then, the guard at the door knows as much, really more than they, only he keeps his mouth shut while this sort of American curator, business man critic, there is no difference, makes a fool of himself every time he opens his, and it is wide open all the time.

My school at the Art Students' League has prospered in every way, save financially, attracting pupils from Japan to Judea and including English, French, Germans and the whole of North and South America, and some have learned a little, a number have taken to teaching what they cannot perform yet, though many have got married and more have failed to learn anything and left a profession they had no business to try to enter. But the financial side is all that counts and while money can be obtained in baskets full for anything except art—I do not mean for artless prize winners to loaf abroad or for uplifting associations here—I have to paddle my own canoe as best I can. I have almost reached the harbour, never to cruise again, I am reaching it successfully and this some day will be recognized. I have learned also, mainly from my students who endlessly experiment, some new methods of work. For example, in stopping out, instead of using liquid ground for a small space, as I have recommended, if a brush is dipped in turpentine and rubbed on a ball of solid ground, a mixture will be made with which the finest line can be drawn or the tiniest spaces stopped out. And it can be worked over and dries at once. A very good dry point has been invented by my most inventive pupil, Mr. Ziegler, who takes a safety razor blade, breaks off with pincers a narrow section which is extremely sharp at the ends, inserts this in a handle, and draws with it. The line made is remarkably sharp and clean and never seems to wear out nor the burr to break off while the tool can be handled with the greatest freedom, and if it breaks another point is formed by the breaking of it. But, after all, it is not really the tools, though the best should always be employed, but the way they are used and the brains to use them that count.

Mr. E. S. Lumsden, who is an etcher, not an amateur or outsider, has published the only up-to-date and useful treatise on Etching issued in England since Short's and Strang's which are out-of-date. Lumsden's book actually contains some references to American methods, and he even mentions, beside myself, one American Etcher, while clerical authorities like A. M. Hind can now use Lumsden when they never would refer to me, in those parts of the book where Lumsden gets his information from me.

Etching societies, etching schools, etching dealers and collectors are multiplying fast, but I have not noted a new living etcher. Even loan exhibitions of etchings are being sent round the country on some sale or return scheme. But the same benevolent benefactors who are doing this good to the poor people are dumping, at the same or higher prices, chromos, colour prints, and all sorts of just as good mechanical reproductions on them, the promoters being unable to distinguish either artistically or financially good from bad, to the incredible damage of the creative original Graphic Arts. But the world must be uplifted even if the artist is downtrodden.

It looks too as if the inflated balloon of commercial etching will have its periodical burst again before long. And again for years the works of the real etchers of the past— the men in this book—will be alone sought for, collected and preserved. Now it is a toss-up who is collected, but there is no doubt who the true etchers are. If collectors trusted the very few other etchers who know and myself, they would not go wrong, but they prefer to trust those who have wares to sell, and some of them are not to be trusted. And as the book is going through the press I find that a group of ad. men, business men, and I suppose women, describing themselves as an Institute of Graphic Arts, are going to decide which are the best fifty American etchings of the year. I was asked to select twenty-five, and some one else another twenty-five, as though in the whole world fifty good etchings had been made in a year, and I was told it was good advertisement, and it is said it pays to advertise—but it has nothing to do with art.

Poor Zorn has virtually vanished as a profitable investment, a proof that the knowledge of etchers, rather than the notions of business men and oil painters, should be accepted by amateurs, collectors, and etching societies.

But I am sure all the great etchers are now included in this book, and the right methods of work are described in it. And the art writers cannot prevail against it, or make people who practice etching, or understand etching, or any sort of art believe in them. But today this country is filled with faddists and fanatics, and even a fool may and can do harm, especially to the cultured, but even to the people.

BROOKLYN, JULY 4, 1925.   JOSEPH PENNELL

PREFACE TO THE FOURTH EDITION

FEW things would have given Joseph Pennell more pleasure than to know that a Fourth Edition of his *Etchers and Etching* was to follow the third in the short space of a year. The Third he welcomed for the opportunity it afforded him to pay the tribute he had hitherto denied to Alphonse Legros, and also to answer certain of his critics. The book was then made so complete, within the scheme he set for himself, that it seems as if he could now have had nothing to add or change. And yet, his interest in his subject was so inexhaustible, his knowledge and eagerness to increase it so great, that if he were here to-day he would most likely have found new material to include, statements to correct or modify. For he never believed in his own infallibility, never thought himself too old or too accomplished to learn.

This was really the secret of his strength and, as I can say though he probably never would have said it, the reason the book has been an inspiration to many. Etching was an art and a craft he practised all his life. There were periods when he spent more time in drawing in pen-and-ink or Russian charcoal for illustration, periods when he devoted himself above all to lithography. But he never ceased altogether to etch from the days when, a mere youth, he made himself known by his etchings in Philadelphia and Italy, to his last years when he was increasing his reputation by his fine plates of New York and its sky-scrapers. The amount he did in this medium alone is enormous. But he was never indifferent to the quality of his work, never careless. He was the most conscientious of craftsmen. He took enormous pains with every detail of the craft of etching, would have the finest, the most perfect tools no matter what trouble obtaining them entailed. The exact and minute information he gives in his chapters in *The Materials Necessary for Making an Etching* would explain how tireless was his pursuit of perfection even to those who never saw him at work in his studio or classroom, who were never witnesses, as I was, of his perseverance and patience where his work was concerned. If, throughout his chapters on *Methods of Making an Etching*, he insisted upon the artist doing it all himself, from grounding the plate to printing it, he was only preaching what he practised. Now and then at the beginning of his career, scarcely ever at the end, circumstances forced him to entrust his plates to a professional printer. But he always regretted it, feeling that the printing was as much a part of etching as the drawing of the design on the plate, and that the artist had no right to shirk it, however laborious it might seem. And, indeed, it may well be regretted that anyone save himself ever touched one of his plates. No contrast could be more striking than between the etchings of his own printing and the etchings printed for him even by the printer of exalted reputation. After all, the artist knows best what he puts in his plate and what he wants to get out of it. Long experience made a wonderful printer of him, and from the many undestroyed plates he left no one could ever be able to obtain the same results — prints with the same color, the same delicacy and strength, the same life in the nervous line.

He was as keen, as rigid in his attitude towards the art as towards the craft of etching. He believed, he knew there were some things it could do and some things it could not do, and he had no use for etchers who aimed to achieve the impossible or the undesirable. He never ceased to protest that the end of etching was not to reproduce paintings, amazing as these reproductions sometimes were — not to build up in the studio stilted and mannered designs from sketches and studies — not to draw laboriously on the plate with a line as mechanical as the bank-note engraver's — not to imitate wood or steel or any other sort of engraving. He considered spontaneity an essential virtue of etching, though critics, in search of something new to write, may begin to denounce spontaneity as an evil and declare themselves in favor of "careful work" — as if it were not by increasing care that the artist gains the power of being spontaneous.

All this, I admit, Joseph Pennell has written with a force and an enthusiasm which I cannot attempt or hope to rival. If I re-echo in a few words what he has said in many, it is simply because I want to emphasize the fact that he was scrupulous to a degree in carrying out himself every principle he upheld. He spoke and wrote wholly from practical experience and experiment. When he did not know — but there were few things about etching of which he was ignorant — he would say so frankly, and he only increased his authority by the admission. He was always, to the last, willing to learn from others and to acknowledge it. A fellow artist or one of his students had but to bring him some new device or new tool, and he could not rest until he had tried and tested it. If it pleased him, he said so, and several acknowledgments of the kind are included in this volume. There was nothing narrow about him, and the reason of the respect and love for him of his students is that he not only taught them, but worked with them, their fellow student and their master. Their faith in him was the more complete because he disdained all pretence to ominiscience.

To me, this Fourth Edition seems a fine tribute to his sincerity in his art and in everything he wrote about it. No one can mistake the honesty of his opinions. He was never prejudiced. If he was as fearless and outspoken in criticism as in praise, the sole reason was his determination to accept none save the highest standard. He was jealous of the fair fame of the art and craft of etching and, by the lowering of this standard, he would have believed it dishonored. I, who for years watched him at his press, realize what the art meant to him. And I often used to think that, with something of the old spirit of the Friends, he felt a "weighty obligation" to speak the truth about etching as he understood it, and to proclaim to all the world that cared its unlimited beauty within its technical limits.

ELIZABETH ROBINS PENNELL

BROOKLYN HEIGHTS, AUGUST, 24, 1926.

CONTENTS

CONTENTS

CONTENTS

CONTENTS

LIST OF ILLUSTRATIONS

LIST OF ILLUSTRATIONS

LIST OF ILLUSTRATIONS

HAMERTON, in *Etching and Etchers*—and with all its faults it is till now, the most important work on the subject[1]—discusses Etching under several heads, and it is just as well to discuss him after a lapse of fifty years. How many other modern technical art books have lasted so long? He begins by comparing Etching with Oil and Water Colour Painting, and Drawing in Monochrome. Such comparisons are futile—there is no possible comparison to be made—the Etcher who should try for lines in oil paint, or tone in etching, save in aquatint and mezzotint, which Hamerton was not discussing, has no knowledge of the scope or limitations of these arts. Nor is there any comparison to be drawn, as he does, between Etching and Pen Drawing, or Etching and Lithography. Unless the etcher gives to his work, or gets out of his methods, their distinctive qualities, he is not their master—not an artist. In discussing the technique of the Graphic Arts, with which Hamerton had but the passing familiarity of the amateur, he speaks of Etching being quite as autographic as Lithography. Etching is not autographic at all, Lithography is the only autographic, graphic art, and lately I have seen that charged against it by another amateur. A lithographic print is an original—the multiplication of the artist's design. Every line that he draws is printed as he draws it. All this is fully explained in the volume on *Lithography* in this series. An Etching is a print from the etcher's lines, scratched or drawn on a plate, through an acid-resisting ground, then bitten or dug into the plate, and finally printed from it: the lines in the print are absolutely different from those drawn on the plate.

Hamerton further discusses the relation of Etching to Pen Drawing; rightly used there is no relation. An etched line, and a pen drawn line, should show immediately, to the intelligent, what they are, how they are made, by which method. The artist —or rather, the clever one, and the swindler, can make a pen-drawing, put washes on it to imitate the tones of printing ink, spatter it with drawing ink to imitate foul biting, have a photogravure made of it so well as almost to deceive the elect, and, if that is his aim, scribble a few lines with a needle on the plate, and he should have a very good imitation etching. But the man who would go through all this to deceive, could make an etching of the subject with half the trouble, delay, expense, and certain subsequent exposure of his deceit and tricks, as has happened. If such an etcher took to forging bank notes, he could make governments sick. I have often wondered why it has not been done.

Hamerton's most absurd comparison is with "Black Lead." Any artist who wants to get the effect of "Black Lead," can get it by Soft Ground Etching, which is described in this book, as soft ground etchings are made with lead pencil or charcoal, and give in the print the effect of that sort of drawing.

---

[1] Though Professor Singer in his excellent *Moderne Graphik* never mentions it, nor Hamerton either. Equally—even more important—was Hamerton's work in the *Portfolio* edited by himself and published by Seeley, to which almost all etchers contributed: a delightful and remunerative contrast to the blackmail, if you don't give me a print or loan me a plate I won't notice you, process-block illustration methods of the present.

There is another section devoted to comparison with Wood-Engraving. In this there are some valuable hints and suggestions. Hamerton rightly objects to the modern wood-engraver copying etchings—a most useless labour—though marvellous results were obtained by American wood-engravers thirty-five years ago. But all this copying is now abandoned, and rightly, for process, mechanical engraving, which does the work better. Wood-engraving is an art for original artists, and has a character of its own; to prove that the wood-engraver, who is a master craftsman, can express himself perfectly by various methods, it is only necessary to refer to the work of Auguste Lepère: his etchings do not look like his lithographs, nor do his lithographs resemble his wood-engravings; all retain their proper technical qualities. So do mine, I think, and Whistler's certainly did. Hamerton's comparisons are blunders no artist would have made, but he was an amateur—and fell in a pit.

In fact, the only one of his comparisons which is of any real importance, or even relevance, is that between Etching and Line Engraving. But even here is no similarity. Etching, as Hamerton says, is done passionately: Line engraving, I say, ploddingly. Again he blunders and flounders ponderously—loving to discuss and analyze, compare and expound, for the sake of discussion—the result does not matter.

Hamerton points out truly that some of the greatest original work in the Graphic Arts is found in the work of line engravers from the time of Dürer. He says that now it has fallen by the way, because it is "so expensive"—he talks like a canny editor or cheap publisher. That is not the reason; but because line engraving fell into the clutches of the middle man—the hack line engraver, who charged more for grinding out one plate after Dürer than that artist probably was paid for all his own engravings. Dürer did not mind how much time he and his pupils spent over their plates, so long as they got what they wanted artistically; the modern steel engraver, copyist, makes a money contract before he touches a plate, by the inch or the year. Some of the very best reproductive engravers, those who worked for Turner's *Liber Studiorum*, were very modestly remunerated, from six to twelve guineas a plate, and even then Turner fought them and tried to jew them down.

The greatest triumphs of modern steel engravers have been in England. The results are not art, but plodding, sticking at it, muddling through, by which means a steel engraving is ground out. There have been any number of these people and mezzotint and stipple engravers of the same type—amazing in their way. But Great Britain has never produced a supreme etcher, and I do not believe ever will; it is not in the nature or temperament of the people. And if a real etcher—an occasional one—appears, he is not recognized by his fellows, whether native or foreign, during his lifetime—though his followers, when he has any, reap his rewards.

During Whistler's, Haden's and Legros' lifetime, there were no etchers admitted to the English Royal Academy, but any number of reproductive engravers were made members. Whistler was but little encouraged by the leading dealers of England—his aping imitators are boomed and lauded, boosted—financially to the skies.

Now that metal engraving has for the time ceased, the followers, imitators of

J. M. N. WHISTLER: JO. DRY POINT. ENGRAVED ON WOOD BY J. H. E. WHITNEY

The fame of the American School of Wood Engraving was made by works like this reproduction of Whistler's Dry Point of *Jo*, printed in *Scribner's Magazine;* incidentally it appeared in the first appreciative article on Whistler published in America, written by W. C. Brownell, who however described it as an *Etching Joe* when it was a Dry Point of Jo, Whistler's model, and called her the artist's brother; she was scarce that. In the same article and in other articles in contemporary magazines were many other wood engravings, by many other wood engravers, after Whistler and many other etchers. The engravings were wonderful. But it was toil, time, and trouble thrown away, not altogether, however, for the prints will live. This then was the only practical method of reproduction and printing at the same time with letter press. The design was photographed on the boxwood block, and this photograph, in reverse, the engraver cut into relief on the wood, that is, every line was left in relief; to do this the engraver with infinite skill and endless patience cut away by cutting on each side of them everything on the surface of the block except the artist's lines, which were left in relief. Whistler drew with his dry point, scratched each line, on the copper, simply, expressively, quickly; the engraver reproduced every line the artist drew freely, by two cuts, two lines or spaces one on each side of it with his graver laboriously.

Whistler probably made the portrait in a few hours—though he may have taken days—that we shall never know, but we do know that it took Whitney weeks to engrave this block and to engrave it marvellously, yet it was not really a reproduction but a translation, so was similar work by Cole and other contemporary engravers who worked for *Scribner's, The Century,* and *Harper's,* and who made reputations for themselves and the magazines by their work, as the engravers of the Early Nineteenth Century had done in England, France, and Germany, superseding metal engraving, which could not be printed on the same press with type, by wood engraving, which could. Then came Photo Engraving, by which the drawn or engraved line was photographed on to a sensitized metal plate, and the lines so photographed, covered with an acid resisting ground, and etched into relief; that is, the acid did the work of the wood engraver, and in this rare case did it better then the highly trained engraver, as well as more simply and cheaply. This print is a photo engraving of Whitney's wood engraving, twice removed, therefore, from the original. Artists liked the results, too, better; they were closer to the original, and the early photo engraving in the American magazines was better than the late wood engravings. The engravers after this either engraved the works they wanted, did original work for themselves, or copied paintings, though most of them, alas, disappeared or became hacks, for they were not most of them original creative artists. That there still was work to be done in wood engraving was proved by the later success of Cole and Wolf here, Lepère and Florian in France. Alas, however, to-day the American Art Editor cares no longer for the wonderful art of wood engraving, it costs too much for him—art has nothing to do with it, cost and hustle are his ideals, and the artist wood engravers of the world have fallen on evil times. Their work will live, however. The work of the photo engraver now is mostly inferior, not only to the wood engraver of the past, but to the photo engraving of the past. It is a strange but ever recurring fact that when a new method of multiplying arts or crafts is invented, artists capable of carrying it out appear, or rather the new method appeals to capable artists. Just as the best books ever printed, were printed immediately after the introduction of movable type. To-day we are ignorant of what has been done in printing and engraving, don't care, think we do the best work when we do the worst, and have lost mostly all sense of beauty, art, decoration, craftsmanship gone dry, dreary, decadent, diseased, dull.

J H E WHITNEY SC

ETCHING: "JOE."

DURER: THE CANNON
REMBRANDT: THREE TREES

DURER: THE CANNON. ENGRAVING. REMBRANDT: THREE TREES. ETCHING. COMPARISON BETWEEN ETCHING AND ENGRAVING

Haden to prove that etching was a vital art, and engraving a lifeless one, enlarged a small bit from an etching and an engraving. He proved his point but not fairly; the bit of etched work explained itself, the piece of the engraving did not. But it has seemed to me best—in landscape to place two famous plates on the same page and then compare them and the lines with which they were drawn by two masters—engraved and etched rather.

The difference of technique is best seen in the sky. Dürer's is made with a single line simply, firmly, boldly drawn, dug in the metal; Rembrandt's by a multitude of swirls, cross hatchings—scratches— long and short lines all made with the utmost freedom—both artists got their effect—though I have said in the chapter on Rembrandt what I think of this plate—both artists worked in an absolutely different way. But each in his own way, and keeping one's character in one's work is the charm of work.

The distance, the hill side in both are not so different, both artists have darkened the sky to lighten the ground and Dürer has drawn the distance more simply and expressively than Rembrandt, though this is the best part of the *Three Trees*. The foreground in both is beastly, there is no real observation—I do not know which is the worse—Dürer's cannon is fine so are the figures—Rembrandt's are cheap. And as for Dürer's one big tree and Rembrandt's three, they are both vile; nevertheless these two famous plates prove in themselves my point, and show better than I can describe the difference between etching and engraving though I could easily find a worse engraving and a better etching. But one shows masterly plodding in execution, the other masterly freedom of handling. I have since writing this gone through the authorities. Some say *The Cannon* is etched, some engraved. To me it looks like an engraving. Feels like it—any way it is fine and the reproductions show the difference of the two masters' work.

After the artist's design is drawn on or transferred to the plate a steel engraving is made with burins, gravers, gouges of different shapes held in the palm of the hand. The artist uses different sized tools for different sized lines, and with amazing skill, and certainty of hand, he pushes the point from him, and digs his design into the metal plate with it. Any ridges of metal thrown up by it and adhering to the side of the lines are cut off with a scraper and the design cut and dug into the metal, prints with great sharpness and clearness. Heavy lines are made by digging deeper into the metal with broader tools, lighter lines, by using less force and narrower tools. Line engraving is a slow, laborious and most exacting method of work, requiring enormous skill and endless patience. In the etching Rembrandt used his needle held more or less vertically with the greatest liberty and lightness, drawing with the same sureness and accuracy as Dürer but with absolute freedom.

The difference of handling can be best studied in the sky and middle distance. Dürer got his darks with one strong line, Rembrandt with many weaker ones. The deeper the lines are dug or bitten into the plate, the more ink they hold, and the blacker they are.

NOTE: I believe now that *The Cannon* was etched, but that the lines were drawn with a graver and not with a point, and that the plate was mostly bitten, only once. That would explain it. Why, for example the lines look like engraved lines and not bitten lines—why there is little rich depth in the blacks. Rembrandt's lines in the *Three Trees* are utterly different—as lines—the way they are drawn and their variety—and so are the blacks in his plate different in quality and colour from Dürer's. I have shown the two plates together and the difference should be apparent—and my explanation plain.

NOTE TO THIRD EDITION: My original statement has been refuted—that Dürer's "*The Cannon*" is an engraving by "an authority" who never read the above note—So I shall leave it to fool some other f— f— f— for it proves he has not read the book he reviewed. This is the way with some reviewers— others only extract the illustrations and ignore the text, they are too ignorant to criticise.

Haden and Legros, are welcomed to the Academic fold, but that is the way of Academies.

Hamerton ends his comparisons by pointing out that "the strong points of etching are freedom, facility, power." He omits to say the etcher must possess them; and he finishes by saying its weakness is "tone." No etcher, great etcher, however, tried for tone. Etching is a line method, but the great etchers have suggested more colour, tone, and values with a few lines, than the little duffers have failed to do with endless, useless, honest, soulful, stupid, patient bungling.

In a sea of platitudes and commonplaces one comes across grains of great sense in Hamerton's book: it is really in technical matters that he is hopelessly wrong or completely out of date. And he says rightly in his chapter on "The Difficulties and Facilities of Etching" that "it is extremely difficult to detach manual from intellectual qualities," and that "the quality of an etched line depends on its meaning and that alone." He does not, as Ruskin meant, mean inner, spiritual, soulful, precious, or other hidden meaning; but that the etched line made by the etcher, so it will print, should mean a tree, a house, a man, a cloud, or some part of these objects. Now this can be easily proven. Take, as has been done, a portion of a steel engraving, and enlarge it; and take a similar bit from an etching. The former is formal and meaningless; the latter is full of meaning and explains the bit enlarged. If a bad etching is chosen, the lines will probably be more meaningless than those of a good line engraving.

And Hamerton's statements about the highest skill in etching are memorable. This, he says, "cannot be reached at all by the average aspirant. Thousands have attempted etching. In this multitude you cannot find thirty first-rate etchers— there may be ten. If there is any human pursuit wholly inaccessible to men of ordinary powers, it is etching." It is to be noted he never refers to women—yet women now run etching societies, teach etching, lecture on etching, even make etchings. But there never has been a great woman etcher—not one woman is included in Hamerton's book. And Hamerton dares to say that "for ladies to take up etching is a delusive fashion." Haden remarks that, "it has come to be spread abroad that etching, the most difficult of the arts, is fitted only for the amusement of the amateur."

"Patient industry," Hamerton continues, "and some imitative faculty may produce a passable engraving, long training an academic painting; but nobody can be taught to make fine etchings or fine poems." Yet in Great Britain the Government, and the National Academy in America, employ etcher academicians, to turn out etchers, male and female, from Royal Colleges and National Schools and in Germany there are eminent Herr Professors, not a few, engaged in the same work. In America we are all etchers, but here as has been said, "all our geese are swans and all our swans are geese." The fact that there is supposed to be big money in it has nothing to do with the matter.

Etching is not putting down lines, as someone, who cannot do it himself, tells you to, or as he does it, but putting down lines for one's self that will print, that mean something to others, others who can see. Not learned people, cultured people, critical people, but people who can understand etching. Show an etching to the average parson, professor, critic, general, or—the best test of all—painter. It conveys nothing to him; there is, however, no reason why it should. Great etchers do not work for such people, nor have they any desire to educate them. If lines, as lines, mean nothing to the spectator, he is wasting his time looking at them, though the correct thing to do.

Yet it is in this vital, passionate art that the amateur and the artless are nowadays entangled, intrigued, and abandoned, with a collection or a diploma. Haden also says in *About Etching* that "the revival of the art has done harm as it has led many to misapprehend, and in practice to abuse, the true aim and end of etching."

If, too, the mechanical side of etching has no attraction, if the biting does not fascinate him, and the printing ravish him, the artist will never be an etcher—he is not even an artist, for etching has always fascinated the greatest artists. To-day the little painters are turning to it—encouraged and applauded by the little critics—not because they must etch but because they hope it will help them to pay the rent.

A tribe of etchers, tribe is the word, have also arisen who with almost clumsy stupidity, copy the stupidity of the successful. Daumier, Forain, Steinlen, Leech, are all lumped together and their mannerisms copied. All these artists could or can draw though sometimes clumsily, save Leech, the most popular, who could not. Therefore the more clumsily, the more perfunctorily, the more stupidly a drawing, an etching, or a lithograph can be made the more it should be prized. The artists I have mentioned exist despite their mannerisms and blunders—the moderns are praised because they crib their failures or carelessness.

One cause of failure to differentiate between good and bad etching, good and bad art of any sort, is the appalling and incredible ignorance of present-day art critics, who mostly have no technical knowledge, nor to make up for such lamentable ignorance, the power to express themselves by brilliant, memorable, convincing writing backed by their own opinion—an opinion respected, feared, looked up to, looked forward to—by artists.

Another point is that the difference between good and bad art is so slight that few can distinguish it. Most critics to-day have no opinions even of their own; they patter like parrots taking their tips from others with no ideas in their heads.

A man who is ignorant of etching, who is not an etcher, cannot criticize etchings; he can, and often does, blither about them, he can deal in them openly, or on the quiet, catalogue them, boom them, always the wrong ones, unless they and their makers have been recognized by the ages, and even then he blunders. He may have "experienced art"—the latest cant—but as Whistler said, a life passed among pictures makes not an artist or even a critic, "else the policeman at the National Gallery might assert himself." The critic does, and makes himself a spectacle.

Hamerton admits all this (I do not mean Whistler's statement—Whistler was to him the red rag). But he says: "No person outside practical art can criticize, and no practical person living in a narrow clique can criticize justly."

But the greatest critics of the past have always been narrow artists; in the present they are artists, although they mostly no longer trouble to write; they will be in the future, if there are any "art critics," for whom I with others see no necessity—an American advertising writer would serve the purpose better and be more interesting—unless a great artist and great writer and a forceful man—the rarest combination—appeared as critic, and he is not conspicuous in the public press, except as a boomer of exhibitions, the present-day tribe of critics are worthless—or harmful for "even a fool can do harm."

It is possible, as Hamerton says, "to be a connoisseur without having etched a plate, that is a collector, a cataloguer, a compiler, an editor, but no one can be an authority on etching, or even oil paint, who is not an artist." Still he may be on the staff of the most important organ of public opinion or profess the fine arts at a university. But the likes and dislikes of such people, and the public too, are not worth the paper they are printed on, to artists, unless they—the newspaper critics—praise them; nor are the opinions the people utter; they "know nothing about art, but they know what they like," or rather what they are told to like, for the public has no opinions, no ideas, no courage, or there would not have been this damnable commercial shop-keeping war. We hear to-day that there is a great boom in etchings. There is a sort of one. It was only recently that you could buy a Rembrandt or a Whistler much cheaper than the work of the modern genius—but the bottom has fallen out of the boom—and copper has advanced—and many of them will take to some legitimate means of trade—like painting.

Now there never was a real, a genuine interest in etching any more than there ever was an art age. Rembrandt's, and Dürer's prints were cheap enough when made—and few wanted them. And as to their popularity, even now, in artistic America with our hundred millions, it is very difficult for a good etcher to sell fifty copies of a plate—and Whistlers are still to be had—though he never printed more than one hundred proofs from any plate.

As for the amateur, the real amateur, he is one who loves prints and learns about them, treasures them for their own sake, their own beauty, not because they are rare, or the artist was mad, or only made failures, or had ideas he could not express, or because he did not know his trade, or wanted "to make big money quick."

But it seems to me I am not altogether writing "About Etchers and Etching," but somewhat about what they are not.

A great etching by a great etcher is a great work of art displayed on a small piece of paper, expressed with the fewest vital, indispensable lines, of the most personal character: an impression, a true impression of something seen, something felt by the etcher, something that means a great deal to him, which can be expressed only by etching, something he hopes someone may understand and care for, as he, the artist, does—for it is all his own work—and if not, well, it does not matter; he pulls a few proofs, knowing them to be good, he smashes the plate, feeling like a murderer, and then, some connoisseur comes along and tries to get, what he had not the brains to appreciate, when he could have had it, and now can never have it at all.

If even commercial collecting was sensibly carried out, and there are signs of it, the collector dealer, or the dealer collector would collect not prints but drawings. He wants things for their rarity, and for a rise in value : a drawing is always unique ; but he prefers a print which because it was bad, or because the other copies have been destroyed, happens to be unique. But there is no accounting for the collector. He prefers an early inferior state, which is rare, to a later and better, which is common ; he wants a proof with an accidental scratch on it, which the artist immediately removes. He wants in fact mostly all those things in a print which the artist doesn't want. But then that is the way with most collectors, for whom there is no accounting. But the intelligent collector and the intelligent dealer are absolutely necessary to the intelligent etcher, and it is this intelligent coöperation that has enabled us to carry on the art.

OF THE MAKING
OF ETCHINGS

THE artist who can make a great etching makes it because he must, because he feels that the subject can only be rendered by etching, and he goes at it, seeing before him in golden lines, on the bare black-grounded plate, the design as he hopes it will print in black lines on white paper. The idea, the impression he has, is so strong that he does the plate straight off from nature, or out of his head. He does not fumble around making sketches and drawings for it, apparently as studies, actually machines, which he hopes may sell, or working stodgily day after day at it. If a great artist makes a fine sketch on paper, full of vigor and vitality in every line, he cannot copy it without losing all that vitality—he must do it straight on the copper or never do it. If this is not in him, he is not and never will be an etcher, though he may be a most successful person. The real etcher goes at the drawing on the plate with as much fury as care, and dreads the biting and fears the printing, though they fascinate him, as much as the drawing; for it is all an uncertainty; the greatest etchers have made the greatest messes. It is only the plodding manufacturer of plates whose etchings are ground out, not fought out, whose prints are striven for by collectors and dealers; the real etcher never really bothers about such people, though all etchers have used dealers wisely for their own profit. The modern celebrity works up or down to them. Of course the true etcher likes to sell his prints, and he hopes they will sell, and he asks the aid of dealers to sell them, but that is not the reason why he makes them.

Most modern etchers and societies of etchers are made, not born. They are made by schools, dealers, and charters. The modern etcher mostly makes etchings to make money.

Owing to the present boom a tribe of etchers has arisen who can't draw, can't bite, can't print; but by getting photography and other people to do as much as possible for them, can make money and a temporary notoriety; but money is what they want; because after years of toil Whistler did get a living wage from his etchings "for the knowledge of a lifetime," these parasites want a fortune at once, regarding etching as a swift and sure way to win it, having sometimes failed at something else. They, however, like other nasty insects, die almost as soon as they are born, and the only people to blame are those who create them and encourage them; and though they make money, that has nothing to do with making etchings, which are made because the etcher must express himself by etching—because he loves the art yet fears it, and for the pleasure he gets out of making prints.

Though all these things are commonplaces in all real art work, to all real artists, there is so little real art, there are so few real artists, so few real art lovers it is worth while to repeat them.

OF THE COLLECTING
OF ETCHINGS

ETCHINGS are collected for two reasons, and by two classes of people. The first collect etchings because they love to, because they care to. The second because it is the correct thing to do so. The real collector loves to hunt for prints in artists' studios, in auction rooms, in dealers' galleries, in boxes and portfolios at second-hand shop doors, and when he has got them for his own, he loves to turn them over, to carefully mount and accurately catalogue them. Each has a story of pursuit and of capture as interesting, often, as the print.

There are curators, keepers, and directors. Some curate as a business as a means of making a living, usually eked out by other means. Some keep, or get their posts by examinations or promotions. Others by accident or influence. Others are genuine directors who not only direct their galleries but the public, and encourage artists by collecting judiciously modern as well as old prints and back up their opinions by making collections of their own.

There are dealers who have the love of the chase, whose delight is, in some out of the way corner, to find a treasure; and, if they are willing to part with it for a very high price, if by chance they have picked it up for a very low one, they are—this sort of dealers—as keen about their prints as collectors.

Other dealers are genuine collectors. Two names—for they are gone—may be mentioned: Avery and Keppel. These men did in every way, far more to encourage etching and etchers than all the pompous pedants who have written about it, and themselves. Avery and Keppel, it was found too, had enriched libraries and print rooms by the Collections they left. Not like some other much advertised collectors did they sell their collections, or allow them to be sold before or after their death, or pave their way to heaven by advertising what they are going to do with their prints after they shall be done laying up treasures on earth.

These intelligent dealers love to fight for and pay for the fierce struggle of the auction room, and the triumph of possession that comes with it.

But your present-day collector is at times a quite different sort of person. He buys etchings as an investment. He is at times, he thinks, a sharp shrewd investor, but if he exercised no more brains in his dealings on the Stock Exchange than he does in the dealers' shops he patronizes, he would land in the Bankruptcy Court.

Others simply buy etchings because it is the correct thing. They order a print before it is made, or published; it is as correct to have it, as a white undervest, or yellow gloves, or any other fashionable article, and it is bought just because in a certain set the owners do not dare to be without it; and the people who make such things, sell such things, buy such things for such ends, do so to advertise themselves for their own profit —for there is as much commercialism among artists as among the commercial classes.

Certain etchers now simply manufacture etched plates, with or without a photo-graphic basis, with or without remarques, broad-margins, artists' signatures, or other baits, for the benefit of such collectors. Societies are started for them and everything is done in some quarters to encourage them. There never was such an interest, such a boom—a better term—as there is to-day in prints, artistic or photographic, but there are no more real etchers than there were fifty years ago. There are fewer and there is no real boom either.

There are many etching societies, but there are not so many etchers as societies. The whole affair is a commercial proposition. For some reason, a fictitious commercial, and a sort of sanctimonious respect, is paid to a piece of paper on which a few lines have been printed from a scratched or bitten copper plate. Their merit, or want of merit, does not matter. Like the Order of the Garter there is no merit about it. It is really only the same sort of respect that is paid to another piece of engraved and printed paper labelled fifty francs, five pounds or ten dollars by the same sort of people. This sort of collector collects because he hopes he is making a good investment, because he thinks it correct. But out of this collecting for profit's sake, for vanity's sake, good may—and sometimes does—come. It is certainly infinitely better that a man or woman should find it more amusing to chase a print around town, than a ball around a field; and there is just as much, or may be more walking exercise to be had running from studio to shop and to auctions, and more brains in this way may be developed than by driving a ball over a net. It is certainly a good thing to start print rooms, but it is an absurdity to crowd them immediately with prints: a print collection should grow so slowly that those who study it may know and understand the prints in it. It is a good thing to start lectureships and professorships of the Graphic Arts, provided the lecturers and professors know what they are talking about, and command the respect of those who practise these Arts. It is a good thing to have good honest dealers about; but some are ignorant or dishonest. Others know every state of every plate, but can't tell if it is good or bad, by looking at it, or anything about it unless it is in a catalogue. Others are too superior to know anything but the price of motor cars and the states of artless prints or numbers in artful catalogues. The etcher is a necessity to attract people to their shops, but their encouragement of his art commences after an artist's death mostly. It is an abomination to start etching and engraving schools and fill students' heads with the idea that they can all make etchings and sell them to collectors—and make fortunes. Some of the teachers have never etched, others can't draw—and I know of a school where there is no press.

If the collector really cares and really collects, he will learn all these things very soon, learn that there are a few things he must learn. Whether he is going to collect prints because he loves to have them round him, to look at them, to show them to others. Then he will learn, first, whether it is the subject or artist which interests him, or whether it is the state, or the rarity of the print, whether, when he has learned the difference, he wants a good proof, or whether an electrotype of the subject gives him equal pleasure. The great difficulty is what he shall collect. Artists and dealers want him to collect their works, or the works of those they are interested in—their school, or their clique, or—well, themselves—and nobody else. And in these the collector may have no interest whatever. Scheming shop-keepers will work off on him the productions of their docile hacks and tame etchers. If they cannot do so, the work of these tame etchers will be found, in a few weeks after it is published, in auction sales, bringing more than the published price of the unsold copies still in the dealers' portfolios. Of course no one compels a collector to collect in this fashion, but he often does—one kind of collector—and one kind of dealer gives him every encouragement to do so.

But the right sort of collector, if he has it in him, can collect intelligently, and wisely, and well, and cheaply, but he must know, and feel, and see—and he will find intelligent dealers to help him. Some of the most interesting hours of my life have been passed in talk with collectors, curators and dealers, in their homes, their galleries and their shops, where new prints were shown and old prints were again looked at, and we all gained knowledge by relating our experiences and comparing our prints.

I have lived through two so-called booms in etching—the second will be over before the war is finished—and many dealers, etchers, and collectors will vanish with it. We have all been too successful. That is finished. But there will come a more rational, a more sensible, a more intelligent period, though I shall hardly see it. But great work will still be done in etching.

The armistice came suddenly and etching—commercial etching—profited.

But the good etchers survived.

INTRODUCTION

SINCE the world began there have only been two supreme etchers—Rembrandt and Whistler. I am not sure there have even been two—but I am sure the latter artist is the greater etcher. I shall have to drag in several other lesser etchers, because in some way they have done something, because they were etchers—a few were great, but not of the greatest.

The reason why these two artists occupy the places they do is because they employed—Whistler more, Rembrandt less—their genius, and the art of etching in the right way :—That is, for the expression of their ideas, or their impressions, in the most perfect manner, and this means with the most vital, as well as the fewest lines, and these are the foundation of great etching. The greatest etchings being then the result of the choice of the fewest and the most passionate lines, there are artists who are artists, painters, sculptors, but not etchers, for their line, as line, is of no value, and if half the lines were omitted from their plates the results would be better. Others, whether they use a single or multiple point, do not draw lines with it, but paint with it, make tones with it; and this tone work is carried still further, to a ridiculous end, in the so-called colour etchings now published widely. Artists sign these reproductions, but I believe, from what has been told me, have little else, save pocketing their royalties, to do with most of them. For a few years a whole army of etchers who never made, at any rate never showed, an etched plate, in black and white, signed endless numbers of these colour prints. The perfection and rapidity with which they appeared proved that the artists had no trouble to make them, while etchers have infinite difficulties with each plate.

As for line,—what is meant by it,—is expressive line, not a scrawl or a fluke, but a line so drawn on the plate and so bitten and so printed that every bit of it has life and meaning and character—in the print—and a series of such lines make a great etching : a few lines so drawn make a great picture. Many may be so drawn that they are meaningless.

The lines of the greatest etchers are not only in themselves of supreme beauty, but drawn with supreme technical skill. For a great etching is an everlasting proof, a self-evident proof, that a great etcher is a great technician, little as that is understood, or cared about to-day, little as the cataloguing curator, or the intrigued collector understands it, or the blundering, bungling "painter etcher," for that matter—a blundering, bungling name invented by Haden.

The drawing and placing of the lines on the plate is a part of the making of a great etching, and in the biting of the plate there is as much art as in the drawing of it, while the whole is crowned by the printing, and all great etchers have been great printers and their own printers, and the greatest printer of etchings who ever lived was J. M. N. Whistler,—that I know, just as I know he carried the art of printing further, in the right way, than Rembrandt did—and so carried on tradition.

Now Rembrandt's etchings may have, in printing, been as rich and luminous as

Whistler's, when they were printed; to-day they are mostly dry and pale and weak. Either, then, they were always, in printing, dry and pale and weak, or they have become so; anyway, they are surpassed by Whistler's. What Whistler's work will look like in three hundred years, how it will stand the strain of time and collectors, who shall say? Will the richness we now love fade, and the depth beyond depth of tone decay, dry to dust? Well, we have seen his prints in their perfection, and they are more wonderful than Rembrandt's.

I know it has become the fashion to decry skill and thought and care in printing, to decry printing altogether, to decry art and laud clumsiness to-day. It does not matter. The artist, who is an etcher, will pay no attention to such artless prattle, by artless preachers and stodgy, incompetent, ignorant plodders; but shutting himself up with his press will pull his own proofs, trying to make the next better than the last. If he has not this love for his work, this delight in it, this excitement over each proof, he is not an etcher and never will be.

A S to modern etchers, I am not going to discuss living men, but I shall discuss modern men. But the etcher whose name is most in men's mouths, who is most imitated, is a modern, Meryon. That is why I speak of him first. Now "Meryon," as Whistler said, "was not a great artist," but he was a great find, for two or three collector dealers, or dealer collectors. They got up a corner in him, and Meryon was, I believe, the first etcher since Rembrandt to whom Stock Exchange methods were applied. The merit of his plates is nothing to such people, the states, the numbers, and the paper they are printed on, everything; and all is backed by a sentimental story, the story of his madness, which hardly appeared in his art save in the shape of devils and balloons in the skies, and stories and tales on the ground of a few prints. His most famous plates, *The Stryge*, and *The Abside of Notre Dame*, are his worst. The figure of *The Stryge* is not bad, though whether it was anything like the original chimera cannot be known, as the one now on Notre Dame is a copy; but Meryon was totally unable to give any idea of the height where the beast is perched, or of the mystery and confusion of old Paris below—his drawing of the Tower of St. Jacques is rotten—yet if printed, I believe, on green paper—or it may be some other colour—by a professional printer, not by Meryon, it is of enormous value. The *Abside* is a stupid rendering of a magnificent subject, meanly seen, poorly drawn, badly printed.

The bulk of Meryon's work is totally uninteresting, totally uninspired, devoid of spontaneity, absolutely easy to imitate, poor in perspective, without observation, out of scale, faked. The world to-day is full of little Meryons, drawing his subjects in his manner; some do it as well as he did. Only the names signed to the plates, and the prices obtained are different. The few sous Meryon got for his proofs have in the hands of his imitators of to-day grown to dollars and pounds; but the works are the same tiresome, stodgy, uninspired commonplaces, and that is the reason why they are so sought for. Meryon was not an etcher. He never did—at any rate there is no evidence of it in his work—a plate from nature, but he made pencil sketches, or worked from photographs, set up his subjects in the fashion of an architectural draughtsman. Hamerton, who in *Etching and Etchers* writes as though he knew Meryon personally, says he did work out of doors on the copper, "holding both plate and mirror in one hand, laying the lines with the other, and so steadily that the most skilful etchers marvel at his skill." I should think so, and I marvel more at the story, for Hamerton omits the real point that Meryon must have turned his back on his subject to work from the mirror. What a detail this adds! And think of the crowd that would gather to see the wonderful artist who could draw without looking at what he drew. As for his two best plates, in the *Collège Henri Quatre*, the background never existed at all, while the *San Francisco* was done from photographs. So much for Hamerton's story. These two prints are never referred to by—or are unknown to—the authorities. But there is another detail. The man who bothers so much about reversing his prints, as Hamerton praises Meryon for doing, is not an etcher at all. Who knows or cares

* Note: Meryon said himself, " I am not an etcher, Bracquemond is."

whether Rembrandt's little towns are reversed? Whistler's work always was reversed. Etchings are made by real etchers on the spot, and are always reversed, for when the drawing is made the right way on the plate it is reversed by printing. I know some of my aquatints and mezzotints in this book are in the right orientation, but in that sort of work one does reverse when drawing in the studio, never when drawing from nature. The collectors who are worried by such details should collect post-cards, or put their prints before a looking-glass, and they would see them the right way round with a fool behind them holding them up by the corners.

Meryon was an architectural draughtsman and a commercial etcher; everything is in his prints, and all are perfect; but his work has no life in it, it has no go in it; it has most of it little art in it. All really great etchings that have ever been made have been done straight away on the copper and not faked and tinkered from sketches.

Any architectural draughtsman with a few months' training can turn out a fair Meryon, if he is stodgy and careful enough, and if he has any real ability he can surpass most of the master's work. Meryon himself admitted he was no etcher, but that Bracquemond was. Meryon had great love for the Paris of his day and loved its disappearing picturesqueness—that he etched it was an accident—really because he could not paint, which he tried to do. Why, I have known ranchmen, architects, and painters to do excellent Meryons. It is true that Whistler tried to do a Meryon— *L'Isle de la Cité*—from the windows of the Louvre, and failed, simply because he was not a copyist, an imitator, and had something to say for himself, as even Meryon had, who would have made a mess of the *Black Lion Wharf*, which is a work of art—not an exhibition of tiresome, misplaced patience. Work and disappointment drove Meryon mad.

But there are a few plates which save Meryon's reputation. These are: *The Morgue*, which is fine, though it is rare and sought for; and the best of all his plates, which can or could be bought for about the same price Meryon got for them, the *Collège Henri Quatre* and *San Francisco;* the first is the most magnificent piece of drawing and biting of an imaginary view of a city from a height that has ever been done; and the second a most remarkable fake. For Meryon did not, I believe, see San Francisco while in the navy, or anyway, did not make the plate there, but did it from photographs supplied him by two Frenchmen of the town, who wanted the plate as an advertisement. Even the photographs are regarded as something holy—and shown as treasures— the possessors oblivious to the fact that Meryon would grind out any pot boilers that came his way. *Le Ministère de la Marine* is excellent and contains endless devils— even airships—and stories, if they are any help to it—but the palace is finely drawn.

Meryon's biting is so perfect, so utterly devoid of accident, that I have often wondered if he bit his plates himself, if he did not turn them over to a professional visiting card etcher and engraver—one of those people who make copies on the Quais of Paris of Meryon's plates to-day, or did before the war, and, well, sometimes these are sold as originals. There is not a bit of excitement about Meryon, and this is so comforting to the present-day unemotional etcher, dealer, teacher, collector; Meryon is so reliable, so

I have pointed out in the text, Hamerton's inexcusable blunders over Meryon.   But the photogravure proves the wonder of Meryon's rendering not only of a city which never existed, but a city Meryon made to suit himself — for in state after state he changed it till it pleased him.   But because the plate exists or did exist, till lately, this wonderful plate, this wonderful creation, is not appreciated as it should be simply because it is not rare.   Some day it will be, for it will be rare and then collectors will try to collect it, and though they can have fine proofs now they do not want them because they can have them.   That has nothing to do with Etching, however.

Hamerton pretends this plate was done from nature but this is evidently not so.   Meryon describes how it was done from sketches himself and some bits of it finished out of doors.   There are no such wonderful concentric lines, converging to make the composition just as Meryon wanted, in this part of Paris.   The mad figures, some of them the height of the tallest buildings, give the realism away. Meryon describes their size, meaning and purpose in long letters to Burty the French critic.   Everywhere too are the same roofs and windows, the same tricks of *The Morgue*, but the wonder of this plate is the way the town recedes in the distance, street beyond street, house beyond house, and all in perfect relation, perfect perspective, and all have character.   This impression of a city is wonderful and is given perfectly; impressionism does not mean necessarily a sketch or a note, but giving the impression the artist had to an appreciative observer and in this point he has given the feeling, the grandeur, the size of Paris in a wonderful fashion.   Only those who have attempted such a subject know how difficult it is — how long it takes, how hard it is to keep up one's enthusiasm, yet Meryon never tires, never blunders, never makes or leaves the trace of a mistake.   It is so wonderful, that it is a wonder it has passed unnoticed.   In some states there is a sea in the distance so much for Meryon's realism but his imagination which means mastery of drawing is amazing.

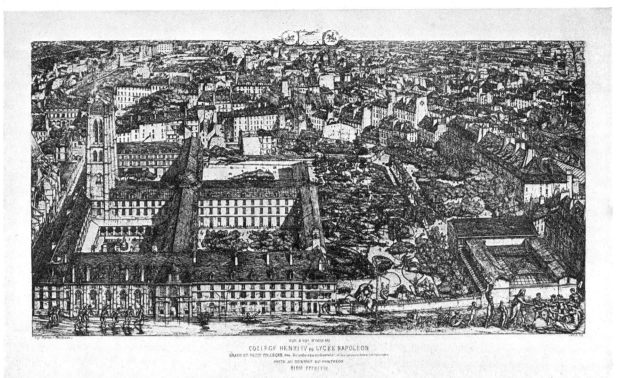

VUE À VOL D'OISEAU
COLLEGE HENRI IV ou LYCÉE NAPOLÉON
GRAND ET PETIT COLLEGES, avec Secondaires en descendant et les constructions environnantes
PRISE DU SOMMET DU PANTHEON

MERYON: THE MORGUE

The finest amongst the few fine plates Meryon ever did — and yet this is more owing to the composition and the lighting than to the line — the drawing is remarkable, almost architectural, almost photographic — yet it is not, and that is the reason why the plate is so fine — and it is in little differences like these that the difference between good and bad work is chiefly found.   Yet even in this plate there are two styles: the light formal hard work — but in this case right work — on the houses, the meaningless scrawled sky and the more meaningless smoke, and weak washing place at the bottom.   And the figures bringing in their dead, are quite different in handling, from those looking over the embankment.   The only explanation I can offer is that Meryon never meant to put them in at the beginning, but added them, to give effect to the finely drawn architecture.   There are two manners of work in the roofs also, those further away more loosely drawn and harmonizing with the sky, in a way, that in the foreground, the morgue, itself done more formally.   This difference in handling, which has not been noted by any of the commentators, is probably caused by his building up his plates from separate sketches, possibly at separate times, this plate almost looks as though two artists worked at it.   The popular belief about Meryon's technique is that it is thought to be so correct — the lines are almost mechanical — yet they are artistic — but not free and full of life like Whistler's — and on careful study it becomes evident that they are all a trick. Look at the open windows they all give on the same black interior — look at Whistler's windows they are all different — as in nature.   Meryon either never drew from nature or never observed. Look at the windows even in a sky scraper, they are all different when open — Meryon's even in these small buildings are all the same.   As I have said too in speaking of Lalanne's work, he is more observant than Meryon, but Meryon is the fashion and a commercial proposition mostly.   And in this plate there are no mistakes, erasures, foul biting, none of those qualities found in all spontaneous, vital etching — Meryon is perfunctory, perfect, pathetic.   He was a strange mixture and this is his strangest plate.

plain, so direct, so clean, so clear, and the few devils and balloons and stories in some states of some plates, give just the snap, the respectable snap, the respectable person wants; Meryon is the respectable person: he probably sketched in a top hat and kid gloves: though with a story of himself, the story of his respectable madness, even being drawn and etched mad in the mad-house. Then too the printing is perfectly commonplace and professional, and all prints, of all states, are all alike; sometimes the paper is changed, and the collector holds his breath, and opens his pocket-book; but Meryon never changes; he once did change his mind and took back his prints when he found Haden, or was it some dealer, collector, critic, trying to make a corner in them.

Most of the prints which are signed were printed by Delâtre.* Whether Meryon had a press is uncertain and the authorities do not enlighten one. One searches the authorities! for technical information in vain, if one wants it; Burty says there was a wooden press in his studio.

Meryon is the fetich of the commercial dealer and the prophet of the manufactured etcher, and the stock-in-trade of the "experienced" critic. There is no one so easy to sell, so easy to imitate, so easy to write about. Following, however, or copying his work, is a good thing for a student—afterwards a better thing for the student to get rid of.

If, as has been said truly, I think by Hamerton, and he did say some true things, that in the best etchings not one single line could be left out without loss to the design, not a line could be added without being one too many. If half of Meryon's lines and his trick shadows, his ovals cribbed from Rembrandt, were left out, his prints would be far better. And as for most of his plates they had better never have been done at all—or called etchings anyway.

I have nothing more to say about Meryon's work save that it is amazing that a man who did two or three such fine plates could have produced such a number of utterly commonplace ones.

I believe the *Collège Henri Quatre* and certain other of Meryon's plates are now preserved in the Musée Calcographique in the Louvre, with those of other etchers and engravers. Prints from these can be bought—there is a catalogue—by artists and students at the Gallery; if they are out of print other copies may be ordered; these vary in price from a few sous to several francs. As the plates or prints bear a government stamp there is no danger of deception. But for students such prints are of the greatest value for study, as they are well, though simply and cleanly, printed, and show the work. I suppose the plates are steel faced. There is a similar Museum in Rome, with a Sales Room, where many of the Piranesis are to be had, as well as works by the early Italian line engravers. These too are not badly printed. In the Academy of San Fernando in Madrid is the Spanish Calcographic Gallery and printing office. Here the works of Goya are ground out, but the printing is vile, and the plates are mostly so worn as to be worthless. There are doubtless similar collections in other capitals. There should be one in the British Museum and in the Library of Congress. These

* NOTE: And signed by him with his address bitten in the plate. Meryon rarely signed his proofs after they were printed. The signing of proofs with pen or pencil begins really with Haden and Whistler.

Museums were formed of copyright plates, and others which have come into possession of the nation, after they had been printed, being turned over to the government print rooms and stamped by the government. As there is an official stamp on each print, there is no excuse for the collector who is deceived by buying them as proofs. They are pulled on ordinary paper and sold—one copy only to artists—and being from the original plates, they are of far more use than photogravures, or copies of any sort, as well as, usually, much cheaper. These Museums and their Sales Rooms deserve to be better known to young artists studying etching.

I AM not going into this Historical Section, historically, as I have said, but artistically, discussing the most important etcher first. Meryon was not an etcher, but a fad, therefore I wished to get rid of him. We are told in historical works that we must await the verdict of time before we can sum up anything; by waiting for this verdict we lose facts. I prefer facts—and that is why I am stating what I know about Whistler and his work before some anæmic hump-back newspaper reporter or professor of the fine arts gets from people who knew nothing for themselves, and would not understand if kicked into them, "the facts" to suit themselves — I prefer Vasari's contemporary facts, to critics and University Dons and Art Masters fancies, to modern commentators versions and mothers meetings and girl graduates and prize-awarding infants and perambulating lecturers explanations of them. But positive—actual—statements about anything are not wanted to-day. What has posterity done for art? I want to record what is being done, and what I know, and that, and not what the future may say, if anything is left after fools have got done knocking history to pieces, is of importance, and if I can leave a record of what I know of my time, it may be useful, even for possible future disputations.

Therefore, James McNeill Whistler being the greatest etcher who ever lived, I shall say what I have to say about his work, and say more about him than any other etcher, and say what I know because I worked with him and talked with him for years, because it is worth saying and his methods worth following; for it is in this way alone that tradition can be carried on.

The first thing I want to point out is that Whistler was trained in three good schools: in drawing, in topographical drawing, at West Point Military Academy; in topographical etching, accurate etching, in the United States Coast Survey Office, where he applied his knowledge of topographical drawing on paper, to drawing on copper plates and biting them—a severe and exact school in which he studied and practised his art (as Meryon should have done in the French Navy); and then Whistler worked in Paris studios and with French artists. And he had the brains to put in practice what he learned, though being a great artist he never ceased to regret he did not learn more. But till the end of his life he was always striving to learn.

Whistler could not be confined to making maps, and the marginal sketches on one Coast Survey plate and the bits of landscape and birds on another showed the development of his West Point style of drawing, and the etched handling reappears in the French series of plates, mostly made in Alsace and Lorraine, and printed in Paris by Delâtre, entitled *Douze Eaux-Fortes d'après Nature par James Whistler. Imp. Delâtre, Rue St. Jacques, 171, Paris, Nov. 1858.*

From the first to the last, it should be noted, his etchings were "d'après Nature."

The only thing is, that in these he developed his power of drawing and his method of biting. But in almost all of the twelve plates there are superfluous lines, meaningless lines, scratchy lines, West Point lines, Coast Survey lines, but never clumsy, stupid, stodgy lines. Now of these early plates I only want to call attention to the best. There are only two which really need be considered: First, *The Unsafe Tenement* (*M. 17*). I am not going into an elaborate description of it. The collector knows the print; the etcher should; and the student who does not take the trouble to look up the originals in Museums or even the reproductions in the Grolier Club Catalogue is not worth bothering about; most are not, but it is the no-goods, the incompetents, who are laboured with. *The Unsafe Tenement* is the complete expression of the West Point manner, carried out and elaborated endlessly. Doubtless, in fact I am sure, he had seen Rembrandt's mills and cottages and determined even then to surpass the Dutchman—as he did in this plate. For Whistler was so big an artist that he admitted his indebtedness to others. It is only the little grabber who has seen nothing, who steals everything. There is great observation of detail—too much—too great an attempt to render colour and surface, too little thought of line. There is endless care, endless trouble to get things right, just the right sort of way to start. The second plate, the *Street in Saverne* (*M. 19*), is notable too, for it is one of the very few nocturnes Whistler etched; yet here is evidence that from the beginning, he loved the beauty of the night. There is scrawling, but he got the effect. It might be noted that the price of these twelve proofs was two guineas. Twenty sets of artists' proofs were printed. *The Kitchen* and *The Miser*, the best of all, were not issued in the French set. Between 1859 and 1861 Whistler made many plates including most of the *Thames Series*, and a number of figure etchings. In these he carried on tradition, and still further improved his style. In landscape, rather townscape, there is nothing that ever has been done in this world to approach the *Black Lion Wharf* (*M. 41*). I have been repeatedly criticised for making statements strongly, but one should only write of what one knows and believes, and then it is not possible to write too strongly. Critics don't know because they can't do—and take their beliefs from someone else. I know that Whistler himself preferred his later work, but, if he had not acquired his command of his materials, by this elaborate work in the beginning, he never could have expressed himself with such sureness, freedom, and simplicity in the end. The statement has been made that these plates were done from sketches; most of the so-called sketches were made after the plates were finished to show his friends and relations what they were like; they were drawn, he told me, straight on the copper, and he has etched the fact on the cover of the set.

In the *Black Lion Wharf* every single line has a meaning—and there is not one too many—and if one were taken away there would be a break in the design. Here and there are reminiscences and traces of his earlier handling, yet every single line is more expressive than a dozen of his earlier ones.

He gives in this plate the impression that he has drawn every brick, every tile, every plank, in every roof or wall, and some imbeciles have said so; he has done nothing of the sort, but he makes you think so; and this is the art of concealing art by art; not only this, each brick wall is built of a different sort of brick, built at a different time and in a different way, and even the white untouched paper shows plaster of different ages, and the single line of bricks, by reinforced biting, gives shadows, modelling and relief.

48

WHISTLER: STREET IN SAVERNE

A remarkable example, a memorable proof that from the beginning Whistler saw the beauty of night and was able to render it though he saw more beauty and rendered it more subtly as the years went on.   Yet even in this plate he gives the effect of lamp light — though with many lines and in his earliest manner, but rarely in his latest period did he etch nocturnes.   Two or three in Venice, and one or two in Holland and Belgium.

Even in this early plate from the *French Set* there is, with the scrawling sureness and freedom of line, the real etched lines, and each of the lines means something.   Yet it is not immaculate, perfect work like Meryon's, there is a big mess of foul biting in the foreground and there are passages of overbiting and underbiting all over the plate.   But Whistler with simple lines, though some are unnecessary and scrawled, got the effect of night, which he was after.   I do not know how this plate was bitten, but I imagine the whole subject was drawn, then the plate put in the bath and then when slightly bitten the lighter parts stopped out, bitten again, in the old fashioned way, the darks bitten the longest.

One of the best of Whistler's early plates from the *French Set*—records of a little town in what was then, and now is again, France—Alsace. These plates, his first, were, as all his work, all drawn on the spot, and etched better than any one had etched such things before, and, it may be news to moderns to know, that in France and England Whistler was ranked with Rembrandt, even from the beginning.

There is no meaningless scribbling on the house. Every line is expressive of plaster, of wood, of brick, you can't tell what Rembrandt's house by the mill is built of—of course this is rank treason— but it is a fact.

The shadows in *The Unsafe Tenement* are full of reflected lights and darks, and there is, save in the foreground, no scribbling and this is the remnant—the reminiscence of the Coast Survey days—a mannerism he outgrew, for he always went on growing, developing in his work.

His care for, and endeavour, to render the character of surfaces can be most plainly seen in the drawing and biting of each panel of the plaster on the walls, no two are alike, each is different, each is studied, and note also how the old tiled roof is drawn and modelled, yet it—save in the shadows —is all in outline.

From the very beginning with Whistler everything that was worth doing was worth doing well, and he etched even in the early days better than anyone had before him, yet technically he was only carrying on tradition.

WHISTLER: BLACK LION WHARF

Whistler used to say to me, "You like the plate better than I." I do like it, and he even was not ashamed of it—and no one in this world has approached it—how hard I tried years ago. But it is the most perfect of the London Series, done on the spot, and just like the place, only there is selection and arrangement in it all, though that is not evident, yet I know there is, for I know the spot, I shall never see again, another of the horrors of war. But Whistler has made this corner of Cherry Gardens live for ever. He told me he spent three weeks drawing on the plate. He spent most of a year down the river to learn it, but by this, the greatest rendering of the poor mean houses and the warehouses of London, this American gained immortality with Rembrandt and Hals and Velasquez — and the critics don't understand him yet in this country.

I have in the text pointed out how every line means plaster, bricks, wood, and tiles in every house on the other side of the river and how every line shows what the buildings are made of and how they were built.

And all over the plate the same simple vital expressive line is used, every line means something, and is drawn with a purpose. But how few see this or know it—especially the modern art student who is too blind to see, too lazy to learn. Whistler and Hokusai and all great artists, spent their whole lives, however, trying to learn to draw and regretting that they could not draw better.

But in this plate done by a young man of twenty-four there is wonderful drawing, biting, printing.

One authority solemnly has announced that Whistler exhausted all his blacks—put all the depth possible on the distant buildings and had no colour left for the foreground. That this was the artist's intention never occurred to the fool. Of its kind, this is the greatest etching in the world. Rembrandt never approached it. If Rembrandt's *Mill* (*B. 223*) is placed beside it, this will be proven. Whistler was always looking at Rembrandt, as he looked at and admired the Japanese, and admitted it ; it is only, as I have said, the little thief who denies he stole everything he has done. Whistler told me he took about three weeks over the *Black Lion Wharf*.

During the succeeding years came the bitten and dry point portraits. Here too he was consciously competing with the Dutchman and although not too much reliance or confidence should be placed in the sayings of most of Whistler's cataloguers, it is a fact that he praised and wrote the praise on the print—and for the life of me I cannot see why—of the portrait of *Clement de Jonghe* (*B. 272*)—for many another is finer. Rembrandt's portrait of his *Mother* (*B. 343*) in her widow's weeds is the finest of all. In nothing else does Rembrandt approach Whistler's portraits—nothing that has ever been done, is so beautiful as *Weary* (*M. 92*). In this, in the *Bibi Valentin* (*M. 50*), *Bibi Lalouette* (*M. 51*), the *Annie Haden in the Big Hat* (*M. 62*), there is a freedom in the few lines that Rembrandt never attained ; while if one compares the niggled, laboured, elaborated *Burgomeister Six* (*B. 285*) with *Finette* (*M. 58*), a similar design, those who can see, will see immediately, which artist was the greater etcher, but most will not see, or do not want to see, if they could, and the *Six* brings more money.

Again too in the *Annie Haden in the Big Hat*, which Whistler, this time rightly, thought one of his best plates, there is a largeness of design and drawing which gives the bit of copper, a foot high by little more than six inches wide, all the dignity of a full-length canvas. And one proof of the perfection of Whistler's work, is the wonderful way in which it stands enlargement. Rembrandt stands it too, and so do all other real etchers. There were for some years after these portraits, comparatively few plates by him, but amongst them is a most interesting one—*The Adam and Eve Old Chelsea* (*M. 172*). In this, one may see a further development ; here and there are the lines of the *Black Lion Wharf*, sharp, firm, defined, just as in that were a few of the West Point scribblings ; but now there is a further freedom—a painter-like quality that no one had even tried for previously—no one has succeeded in getting since.[1] Then too by this time he had learned to print. The first proofs were the work of Delâtre, by whose side Whistler stood, and on whose press he worked, before he had one of his own, and from whom he learned the art. It is said by those who either know nothing about the matter or conceal what they do know, that in his earliest and latest proofs there is no artificial printing, nothing but a clean wipe all over. There is the most complicated wiping, as a clean wiped proof by Goulding, and a proof of the same subject by Whistler, will show, if they are placed side by side.

---

[1] The latest attempt to deprive Whistler of his work is to say he derived much from Jacque. If this was so, and he copied Jacque's scrawling, it would account for the meaningless lines in his early plates—for all Jacque's line is meaningless.

He perfected his printing in the *First* and *Second Venice Series;* a few of these prints depend altogether on the printing—notably *Nocturne Shipping* (*M. 220*), and *Nocturne Palaces* (*M. 199*). The *Nocturne Palaces* is a very poor drawing, made into a fair etching by printing; the *Nocturne Shipping* is made up of but a few, a very few lines, well arranged, woven into a thing of beauty, by printer's ink, used like paint; it was rarely that he did depend on ink so much as in these plates, which are really monotypes; but he printed, that is painted, on the plates himself; each proof was a new problem, sometimes magnificent, sometimes a mess. There is nothing mechanical about any of the proofs, he did all the printing, each is different. One authority says "a night effect is given by extensive inking of the plate." The inking when right, was what he wanted when he got it. There is no parallel between such plates and the underdrawn, overbitten, badly inked, huge machines—the combined misdirected struggles of painters who can't etch, and printers who can't paint—performances, all as alike as two peas, all devoid of merit—save to the artless and the commercial collector. As someone has said of these affairs, if the paper was only good, one might cut off the edges to print on, but even it is not. The other plates in the two *Venice Series* are most of them triumphs of printing, notably *The Traghetto* (*M. 188*), and *The Beggars* (*M. 191*). The great deep rich shadows in each, would be a mass of scratches in any other printer's hands. The effect is altogether due to the printing by the artist, and there are half the lines in them that Rembrandt would have used. But the lines themselves are wonderful, not meaningless like Rembrandt's endless hatchings, and it is only that Whistler has strengthened and supported them by painting on them with ink—it is not the accidental smearing about of retroussage, but painting on the plate with an inky rag, and the palm of his hand, that has produced the effect—the effect he wanted and that is right—the man who does not obtain the effect he wants can't print—that is why he does not—and if his faked-up plate is pulled quite clean, it becomes evident that he can't draw or bite either. And the artist printer, too, must be able to follow his proofs, and improve on them, know how he made them, and repeat them. For as Whistler said, " if you don't know how you did a thing, and can't do it again if you want, what was the use of doing it at all."

Even more elaborate was the printing in some of the *Dutch Series* where the drawing and biting were more complicated. *The Embroidered Curtain, The Lace Curtain* (*M. 411*), for example. In this the lines are so close together that with the biting they almost collapsed apparently, bit almost all into a hole, but he stopped biting them at the right moment, and they gave the effect he wanted of old bricks and old woodwork. Only those of us who have tried to print such a plate know what care and labour are necessary to get any result save mud, or crudeness; but the average etcher knows nothing about that, he leaves the difficulty to the printer.

Later on Whistler depended less on printing, but the reason, unknown to those who have, with the least experience or knowledge, discussed this, and pointed out, that he eventually gave up the elaborate printing, that is, painting on the plate, is not the reason they allege—the real reason was he wanted to be more simple and trust more to the line

Nothing so beautiful, so weary, so true has been done in ancient or modern art as this dry point, a study of Jo Heffernan, Whistler's model, for the White Girls, and Courbet's also, and probably other artists'.   But this plate was most likely done when Jo, tired out, threw herself back and refused to pose any longer, and yet Whistler, never tired, always with so much more to do than he knew he ever could do, seized the chance and made another masterpiece.   Every line is vital and meaning and all show what they mean, the hair is golden and the bodice black—and the 1860 skirt conceals and reveals the figure in the great easy chair where Jo has sought rest.   It is in things like this that Whistler proves himself among the greatest of the great.

All is dry point commenced feverishly, on a handy plate, yet it may have taken days to finish, but "finished from the beginning"—that is, the momentary pose he saw accidentally taken, he has made to live forever; this is great art.

He probably with a very sharp point sketched in the whole subject, going over it most delicately, just caressing the copper in the lighter passages holding his point almost vertically; in the darker notes bearing on more heavily and inclining the point at a more or less acute angle so that as he scratched or rather dug a furrow in the copper with the point, a ridge of metal was thrown up at the side and the more the point was inclined, and the more it was dug into the plate, the bigger ridge of metal, the burr was thrown up, and it is this burr which holds the ink rather than the lines from which it is dug.   The heaviest work is in the background.   Often Whistler used old plates; look at the head at the bottom of this print which shows the way he started work and then for some reason discarded a plate.

J. M. N. WHISTLER: ANNIE HADEN IN THE BIG HAT. BITTEN LINE AND DRY POINT

Whistler always liked this plate and he was right. Every line tells and goes to make up a subject as fine in arrangement as anything in paint by Velasquez or Hals, an everlasting proof that one form of art in its finest flower, is as great as any other.

This plate is a specially good example of Whistler's care in placing a figure so that it shall tell to the best advantage. The whole subject stands, as he said it should, within the plate; this is the European convention known and understood by the great masters; in Japanese work the design is carried outside the frame; and the plate is also a refutation of the statement that the 1860 costume was inartistic. Compare the big flowing lines, the simple folds of the cloak, the clustering curls, the solemn face of his niece, whom he has immortalized, with the grinning, ogling, vulgar, strutting, muscley frumps, who smirk at you from the picture pages of the papers, to-day. The modern girl—a caricature—yes, compare her with this tranquil, beautiful creature—a girl—not a guy.

Note too the variety of handling, of line, of touch he has used in the different parts of the plate, yet they are all in harmony, all expressive.

There are a number of etchings of children by Whistler who used to say he "loved the babbies" and this plate with that of the other small child, *Bibi Lalouette,* are among the first he did in Paris, and are as good as any he ever did after.   It has been frequently said that he could not draw hands, yet this print shows he could, and give the weight of the small body supported by the hand ; it is all delightfully done even to the tiny tired bored little face.   There are also to be studied the various portraits of Annie Haden, and of the Leyland Children, as well as the exquisite little figures which appear in many of his many plates and give life and movement to them.

Probably drawn and bitten in his early manner, that is, all drawn on the plate at once and bitten from light to dark in the bath.   These early plates were mostly not printed by Whistler, but by Delâtre, from whom he learned printing.   These two French " Bibis " were children of his landlord and restaurant keeper in the Latin Quarter in Paris.

in his drawing as he did at the beginning, and so when he succeeded he did not need elaborate printing; but the failures he made are not recorded.

The reason is that he gave up making elaborate plates and used the fewest lines, and therefore simpler printing to show them. Anyone who knows Whistler's later work knows this. Look at the Belgian Set, *Brussels Series*, where all the elaborate buildings of the Grande Place are rendered with the fewest lines. *The Naval Review* (twelve, more or less, plates, done in a day: he had to do them in a day or not at all). The *Touraine Series*: again simplicity, directness, economy of work—he was travelling and sketching.

And the final *Paris Series* done standing in the streets. These were treated simply in line—therefore they were printed simply. As in his painting for several years before his death, he attempted, or rather finished, few large canvases, so in etching he attempted few elaborate plates; and the same is true of his lithographs,—save one of the last, *The Thames, Lithotint*, worked out of the window at the Savoy—where he had time but trouble; he adapted his method to his surroundings.

Now, these later etchings being drawn with few lines, he wanted those lines to tell; therefore they were, in a way, printed cleanly; but to say, as has been said, that he had renounced elaborate tone, and therefore all others should do so, is nonsense, the nonsense of the professor. The person who first made this pronouncement about the *Paris Series* only worked one morning with Whistler over these prints. And Whistler went to him as a good printer to see what was in the plates, for he thought them underbitten, yet he was afraid in this matter to trust his own press,—fearful that it was not powerful enough, and fearful also of having to reground, and so possibly ruin them. Truly a little experience is a dangerous thing. Another matter worth noting is that though every little Meryon, or penny Whistler, can either have all his works in series subscribed, or the single prints purchased before they are issued, or cornered—or underwritten, Whistler never found any dealer willing to issue any series after the Venice plates, and these did not sell for years, and as for the single plates, till almost his death there were plenty of unsold proofs in the studio; and of some of the later plates scarce any were printed by him, and the price for these Venetian masterpieces was about $7.50 each.

Another subject is Whistler's method of work. I know nothing about his earlier methods, but I do know his later ones because I worked with him. He usually, if possible, got someone to ground his plates—I grounded the last, and the ground came off, when he bit them. Whether this was owing to his taking them away before the ground was properly set, and packing them in his trunk, the change of temperature between London and Corsica, the acid he used, or that the ground was bad, I do not know—all artists have had such accidents. So far as I know, he only bit one or two plates; his Executrix must still have a number unbitten, or unprinted—at any rate unexhibited. Anyway I grounded them, and I believe he drew on them, and when I saw him at work, he usually drew on a number of plates before biting any, the artist always dreads the biting, and if he had known what we now know nothing would have gone wrong.

His method of drawing on the plate—"the secret of drawing" as he called it—was to fix on the copper, when grounded, the spot, or the subject, of greatest interest. This he drew first, making a little picture complete on the plate, but so placed that he could add to it the rest of the composition. Now as nothing can be added to the size of a plate or lithographic stone, as to paper or canvas, the artist is bound to think out his composition most carefully within certain fixed bounds, and to think how it shall be best placed on the printing surface. This is one of the most difficult things in Engraving. After Whistler got the "heart of his subject," as he called it, on the copper, he sometimes slightly bit it, sometimes drew the secondary portions around it, only enlarging the composition, which, as he said, "was finished from the beginning," and so he continued till the work was complete.

The drawing was done with a tiny double-ended steel point, made for him by an instrument maker in Paris.

The biting was, as I have seen it, most primitive. A small bottle of acid, nitric and water, was mixed. The plate was placed in a wash basin. I remember one Sunday summer afternoon in the *Rue du Bac*, he bit the copper plates in his garden, to escape the fumes of acid; and a few drops of acid and water were taken out of the bottle on a feather. With this feather dipped in the diluted acid the darkest parts of the design were painted, for he maintained that a drop, when it commenced to bite, was as strong as a puddle, and also he said that as the acid put on in this way had a tendency on the plate to gather in spots, by means of his feather he could coax and paint it about, both removing the bubbles, which form over the lines, and making the biting varied.

By means of the feather too he dragged the acid around and removed it from, or painted it for a moment, on delicate passages, and so got over, to a great extent, stopping out—at that time a most difficult operation. He took ordinary stopping-out varnish and thinned it with turpentine, and painted over the parts he thought enough bitten, with a camel's hair brush dipped in the mixture; but although it worked fairly well and dried pretty quickly, the turpentine destroyed the ground under it, the varnish was supposed to protect, and this was a cause of great trouble, the ground coming off sometimes in those places it was intended to preserve. He also between the bitings drew with his tiny needle on the plate. These needles he carried in his pocket in a little silver case. The ground was bad on all these plates, and broke up. His methods of printing I don't think were much changed from those taught him by Delâtre; the plate either hot or cold as it required, was wiped either with the hand, or rag, so as to get the best result. He was not tied to any method—all he wanted was the best proof he could pull, and he was the best printer who ever lived, of his own work, and he never, so far as I know, printed anyone else's.

He had no secrets. "The secret," as he used to say, "was in doing it."

Whistler put the ink on with a dabber, often working it into the lines with his fingers. Instead, however, of roughly wiping the ink off all over, as the printer does, without regard to the design, he coaxed it off the plate, playing with it, getting a lighter tone on some parts than others, either with a rag or his hand, which he cleaned on the shoulder of his blouse. This spot grew into an epaulette of ink. He was longer over the wiping than any professional, and when either all over, or in parts, the plate took on

Of this plate it should be said, as Whistler said of Rembrandt's *Clement de Jonghe*, "without flaw, beautiful as a Greek marble or a canvas by Tintoret, a masterpiece in all its elements beyond which there is nothing." This is a true definition of Etching, because it maintains the fact that Etching ranks with Sculpture, Painting and Drawing—is one of the arts and the equal of them. And when he says "without flaw a masterpiece in all its elements" he describes *The Bridge*.

For perfect expression, by the simplest, fewest, yet most expressive lines, this is one of the greatest works of art in the world, only equalled by other plates by Whistler. I know these are strong words, and I know most to-day, are afraid to have the courage of their opinions — usually the opinions of others — but Whistler is the greatest etcher who ever lived. I have always known this, always said so, and I shall continue to say so as long as I live. And why is *The Bridge* a great masterpiece? Because every line in it is exquisitely drawn, exquisitely arranged, exquisitely bitten, exquisitely printed. There is the story in the plate, of the life on the little canals. Those who know them, know that that life, that movement, that architecture is perfectly expressed.

To begin with the sandolas are being rowed home. You know this because in the bow of the nearest lies a boy asleep, tired out after a night's fishing. The line of the boat carries into the design and this is continued by the line of the reflections of the shadow of the bridge. Then the railing of that carries the eye back and up the riva to the group of houses in the distance, "the heart of the picture," as Whistler called it. Every line is placed with the utmost thought and care and observation. Note how the reflections are not only studied under the bridge, but also how Whistler has studied the breaking up of them, by the wake of the boat, which has just passed through the shadow and these ripples also carry the eye into the design. How carefully the clothes are arranged on the railing, hung out to dry, and how full of character is every one of the figures loafing or going about their business! And the drawing of the poor, mean houses is marvellous, and the line on which the composition is based leads past the houses, to the trees in the extreme distance. This use of line to carry the eye into a composition, is not the property of Whistler — Ruskin points it out in connection with Turner, devoting much space to the subject and illustrating it with diagrams. And to explain what I mean I have drawn one which I hope explains itself and shows the way in which the lines carry the eye into the composition.

The Doorway is amongst the greatest of Whistler's triumphs, the exquisite suggestion of the time and water-worn stone, the rusting wrought-iron work, the dim interior of the palace turned shop and work room, and the amazing printing make this in their perfect combination a great technical masterpiece of etching.

It was the correct thing with critics to say that Whistler could not draw architecture, was afraid to try. But as he himself would say " why repeat a masterpiece ". That he rendered great buildings he proved in *The Palaces* and *The Salute* and that he understood detail is shown in this plate which, like the others, was published in the *Venice Sets*.

The difference of stone and iron is lovingly studied and perfectly expressed and note how all the crumbling flower-like decorations have rather become like butterflies and how *The Butterfly* harmonizes with them.

In the original, the interior is but a mystery in the shadows drawn with the utmost elaboration—while to get the effect of the reflections—he gives up drawing with the point to concentrate the eye on the architecture and draws the water with printers' ink, the most perfect printing that was ever done, all the water is painted on the plate with a rag and ink. This plate was bitten, not in a bath, but, so I have been told, by drops of acid poured on it and then painted about with a feather, the acid left longer where the darks were wanted, brushed away for the lights; this method gives the endless variety of the surface of the plate from the greatest delicacy of the shadowed interior to the overbiting under the windows. The grace of the figure is adorable.

WHISTLER : THE RIVA
DUVENECK : THE RIVA

J. M. N. WHISTLER : THE RIVA.   F. DUVENECK : THE RIVA. BOTH BITTEN LINE

Whistler's *Riva* is one of the most Venetian of the Venetian Series—a study of the Riva Schiavoni from his window in Venice.   Every figure is full of life and character, and so is every building and every boat. Duveneck's *Riva* is one of the plates which were attributed to Whistler, and although the subject is the same the difference in the two men's handling is perfectly evident.   But it is most interesting to compare the different way in which the two artists worked, and worked about the same time. Duveneck etched this subject from the balcony of the Casa Kirsch where he lived and Whistler etched the Riva from the Casa Jankovitz where he lodged, high up, looking out also on the Lagoon, and it is quite probable that Duveneck showed the plate to Whistler and he saw how fine the subject was and did it from his own rooms in his own way ; it is equally probable that the reverse is the case, no one will ever know, no one ever did know, save Otto Bacher, and he forgot to tell. There is, however, no resemblance in style, handling, biting or printing in the two American Etchers' works, as these reproductions prove.   Haden and Legros knew this perfectly well, but anything was good enough then to try to kill Whistler, and this endeavor to belittle him goes on still.   The two prints are remarkable proof that when artists etch the same subject they must put their character, their individuality into their work, and etching is the method by which this can be done.

a golden glow, and when finally he could see his face in it as in a mirror, he folded up in his hand a soft ink-charged rag, and, not like the printer with his clean silk, wiping the ink out of the lines, wiped more ink into them and on to the surface, painted the plate with the ink-soaked rag. That was the only special thing I ever saw him do, but it is the basis of his printing, and no professional printer knows of it, or could do it if he did. Even Goulding admitted Whistler's mastery, and said that Whistler was a better printer than he, which was really a tribute from Goulding.

As to trials and states of Whistler's plates, some of the cataloguers have found as many as ten or a dozen states of some of them. Now the facts are these. As Whistler pulled a proof and lifted it off the press, he looked lovingly over it, as carefully as every printer etcher does, and if he saw in any part a line too strong, he scraped or burnished it; if too weak, he added to it with dry point; and this went on, whenever I was with him, with almost every proof. Rightly speaking, in most of Whistler's plates, there are no real states at all—that is in the sense that Rembrandt made states. Rembrandt took out whole sections of a design and replaced them by another composition; this is a genuine state, done for, mostly, the genuine collector's delight. It is rare indeed that Whistler did anything of the sort, or made changes so sweeping, for example, as those in *The Beggars*. This and *The Traghetto* as published, are new plates. What he did was to try to improve the design and the print; and I have heard him say, after pulling a first proof: "I don't like that, but someone will because it is the first," and he wrote "first proof" on it. The plate was then taken up and lines with dry point added or with scraper taken away. If these are states, I believe of some of the first series of Venice plates, instead of a dozen as the cataloguers find, there are seventy-five, in the hundred pulled. Again, some of these people solemnly criticize dry point, which is not strong enough, or which has had the burr scraped off, as a late state because of the appearance—not aware that if Whistler did not like the burr he removed it, as all artists do before printing—not aware that dry point may be added to. The compiler of a catalogue is a dangerous person to lean upon for artistic facts.

Whistler always used old paper, and in his hunt for it he hesitated at nothing—no price was too high for it, no search too long. I made a find with him once at Fontainebleau of two folio volumes, with pressed flowers in them; the paper was of no use to the dealer, the flowers of no use to us. But we eventually got the books, but the dealer got her price. As he knew the value of the paper, he did not waste it, cutting it near to the size of the plate; then he trimmed the edges, leaving in later years the little protecting tab, with the butterfly and imp, on it alone.

There is no question that cut down proofs look better than those with margins; the untouched, unprinted paper is distracting, and often cockles, and mounts are rarely satisfactory; but there is also no doubt that trimmed prints are easily ruined; there is nothing to hold them by save the print itself when unmounted, and damage or tears occur to the cut-down print, when a margin would save it.

He trimmed the prints after they were dry; he took them from the press, placed each between a folded sheet of blotting paper, and threw them on the floor, changing the

J. M. N. WHISTLER: THE BEGGARS: EARLY STATE   BITTEN LINE

It was in plates like this, *The Traghetto*, and *Nocturne Shipping* that Whistler carried his system of printing further than any one else.   Not only is there in the dark archway the same elaborate, but much freer work than Rembrandt put in the *Burgomeister Six*.   But Whistler added richness by covering the lines, painting on them a tone of ink and so obtained a quality and depth that no one had achieved before, scarce attempted.   In the *Nocturne Shipping* the whole effect is got by painting ink on the plate.   The lines are few and not very well done, but the painting has brought the design together.   In *The Beggars* there were many lines and close and they would have been hard and dry if Whistler had not bathed them with color and brought them all together by his wonderful printing in the manner and by the method which I have explained.

It is most interesting to compare Rembrandt's *Beggars at the Door of a House*, or any of his other beggars with this plate.   Both artists were perfectly independent of each other in treatment of their subject and in handling.   But both have made great etchings of the same subject.

There are said to have been two plates, each made of *The Beggars* and *The Traghetto*, and Otto H. Bacher, in *With Whistler in Venice* describes how they were done.   At any rate there are enormous differences and I am willing to take Bacher's statement, as this would have been easier than to make the changes.   To show these changes I have included early and late states of the plate.

THE BEGGARS: LATE STATE

This is the final state of *The Beggars* and shows how Whistler developed the Venetian plates from ghosts to realities—as is proven by comparing the two states but this was not done as Bracquemond did it deliberately, but experimentally by Whistler, he carried on in every way he could, always experimenting—as Bacher says, making in this case a new plate—at any rate changing it completely—but always trying to get what he wanted though he did not always know how to get it.

Bracquemond knew how to do it—and did it—apparently with ease—Whistler with difficulty—but Whistler worked things out and eventually succeeded in making a great work of art as this is.

Bacher, in his book *With Whistler in Venice*, says, or I understand him to say, that Whistler inked the plate and *The Traghetto* with white ink or paint and either pulled a proof of it and transferred that while wet to the new grounded plate, or ran the inked first plate laid face downward on the second plate through the press, and then went over the lines with a point, making what changes he wished.   I regret Whistler never said anything to me about the method he used.   If he did make two plates, these prints are both from the same copper.

NOTE: For illustrations see two following pages.

blotters every day. Once a charwoman threw away a whole set of Venice proofs without looking in the blotters. When sufficiently dry he trimmed them with a pair of scissors, following round the plate mark just outside it. Mr. Menpes says that he cut the edges, after placing a sheet of glass over the print, with a razor. I never saw him do so.

There was still another reason for trimming. In some matters of printing he was like all of us—who are not professional printers—not quite sure of himself, and at times, as this old paper is often brittle or soft, the edge of the plate when going through the press, cut the paper in places right through; the edges then have to be trimmed, or the paper patched up—a vile practice which leaves marks. And also he at times would get creases in the print caused by the blankets, or the paper not being perfectly wet, or flat or slipping, and after the print is pressed these show as white lines and nothing can be done with them save by painting or drawing over them—and this shows, so he let them alone. Had he, however, been a perfect mechanical printer, a perfect master of the professional side of printing, he would most likely have been a poor etcher. He often on his proofs wrote his own opinion of them in a word or more, and on specially good ones at times, on the backs, put, in a circle, little letters or numbers signifying that he was pleased with them.

I have gone at some length into this discussion of Whistler's work because I know how he worked, and a personal statement of this sort is worth any amount of theory, and posthumous history, and I have stated facts concerning the man and his work which I know.

I had something to do with making the world, which laughed at and despised Whistler, admit its blunders and errors, and acknowledge him to be the greatest master of modern time, that is something I am proud of. The world now admits his greatness, I always said he was the greatest etcher of all time, his work proves it.

Finally every etching by Whistler is a direct study from nature of something seen —which could only be rendered by etching. And such work alone is etching, and in real, vital, genuine etching James M. N. Whistler is the greatest artist who ever lived.

REMBRANDT: AMSTERDAM
WHISTLER: ZAANDAM

REMBRANDT : AMSTERDAM.   WHISTLER : ZAANDAM.   BOTH BITTEN LINE

These two plates show the two great artists' methods of work, and they might almost have been done sitting back to back on the same spot—for I have seen the place and worked there myself—on the spot where the etchings must have been done.   The plate is a fair comparison of the two men's methods.

REMBRANDT was a great artist, but he is now a great bogey. Rembrandt made the biggest plates in the past, the only prints that brought a high price, and that is one of the reasons why he is considered such a great etcher to-day, why he was respected in his own day. Carry out the same comparison now. Who is the greater artist—Whistler, or the dealer who runs the hack, who hires the printer, who pulls the biggest and the most expensive copper plates? Rembrandt was fully alive to the importance of proofs, states, dealers, and collectors: he was in these matters most modern, or the moderns are most imitative. Rembrandt's best plates are his smallest—in fact most of his large compositions are only etchings in name; they are magnificent, some of them, but they are not etchings, in the true sense. They are mostly machines and pot boilers.

I will again define an etching as an impression set down on a copper plate from nature or life—not a built up, elaborated composition. Rembrandt sometimes reproduced his own compositions. Whistler never did. That, as Whistler said, "was as impossible as for the hen to lay the same egg twice."

But Rembrandt did make magnificent pot boilers by etching. Whistler did not. It is said Whistler could not: he never tried, for he knew such things were not etchings, they were machines by which Rembrandt gained his living. Rembrandt knew it too, but apparently they paid. Yet Whistler also had money troubles.

Whistler has stated it all so clearly in the Propositions:

"The huge plate is an offence."

I do not mean to say that Rembrandt's plates, the huge ones, are offences, and I do not think Whistler referred to him, but they are not spontaneous vital expressions. Whistler was, when he wrote the Propositions, referring to the huge manufactured machines, then coming into vogue, with which the world is to-day flooded.

Now Frank Duveneck working with Whistler and Otto Bacher, while they were all in Venice, 1879–1880, did make some very large plates, but Duveneck's were all done from nature, and I believe mostly made on zinc; they are but little known, but several of them are very fine: the only very large plates that I know which really are fine. Over these plates, when shown for the first time in London, there was the usual row kicked up, this time by Haden and Legros, from which, as may be read in *The Gentle Art*, the "enemies" did not emerge with much distinction. Whistler was accused of having made the etchings and signed them with Duveneck's name; there is not the faintest resemblance to Whistler's work, but despite their size, owing to the fact that they were done from nature, they are fine, and two or three of them are of very great merit, especially *The Rialto* looking under the arch, and the *Ca d'Oro* from across the canal; but there is no suggestion of Whistler in them, either in the subjects of most, or the handling of any, nor do they technically approach Whistler.

As to Rembrandt's large plates, nearly all of them religious subjects, they are fine; but in the sense of real etching, they are not etchings. They were published as religious prints and to that class of work they belong, and not to original spontaneous etching.

The finest portrait Rembrandt ever did is that of his *Mother* (B. *343*). This is exquisite. It is extraordinary that Whistler never etched his mother, or rather failed in the single attempt he made to do so.

As I have said, I do not place the *Clement de Jonghe* (B. *272*) so high, by any means, amongst Rembrandt's portraits of men, as Whistler did. On a proof owned by Mr. Wrenn of Chicago, Whistler wrote: "Without flaw! Beautiful as a Greek marble or a canvas by Tintoret; a masterpiece in all its elements, beyond which there is nothing."

Far finer are the—as I have said—exquisite *Mother* (B. *343*), the *Young Man Musing* (B. *269*); but how much better the latter would have been had the badly drawn black arm been omitted, and the meaningless shadow behind left out. It is the same as with Van Dyck's wonderful heads just sketched in, all ruined by the mechanical human machine that got hold of them afterwards and finished them in every sense. The *Rembrandt Leaning on a Stone Sill* (B. *21*) seems to me with its great simplicity of line, yet great richness of colour, one of the best of his own numerous portraits. Curious is the *Bust of Rembrandt when a Young Man* (B. *338*), for a curious reason, a large part is drawn with a multiple, or double needle point, described in the technical chapter (Etching Needles); by the use of this needle he has got a brush-like quality in the coat and background.

Though much more elaborate, good too are the *Juan Lutma* (B. *276*) and *Arnoldus Tholinx* (B. *284*), but they too would have been better with half the work omitted; doubtless the sitters made him put it in, though I am not sure, for in his own portrait, *Rembrandt Etching* (B. *22*), there is the same over-elaboration; but after all, when one has gone over these things it becomes evident that his *Mother's Portrait* (B. *343*) is the best, and that is not so good as Whistler's *Annie*. The nudes, mostly clumsy, do not interest me, and I do not think an original etcher or engraver ever has rendered satisfactorily a nude figure, at any rate not since Mantegna and Dürer.

Of all Rembrandt's Landscape Etchings I believe the literary authorities pronounce the *Three Trees* (B. *212*) to be the finest—it is one of the worst; it is an over-elaborated, faked up, unspontaneous bit of story-telling. There are only two things in it worth study: the distant fields with their finely arranged lines and spaces; and this I imagine is the only part of the plate done from nature, one of the only portions certainly, with real feeling in it,—probably there was another subject done on the same plate,— while the trees, stories, and storm are an afterthought. And the other bit is the rain. There is a curious thing about that. Rembrandt has rendered a rain-storm, with the same convention as the Japanese, or what is probable, the Japanese stole the convention from him. Yet no authority has noted it. Besides there are the clouds, fine clouds, but put in with no relation to the design or atmospheric conditions, for they are flying each every which way. As to the endless stories, anecdotes, and occurrences in the shadows, I am not sure whether they were added as a concession to contemporary collectors (as Turner did for the pen makers, Ruskin, and the pill people) or whether this,

Duveneck was one of those rarest of artists who attempted etching once, and succeeded in making good plates, and so did he attempt painting, and succeed in making good pictures, but he kept on with his painting, though he never surpassed his early, his earliest works. Many are the contemporaries of Duveneck who have, as etchers, eclipsed him in popularity; no one has approached him in beauty and meaning of line. Bauer, whose large plates mostly, surely are an offence, has been boomed, Duveneck ignored; both were big artists. Duveneck was far the bigger etcher—and he is scarce known even among artists, and when he was given a gallery at the San Francisco Exhibition in 1915, and filled it with his paintings, etchings, and sculpture, scarce any of his American colleagues, of the younger generation, had seen his work or heard his name, but he was not a best seller, and a best prize winner—the standards of American art—but just an artist who had done what he wanted in his own way and for his own pleasure. Duveneck's interest in etching was inspired by Otto Bacher, one of his pupils in Munich, Venice, and Florence, for Duveneck, going to Munich to study painting, found shortly that he was a master, and hailed by the professors as the modern Rembrandt. He and Chase were there together studying. At the end of a few years Chase had, or soon after he returned, attracted to his studio, as pupils, all the young lady amateurs and a few artists of the country. Duveneck drew to Munich most of the artists who to-day have done the best art work in America.

In Venice he took up etching in the late seventies, I believe before Whistler went there, at the suggestion of Bacher, doubtless. Whistler was a far greater influence after his arrival—and a number of plates of the city were done by Duveneck. They were all made out of doors, mostly on zinc, and bitten in a primitive fashion—in one, he told me, the acid made a large hole before he learned how to control it —all were printed on an old press, with a wooden plank bed—which Dürer may have used, when in the city; and I have no doubt it served Canaletto, and Whistler certainly pulled proofs on it. I worked on it once. It should better have been preserved than many of the objects in the museums of Venice. When Duveneck's proofs were pulled they were sent to London, to the first, or an early, exhibition of the Painter Etchers, but before being shown they fell into the clutches of Haden, Legros and a Mr. Drake, the Secretary of the Painter Etchers, all eager to demolish Whistler, and these plates were pronounced to be by Whistler, but signed by this false name Duveneck. Whistler was breaking his contract with the Fine Art Society, who had sent him to Venice and paid him 1000 guineas for twelve plates and he was making more plates to make more money. However, the authorities only made themselves ridiculous. But Duveneck's plates, abominably printed, were the success of the season; later I induced Keppel to print a number of them decently, and this *Rialto* is one. It is in the Avery collection in the New York Public Library. It is a genuine etching, every line is vital, the point of view is personal, and the arrangement individual, and this is the case with all the rest. Only in one or two, so far as I remember, is there in composition any similarity to Whistler's work. Those are of the Riva, and I am not sure that Duveneck did not make his plates before Whistler came to Venice; at any rate, he showed them before Whistler exhibited his. Duveneck, so far as I know, only worked for a short period in Florence and Venice at etching, but this *Rialto* and his *Desdemona's House* and the *Ca' d'Oro* are masterpieces. He too discovered the beauty of the flag poles in front of St. Mark's, with their floating, flaming banners swung up on a festa. There are two *Rivas* by each artist, similar, as I have said, in being taken from an upper window, the window of the rooms where both artists lived, and which gave on that wonderful, ever changing, ever moving life of the city. A few by Duveneck were done on the Zattere, and by the Dogana, and one or two in Florence, they are masterpieces. But Duveneck found it easier to teach, than to paint or etch. Chase found it paid better, yet he painted more and more and made some plates as well. Duveneck for years did little and showed less—fell out of sight in this country—lived his own life, in his own city, in his own way, beloved and respected by all who knew him—and then just before his death found himself a great man—to the little men in American art, as he always had been to those who knew. I had, as Chairman of the International Jury of Awards for Engraving, at the Panama-Pacific Exhibition, the honor of proposing a special medal for these etchings being awarded Duveneck—as he was a member of the Jury he was *hors concours*. Immediately the painters and sculptors took up the idea, though they would not have dared to propose him, and Duveneck had his reward and came into his own in his own country. There is a collection of Duveneck's Etchings in the Cincinnati Art Museum, but I do not know of any other complete one.

REMBRANDT: THE MILL

The only really good landscape and architectural subject Rembrandt ever did — and yet this does not for a moment compare with Whistler's *Unsafe Tenement* or numbers of the *Thames Series* — but Rembrandt is a fetish and it is treason to criticise him and his work.   W. M. Chase used to say he was sure the Dutchman was a Jew, and there are certain things about his work which seem to prove it.   But if the drawing of the tiles on the roof of the house is compared with those on the roof of *The Unsafe Tenement* or *Black Lion Wharf,* all who can see, will see, who is the more expressive etcher, and this is true of all the two men's works.   Half the time Rembrandt don't get the strength he wants, and to get it scribbles over the weak spots and shadows with meaningless lines ; look on the roof of the house, the shaded side of the mill and the shadows under it, and I never saw in Holland a mill with sails like this.   Still it is far the best thing in architecture Rembrandt ever did and the little bit of the big dyke is good too.   And there is another thing about this plate ; it is so far as I know the first example of Work being used as a subject in art and for its own sake, not as an adjunct or background.   Rembrandt was the first of artists to see and render the Wonder of Work.

The biting is very good and direct, probably Rembrandt built a wall of wax around the edges of the plate, that seems to have been the original fashion as may be seen in Bosse's treatise on engraving. Then when the wax was hard and water proof, acid was poured all over the plate and the wax acted like a dyke, there was a sort of a spout modelled at one corner to pour the acid off, when the plate was sufficiently bitten to stop out, and the process of pouring on acid, letting it bite and stopping out till the greatest darks were obtained, by the longest biting, was the method of the past — But we have changed all that.

Whether Rembrandt used the Dutch Mordant, a mixture of acids, or nitric I do not know.   The Dutch Mordant bites very slowly, turns the lines black, does not give off bubbles, but in its way works very well.   The Dutch Mordant made today is much better in every way.

Rembrandt's best portrait, for he like Whistler, loved to make his " mummie look as nice as possible." Whistler failed and had the sense to destroy the plate he attempted; Rembrandt succeeded and the old woman lives forever — a son's tribute to his mother and his art. Still, fine as it is Whistler's other portraits are better as etchings for he got his effect with fewer lines. Rembrandt has rendered admirably the wrinkled old time worn face, and the tired hands, but he has so much cross hatching on the dress to show it is black, that he has lost many of the vital lines with which he must have commenced the figure, but he has well distinguished between the textures of the lace, the cap, the shawl, and the dress.

REMBRANDT: THE GOLD
WEIGHER'S FIELD

REMBRANDT: THE GOLD WEIGHER'S FIELD. BITTEN LINE AND DRY POINT

The greatest of Rembrandt's landscapes — the only one — for save that of *The Mill* and bits of some of the others, the distance in the *Three Trees*, there is nothing to approach it, by him. It, in its way, is perfect in every part, and every line has meaning. If you are not able to see this — to feel that each line delights you, expresses the lay of the land, the undulations of the ground and that there is not a wrong line in it — and that a surveyor could work from the print — well you can't — and it doesn't matter — but the plate is a master work — Rembrandt's greatest landscape.

Various authorities and various artists have asserted that this plate is dry point with the burr taken off, others that it is bitten. I believe it is the latter with dry point added.

REMBRANDT : SIX BRIDGE

This reproduction confirms everything I have said of this plate.   There is no reason to take it seriously — Rembrandt did not do so himself — I am sure — so why should we allow respectable antiquity to overpower us, or even modern critics' estimates?   The plate is poor.   If done by an amateur, and an amateur could do it just as well, it would be dismissed with contempt.   But it is by Rembrandt, or is said to be, and so it must be taken seriously; it is this preposterous praise of rubbish which has bred anarchy in art.

From the story, which is told in the book, it must be evident that Rembrandt did not take it seriously.   Why should we?   It is bad and so are most of his landscape etchings.

REMBRANDT: BEGGARS AT THE DOOR OF A HOUSE. BITTEN LINE

When Rembrandt wanted to, he could do things; and in this plate, he — in his own way, and in his own time — rivals Whistler's *Soupe à Trois Sous* or *The Longshoremen;* both artists were doing the people of their day and generation, and they have made the people live when peace congresses and Leagues of Nations have let them die and rot, or make fools of themselves.

Another plate of Whistler's which may be more appropriately compared, though in subject only, with this is *The Beggars* of the *Venice Set.*   Technically, however, the other two mentioned are more similar to Rembrandt's work.

Even this fine plate may only have been worked on by Rembrandt, there is so much unlike him about it — Especially if the rotten *Six Bridge* is by him — and that is not so bad as lots of his other signed landscapes — but a signature is the easiest thing to forge.

like some of his other plates, is a worked up Siegers plate bought at that artist's sale, or as I have said a faked up thing of his own. As to the absurdity of the whole storm effect, Michel describes the rain as coming on, Binyon as passing away, Hamerton says nothing, Hind hedges, Haden says the "Sky (is) full of angels' wings"—a perfect proof that Rembrandt's "greatest" etching is an utter fiasco in really rendering a dramatic effect. In fact there are not more than six, out of his twenty-six (I believe) landscapes that are worth much artistically. *The Gold Weigher's Field* (B. *234*) is very fine, the finest of all, for here Rembrandt was drawing the lines of the fields, the distance, getting perspective, trying to put down what he really saw, what really interested him, not telling a story. So too in the foreground of the *Amsterdam* (B. *210*) there is fine work, but the distance is poor, mean, hard, and crowded. I have put it and Whistler's *Amsterdam* on the same page as proof. The big tree in the *Omval* (B. *209*) is wonderfully drawn, but the rest of the plate is worthless. Most of the farms, barns, and towers are perfunctory, clumsy, full of meaningless lines, put in any way; if one has a rabbit in one proof, that ruins the rest of the plate, that is the state to be sought for — the fact that Rembrandt knew it was bad and scraped the rabbit out, doesn't matter, but the hunt for the rabbit proof does. So too with the *Hog* (B. *157*), as Hamerton points out. This was done on a big plate, intended for something else, and cut down at once, yet the collector regards the white untouched paper as of more value—cash value— than Rembrandt's work on the corner of it.

Then there is the *Six Bridge* (B. *208*),—a missing pepper pot, mustard tin, bottle of schnapps, or salt cellar at dinner-time; Rembrandt was visiting Six; the Burgomaster must be amused, so Rembrandt makes a bet he can do a plate before they are found. He, the Burgomaster, seems to have lived on the very side of the road, anyway they were dining in the gutter. There is a copper on the premises. The story-telling historians should have added grounded. It is drawn on, probably with a fork, bitten in with vinegar and printed from, before the schnapps is brought; either the servant was slow or it is a yarn—as bad a one anyway as the plate; and when Rembrandt was visiting Six he evidently carried his printing press in his pocket—another detail omitted by the historians. Yet all the authorities take story and plate seriously, and all blither seriously about a print that could have been done by any of the pupils—and probably was—to play up to the story. To go carefully over the print is to prove this. The authorities rave over the "pure line"—trying to be on the right side. The line is pure enough, that is bitten, but look at the trees on the left—the foliage scribbled in, while it is impossible to tell on which side of the stream they are growing. The drawing of the grass and weeds on the right is characterless; the boat is careless beyond words; the bridge is well drawn; the distant trees without form. Rembrandt has got the flat distance, but it does not equal any number of other of his plates of the flat country. Compare with it, for example, *The Gold Weigher's Field*, that I have mentioned, in which every line has a meaning and it is pure line too; it makes no difference, however, whether the line is pure, the critics mean bitten not dry point—the all-important thing is: is the line good? is it expressive? is it absolutely necessary? No critic knows or could know. In the *Omval*, which too is pure line, there is a nasty black hole in the left-hand corner, put in to draw attention to the little scene under the trees, all out of scale however—probably another subject which the old story-teller did not want to waste and so drew the design around it for the dealer and the clients. Some people say Rembrandt was a Jew, which would account for things, but his art is against this. But the best of all, far the best, is *The Gold Weigher's Field;* and I return to it, again and again; here Rembrandt really did try, here every line and every spot is right and full of meaning, and indispensable; it is the best landscape he ever did, and that is enough, and it is safe to study from. It is the one plate that approaches Whistler's many.

The Mills disappear in mannerisms when compared with Whistler's. Compare the *Mill* (*B. 233*) with Whistler's *Black Lion*—only there is no comparison.

There was one other crime that Rembrandt committed—and in the case of such a great artist to be inartistic is a crime—and that was to make an oval line across the top of his plates utterly destroying the shape of the design already fixed by the straight plate mark, or to make an oval frame on the plate itself, a sheer vulgarity; it is incredible that he should have done so; it is comic to see little Rembrandts carefully prigging his artless trick, though they struggle vainly and clumsily to imitate his art.

Rembrandt's Beggars are most of them most interesting and evidently done straight from life, and the most elaborate,—*Beggars at the Door of a House* (*B. 176*),—is one of the best, but the numerous single figures are brim full of character as well as delightful in line. Of Rembrandt it may well be said in Whistler's words: "The man who can draw anything can draw everything," and his *Hog* and *Shell* are most interesting, but even more interesting is it to find Whistler competing with him in his *Dog on the Kennel* (*M. 18*) and the *Wine Glass* (*M. 27*). Yet here is just the difference: Haden imitated Rembrandt's handling and style: Whistler evolved a style of his own and applied it at times to subjects somewhat similar to Rembrandt's; he was carrying on tradition, Haden only imitating. This *Wine Glass*, and the drawings by Whistler in Sir Henry Thompson's Catalogue of a *Collection of Blue and White Nankin Porcelain* prove that Whistler practised what he preached. Compare the laborious way in which Jacquemart works to get his glass, with Whistler's simplicity. Buhot is to be studied for this too. Whistler got the feeling, the quality of things, as well as their surface and detail; Jacquemart only got the last and least.

To return again and finally to Rembrandt's large plates and his subject etchings, I should be a fool to say the *Christ presented to the People* (*B. 76*), *The Three Crosses* (*B. 78*), *Wedding of Jason* (*B. 112*) are not fine : they are. But I also say that these plates were an attempt on Rembrandt's part to substitute for religious engravings, religious etchings, and fine as they are, they are not genuine artist's etchings but worked up compositions. Rembrandt, in every way, even though he did go bankrupt, was a clever man of business, and from the beginning was always exploiting his prints, producing states, and so running up prices as in the *Hundred Guilders Print* (*B. 74*)—even the title proves this. And he did endless work in scraping out; re-drawing and re-biting never seem to have bothered him; probably the pupils did the scraping; and even from the

REMBRANDT: CHRIST
PRESENTED TO THE PEOPLE

REMBRANDT: CHRIST PRESENTED TO THE PEOPLE. BITTEN LINE. PROBABLY ALSO DRY POINT AND BURIN

This is the best by far as an etching, the best of Rembrandt's big plates, and the best state of it. He repeatedly changed it all about, but it is made up of fewer, more vital, more meaning lines, than any of the others of his large plates. It is a masterpiece and it is one of the plates by which Rembrandt lives. It is a large plate but not an offence.

The character in each of the figures is marvellous, and they are in this state mostly in outline, but there is endless variety in the outline, from the strength at the sides to the delicacy in the centre, and this arrangement brings the whole composition together.

Another interesting matter about this composition is that Rembrandt did not go to Jerusalem for his Jews or his architecture, but used the buildings and the people and the costumes about him, there is nothing of Palestine in the plate, it is all Amsterdam. I am not defending this sort of faking. I only want to point out that Rembrandt did it, but it was the custom of his time and all previous time. It is only we moderns who have become accurate topographically and historically, but we have advanced little artistically. The old men etched as they wanted and the people accepted their work; now the people tell painters how to work and the painters accept their piffle, we are dominated by Cook's Tours, college culture and photographs.

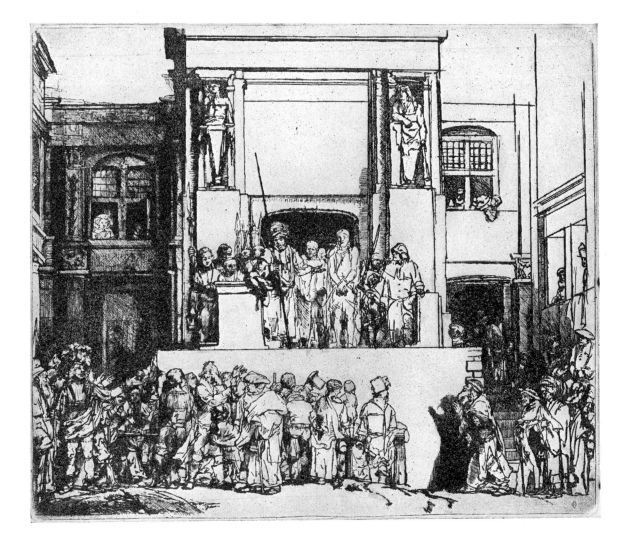

REMBRANDT: THE
THREE CROSSES

REMBRANDT: THE THREE CROSSES. BITTEN LINE AND DRY POINT

The *Christ Presented to the People* is the best of Rembrandt's simple machines — this *Three Crosses* is the best of the complicated ones; he has carried light and shade in this print and in the various versions of it to the utmost limits; it is magnificent and it is art — but it is not spontaneous etching like *The Beggars* and *The Gold Weigher's Field*. They are greater etchings than this. It is more impressive and imposing — they are more subtle, more restrained, more what etchings should be — they are truer than this.

But technically in drawing, in biting and especially in arrangement of the composition and in the light and shade it is magnificent and this is the finest, simplest state.

Curiously too there is an attempt at Oriental and Roman costume in the figures, but they are not half so good as those which he has seen and drawn in the *Christ Presented to the People*. This attempt is a worse fake than the other, doubtless a critic made him do it.

first, as Michel says, his plates were valued as much for their rarity, as their art. He was the first etcher, probably, to print his own plates with tones, and in the large proofs there is as much printing and painting with ink as he knew how to put there. It is quite true that the landscapes and little portraits and figures seem to have been very cleanly wiped, but as Goulding once told me, he had found on proofs he had printed twenty-five years before a fine layer of powder instead of the tone he had put there, and when he dusted it off, the lines sharp and clear stood up, the tone in ink having dried up on the surface of the paper and not sunk in, and then turned to dust. How do we know the same thing has not happened to Rembrandt after three hundred years? Anyway, most of his subjects would have been far better for better printing, for more tone, and Whistler could have shown him how to print better. There was in the possession for a while of Mr. J. Kerr Lawson a collection of Rembrandt's proofs, which came from Russia where they had been hidden for years; so fine, so strong, so rich that, not only because of the large price, but because of this richness and depth of the ink, dealers and collectors were afraid of them—afraid because of their excellence that they were fakes. On these certainly the ink had not dried out to powder.

Rembrandt was a great artist but not so great an etcher as Whistler.

This has now been admitted more or less even in England, and as a compensation Whistler has now been grabbed as a member of the British School. Even Mr. Campbell Dodgson says he was first of modern etchers, and recognises even in the past no greater master of art than Whistler save Rembrandt Van Rhyn.

Prof. John C. Van Dyke has now too commenced a serious study—it has lasted some forty years—of Rembrandt's paintings and Dr. Singer has scientifically treated his etchings.—Both these writers, while not depriving him of one great painting or etching, have removed from the list of his works many oils and plates, which if they were his, prove him capable of doing as bad work as the veriest duffer. That such work is signed only proves the signature was often forged or that he would sign anything. By denying that he is responsible for much that is bad or unimportant and should be lost, forgotten or destroyed these writers have done a great service to the artist and his art.

OF THE FOLLOWERS OF
REMBRANDT AND OTHERS

I AM not going to discuss the Engravers and Etchers, the contemporaries, predecessors, or successors of Dürer, the work of Mantegna, and all the rest, nor the prints of the followers of Rembrandt. There was occasional good work done by occasional artists, but to take any sort of old stuff seriously, and discuss it elaborately because it is etched or old is simply a weariness of the flesh and a confusion to students.

For this reason I have not referred to Millet, Corot, Daubigny, Jacque, amongst moderns. Their etchings are either like their pen drawings, or else reproductions of their paintings. Now and again, as in the case of Fortuny and Jongkind, there is genuine, real, and vital work to be found; but in the case of these men it is interesting more because of its personal, than its etched, quality. Jongkind, for example, is a most interesting etcher, but an abominable master for a student.

Again, there is another tribe of etchers, the degenerate successors of Callot and Hollar who were great artists, once in a while great etchers too—masters of vital line— I mean the tribe of Cruikshank, Leech, Doyle, Phiz, and all the rest. Cruikshank had a wonderful invention, and in *Ainsworth's Tower of London* his management of crowds of little figures is astonishing; but the pitiful trash with which he, Doyle, and Leech, and the rest covered acres of copper is appalling, enough to copper bottom a fleet, or build a steel skyscraper, a positive proof that the world of Dickens' time, led by Ruskin, was infantile in its appreciation of art. The story was everything, the method, the technique nothing. Seymour did create Mr. Pickwick, but he is artistically a pitiful creation, and so are the other members of the Club, but it is incredible that such stuff should ever have been discussed as art. Besides which, I am almost certain that these people never, or rarely, bit their own plates—(I am doubtful if even they drew the designs on the copper or steel)—but from the mass of work turned and ground out by them—without a bit of foul or over- or under-biting in it—they must have employed a regiment of hacks and ghosts. Other evidence is that in many of the plates machine-ruled skies and backgrounds are common. While apart from the grotesque figures, thousands of which are like the drawings of children, but not like post impressions made to appeal to a childish-minded generation, there is no observation of any sort in them, nothing but a commonplace rendering of self-evident facts.

If the student can make use of such stuff, it may be of use to him for suggestions; otherwise it should be avoided, as poison and perdition in art. Just as Thackeray, Ruskin, and Dickens who praised it should be avoided as critics. The work of most of the British Academicians of the same period is as bad technically; its only quality is its tiresome boring seriousness; now and again a plate may be found like some of Girtin's or Cotman's soft ground etchings, or Wilkie's or Geddes' figures and portraits, but the rest is a dreary desert to be shunned, especially those oases inhabited by ponderous bores like Samuel Palmer. Of all the men of that time Charles Keene is the only etcher worth study, and naturally he is unnoticed by Hamerton and reviled by Ruskin— with Rembrandt, however, by the latter. Rowlandson, Gilray, and the real caricaturists, the successors of Hogarth, are not worth study technically, any more than are the present-day caricaturists of England and America; mostly they were not troubled by art, or by technique, and so it is not necessary to trouble about them. They were without merit of any sort, and were therefore most popular with the masses and classes.

The Dutch etchers preceding and following Rembrandt are without, as a rule, any technical merit—and the few who have any are feeble imitators of the master. For those who wish to know more, there are all the lives, histories, and examples necessary in all museums, but Rembrandt is the only etcher of his age.

A S for the few etchings by Dürer, they are in their way wonderful and should be studied; the little towns and cities in them are far better than Rembrandt's and are to be ranked with Whistler's Thames plates; but in all it is evident that they are built up from sketches, not seen directly, as Whistler saw and etched similar backgrounds; though technically plates like *The Cannon* are superb. *The Cannon* is said to be engraved, but I have the courage to doubt it—the line is so vital, so superb. These were, it is said, etched on iron, and have, maybe in consequence of the metal, a distinct, strong, firm quality of line which is remarkable, in this plate of *The Cannon* especially, and it might be a good thing to etch on iron again to-day instead of copper, as it can apparently be well bitten, though I do not know what acid was used. However, I have an idea it was more Dürer's ability as an artist than the iron plate which has made the print live. The printing in all the etchings is sharp and clean; the prints look as if the plates had been clean wiped like his engravings.

NOTE: For Durer illustration see plate of Great Cannon, page 11.

IN portraiture, no etcher in the past approached Rembrandt, and he does not approach Whistler. The best was Van Dyck; and yet if one looks carefully at the series of heads done like Turner's landscapes for future work by the professional engraver, one finds the line of little importance, rather with little character in it; it is wonderfully well done, but it is perfunctory. Rembrandt's and Whistler's line vibrates, is sensitive in drawing and biting. Van Dyck's is hard, flat, and dry. Look at any of the Portraits. Van Dyck gets the modelling of the face mostly with a sort of dot, stipple-like, method; the modelling is all right, the method is all wrong; the drapery is all there, but the lines—I am referring to the original states of these plates, where the work is all by Van Dyck if they are by him—the etched lines are flat and stale. The only portrait of his that I know which has any real go and character is the *Lucas Vostermans;* that is fine. Van Dyck, in his way, was trying to rival Holbein's drawings, by etchings, and he did not succeed. There are but two etchers between Rembrandt and Goya who need be seriously, carefully looked at or considered—Callot and Hollar. I do not know if that great artist Hogarth did much etching, on his great plates. Some of the less important ones are etched, but the etching is not vital, and the etched work on the plates was not published—as etching. Callot at times is most spontaneous and passionate; so far as I know the printing of his plates is always poor; rather there is no printing in them—they are clean wiped; but the little figures, the little dramas, the little anecdotes, the little horrors all tell and tell well; in this he was, with Hollar, the forerunner of that amazing contradiction Cruikshank. These two artists, too, are responsible for Meryon and the little Meryons, though most may not know it, at any rate admit it. Callot and Hollar were the first of the commercial manufacturing etchers, though they did their work well, far better than their successors, but horrors, fashions, wars, portraits of people and their palaces, views of towns, sport,—all were etched by them. They were journalistic etchers, illustrative etchers—their like has never been seen before or since—wonderful technicians, wonderful workmen, no fear of overproduction; and even in war time Hollar and Callot did their best work, like Goya. Callot made 1000 plates, Hollar 2500, Cruikshank 5000. One boasted he had etched fifty kilometres of copper, another enough to sheathe the British Navy. And prolific as they were, technically, artistically, historically, for they etched the things they saw and knew, they are far more worth studying than the heavenly hosts and holy families ground out of their inner consciousness, conscientiously for gain, by some of their less prolific contemporaries, and more financially successful successors.

All this talk of overproduction is rubbish—the work of dealers who want to do their business in the most comfortable fashion. Who ever regretted the thousands of drawings made by Beardsley, Houghton, Abbey, Daumier, Menzel? And yet if an etcher has ideas, something to say, the power to say it, he is told, if he do more than a plate or so a year, he is "spoiling his market." Such is the art and commerce of etching as preached and practised by the majority of etchers and dealers to-day, especially if in the employ of the modern up-to-date superior dealer who regards himself as of much more importance than the unfortunately necessary—or rather accidental etcher—whom he lives on.

I have not attempted to make the artists discussed in this book picturesque or pathetic, or to consider satire, humour, intellectual or religious schemes or motives; all these may come into good work, but they have nothing to do with it. If Michael Angelo or Titian or Velasquez paints or draws a religious or historical subject, the student and the artist should study it for the paint, the line, the composition; the fact that it is religious or historical neither increases nor decreases its artistic importance; a well-etched dung-heap is of more importance artistically, technically, than a badly etched Nativity. Whistler has in this matter been most maligned—he never objected to subject—he only protested against badly etched, drawn, or painted subjects being taken seriously because of their titles, or the years of misdirected energy wasted over them, or the enormous sums made out of them.

NANTEUIL: PORTRAIT OF THE DUC DE MELLERAYE
VAN DYCK: PORTRAIT OF SNYDERS

NANTEUIL: PORTRAIT OF THE DUC DE MELLERAYE. ENGRAVING. VAN DYCK: PORTRAIT OF SNYDERS. ETCHING

These two portraits show the difference in portraiture between engraving and etching. The Nanteuil done laboriously with a single line, though there is cross hatching in many parts of it. The Van Dyck done freely with several sorts of lines and dots. The Nanteuil is after a painting or drawing, the Van Dyck is his own design, probably from life.

OF WILLIAM BLAKE

BLAKE should be studied; technically he was a trained etcher and engraver, and what he got out of his knowledge of these arts was wonderful. But his best plates are his relief plates, in which, instead of being etched, his lines, drawn with acid-resisting varnish, are left in relief, the rest of the plate bitten and dug away like a wood engraving, made into line in relief. The colour was mostly put on by Blake or his wife afterwards, painted in with water colour. The lines and the text were printed usually in red, blue or brown. His engravings for the Book of Job are in subject and handling amongst the finest of modern works, but they are not etchings.—I have said his best plates are his "relief plates,"—I should have said his most interesting for his best plates are his engravings and the greatest of them are in the Book of Job. Blake tried all sorts of mediums, wood engraving and even the newly— in his time—invented art of lithography. He was a most interesting artist and craftsman.

It is possible, having made a lithographic pen drawing for *The Polyautographic Album*, that Blake made his drawings in lithographic ink on paper—and wrote the text under them also, in lithographic ink, and transferred the whole to copper, then rolled the design up as the lithographer does, getting it stronger—and as the photo engraver does—to protect his lines, and bit the plate. And then printed it as a surface print on the copper plate press. This would give exactly the effect he got. If he worked in this way Blake was the inventor of mechanical line engraving.

Or he may have made the drawing with Dragons Blood, also used by photo engravers.

OF WILLIAM BLAKE

This artist's books, those he wrote, illustrated and printed are most interesting. Blake was a trained engraver and knew what he wanted and how to get it—as the books prove—he was not one of those "imaginative artists" who reek with imagination and are devoid of expression—he was full of uplift and message which he could put in words and lines—and not merely talk and cackle about—as do so many of his imitators and successors—who if they had been his contemporaries would either never have heard of him or have ignored him. But Blake is now firmly established among the correct, and he was also an artist—as most of his sort are not. So for once the collectors are right—though Blake has been appropriated by the artless too. Blake when he made his books was doing in metal successfully what Senefelder was attempting unsuccessfully in stone—not on stone—to engrave and etch it—before he discovered lithography, Blake knew of Senefelder and his work for he made a drawing in pen and lithographic ink in the manner of the engravings for the Book of Job and it was printed in Senefelder's volume *Examples of Polyautography*—(see *Lithography and Lithographers*).

Blake either drew on the polished copper—maybe, from the look of the prints, zinc or some other metal plate—I never saw in any authority any definite statement as to what he did use and I do not know what became of his plates—with an acid resisting ink or varnish, as a matter of fact, lithographic ink and chalk might have been used, and then bit the exposed, undrawn surface of the plate away, exactly like a wood block, but he inked and wiped the bitten plates like etchings, cleaning the surface and leaving ink in the etched parts. There was in some of them much foul and uneven biting and I do not know how deeply the etched parts were bitten. He also lettered on the metal in reverse, the poems, or some one did it for him, as the lettering is all the same in the same style—I know nothing of this. Or else as in lithography the text was written on paper and transferred to the plate I am not sure that he did it himself. But, because it is probable that the engraved text is his own, but to avoid or remove foul biting in the lettering which, though on the same plate, was printed like a wood block, the two sorts of inking being used—must have been extremely difficult. But the more I look at his books the less sure I am of how he engraved and printed them. The colour is said to have been added in water colour by Mrs. Blake, or transferred to the plates or prints from some sort of painted or inked pad. The method died with the artist, but if Linnell had only paid as much attention to describing Blake's methods of making his plates and his prints as he did to collecting the proofs and the volumes, he would have done a greater service to artists, for he, John Linnell was an artist—as well as a collector and might have left a valuable record, as well as a fine collections of the works of a most remarkable contemporary artist whom he had the sense to appreciate.

The more I look at these prints, in *Jerusalem* especially, the more I am amazed at their technique and puzzled by it. Every line in the figures has been drawn with a pen or a brush and in the print Blake has kept all this feeling of brush work, not turned it into a metal engraved line. Did he use surface printing lithography? I have no certain knowledge as to how the work was done and the authorities know no more. The plates might prove his methods. I do not know if any are in existence.

Leaning against the pillars, & his disease rose from his skirts
Upon the Precipice he stood: ready to fall into Non-Entity.

Los was all astonishment & terror: he trembled sitting on the Stone
Of Londan: but the interiors of Albions fibres & nerves were hidden
from Los: astonishd he beheld only the petrified surfaces.
And saw his Furnaces in ruins, for Los is the Demon of the Furnaces:
He saw also the Four Points of Albion reversd inwards.
He siezd his Hammer & Tongs, his iron Poker & his Bellows.
Upon the valleys of Middlesex, Shouting loud for aid Divine.

In stern defiance came from Albions bosom Hand, Hyle, Koban,
Gwantok, Peachy, Brereton, Slaid, Hutton, Skofeld, Kock, Kotope
Bowen; Albions Sons: they bore him a golden couch into the porch.
And on the Couch reposd his limbs, trembling from the bloody field.
Rearing their Druid Patriarchal rocky Temples around his limbs.
(All thing begin & end, in Albions Ancient Druid Rocky Shore.)

OF GOYA AND ROPS

TWO etchers who have greatly distinguished themselves in the last hundred years are Francisco Goya and Felicien Rops, Goya for his aquatints, Rops for his soft ground plates. Goya, after Meryon, has been of the greatest service to the literary critic—his life, his loves, his mysteries, his sarcasms, have been so dwelt upon by these hangers-on of art, that his art has been forgotten in their anxiety to praise, or blame, or explain his life and his subjects. As to his work, his etchings, considered as etching—as etched line—are of no value whatever. He could, however, in his versions of Velasquez,—they are not reproductions, but sketches of the paintings,—give in a remarkable fashion the look and feeling of the originals, despite the abominable printing. I have never seen a decently printed proof of one of Goya's plates. Those printed at the Calcografica, Madrid, are as prints worthless, yet they are ground out all the time for the benefit of the amateur and collector.

Line apparently never interested Goya any more than Tiepolo and Fragonard, whose etchings all possess the same defects of want of care, thought, or pleasure in line.

By aquatint Goya got wonderful results—that was his medium ; the ground was laid after the etching had been made, and save in the lights, completely ate up the line ; even this aquatint ground, technically, is neither well laid nor bitten, being mostly a flat tone, or an attempt at one, badly printed ; often there are holes in it, and one rarely finds a print which does not look overbitten, while many of the plates have been worked on and patched up with the roulette and dry point, most likely by civil service government etchers. But they are still tremendously effective, full of life and go, as well as mystery and doubtfulness. He was trying, they were mucking up. There are four series of plates, one sketches of paintings, mostly after Velasquez, the *Disasters of War, The Caprices,* far the best of all, and the *Bull Fights,* and even in the vile prints all well worth studying.

Felicien Rops' aquatints, dry points, and soft ground etchings are, on the other hand, of the greatest technical accomplishment, printed by himself or by a capable man. They are of the greatest interest to students ; their morals, or want of them, are not in question. These two artists have carried on tradition, or rather the latter has, in a brilliant manner. Two Englishmen who also did remarkable aquatints and soft ground etchings well worth study, are Girtin and Cotman. But they invented or stole processes, and their art and their methods died with them.

There is another phase of Goya's work which must not be overlooked—his experiments ; the British, Madrid, Berlin, and other Print Rooms contain a large number of these ; whether they are original drawings in lithographic chalk and ink or transfers from etchings to stone, or transfers from drawings on paper to metal, it is impossible to say ; they have been catalogued by one authority as drawings, and the same subjects in another collection are described by another authority as prints. As an etcher, I am unable to say what they are, except this : they are mostly as bad as interesting technically, and I am sure copies or forgeries, nearly all of them, and unworthy of the artist or of preservation save as curiosities.

There are, however, several subjects in the British Museum, notably a drawing called, or I have so called it, *The Garrotted;* it may be a print, an etching of the same subject, or a lithographic transfer worked on. There is also a *Duel*, very poor, most of it, and a reproduction, or rather copy of it; but how this was done I cannot say. And lastly a series of small figures, heads with numbers on them, which I believe to be forgeries, or copies, only I do not know where the originals are, drawn in lithographic chalk; or else they are extraordinarily good prints from chalk drawings, or soft ground etchings; they are variously catalogued by various authorities; there is no doubt that most of them, as drawings, are beneath contempt; even the gentle Hamerton describes some of Goya's work as "rotten," but he had never seen these, I think, which are worse.

A very brilliant technician of whose work far too little was known during his life was Felix Buhot, a master craftsman.

His studies of Paris and London were an inspiration to many moderns. He it was who first showed that there was picturesque material for etching in a cab stand, a kiosk, a landing stage.

His prints of boats arriving at Dover or Folkestone had the rain and the wind in them, but he was never satisfied with leaving things alone, and the design wandered often all over the plate. There were edges of bare copper to begin with, and these got remarques, and attempts, and essays, scribbled all over them. I am not sure how much this was done for the collector and how much for himself, but it was most amusing. In his printing—for he printed his own plates—there were all sorts of experiments with coloured inks, and the plate was printed on coloured paper; he too was a mighty hunter of paper, and when he found it, most generous with his find; but not content with the beauty of the old paper, he tinted that with tea, with tobacco, with anything that would give tone. Then there were inscriptions on the margin etched in, and dedications written on, and finally a monogram in red appeared on those proofs he was pleased with. It was, as I say, amusing, but that part of it scarce art, though at times these little bits were artfully put in. Buhot also made etchings of Chinese and Japanese objects as Jacquemart had done, though they more resemble Whistler's Blue and White China drawings; there are ten of these designs, the subjects taken from Philip Burty's collection, and they were published as a set, and they vary in merit. He worked by all sorts of methods; some of his smallest sketches of country life are the best, especially the old man and woman on a rainy evening staggering home under their wind-blown umbrella.

Another artist who devoted some time and plates to rendering articles of *virtu* was Bracquemond, but to me at least Bracquemond is far more interesting as a reproductive engraver and etcher of his own and other men's work. His portraits of himself and de Goncourt are magnificent, but not real spontaneous etching. In portraiture, in reproduction, he might have reaped fame and honours which were absolutely denied him; but it is a dangerous thing to be a prophet or an artist in this country—the best, the safest thing is to be a follower, an imitator.

Legros' trick, which he played hundreds or thousands of times, was a feeble imitation of Mantegna's vigorous line: in relief or shadow—straight lines drawn at an angle

GOYA : MALA NOCHE

Goya like other great artists was a master of many mediums—or worked in many—and he is one of the few great artists who used aquatint to any extent for original work.   Felicien Rops is another, but it is rather difficult to say how much of the work Rops did himself, and then maybe heard of Goya. This is a very good example in arrangement and colour, as it ranges from intense black to shining white. The print was made from a good proof and good proofs of Goya's are rare, the aquatint having quickly worn and then been patched up ; probably later, by some bungling duffer, possibly in the Calcographic Gallery at Madrid where modern prints can be obtained—or could—before the war.

As in mezzotinting there is an outline etching of the subject under the ground etched before the aquatint ground was laid—as described in the text—and the etched lines in black can be plainly seen in the whites and grays of the finished plate.

When the etching has been made, as in the plate, the aquatint ground is deposited all over it either by the dust or resin process.   The high lights are then stopped out, and the plate is put in the bath ; the first tone bitten and then stopped out, and the same process repeated, till the extreme darks are reached.   The tones are usually rather flat, it is difficult to get variety in them, but they have if flat, a rather decorative quality.

FELICIEN ROPS

FELICIEN ROPS: THE DEVIL SOWING TARES OVER PARIS

It is difficult to get a plate of Rops which shows his methods and at the same time can be shown—but —though it does not reproduce well this is a magnificent example in biting and soft ground and aquatint—which are described.

of forty-five degrees, a useful background, but quite meaningless. Legros is even more meaningless and much more mannered. In England he is taken most seriously though Hamerton scarce mentions him. He was never accepted by the Academy which has accepted his imitators; but he is so easy—easier than Meryon—to imitate. He had nothing to say of his own; he was overpowered by the past, carried on no tradition, and save for a few paintings, will not be recognized or remembered in the future. Possibly the fact that he gave up his country for another—as no artist, no patriot would do—may account for his failure, save in popularity. There are a few goodish portraits—but much better have been made by his students—there are a few goodish figure subjects and landscapes, but there is no feeling for real character or actual modernity in them. He has not carried on tradition.

Jacquemart was a most amazing technician and glorified articles of *virtu* and immortalized old shoes with incredible surface accuracy.

TURNER'S Etchings for the *Liber Studiorum*, for the mezzotints, though never intended to be seen or rather published—at least it is said only some twelve sets were printed—are very fine, some of them. Etchings such as these are merely a guide to the engraver who is a copyist. If the artist, the original artist, scraped his own plates, there is no reason, in fact it is frequently a defect, to put in the etched lines beneath the mezzotint. They are supposed to strengthen the work, or to guide the mezzotinter; they frequently show through it. Turner, however, etched these lines with great feeling; he gave the bigness of his design, the bigness of nature, with the fewest possible and the most expressive needle strokes, and was the only great British etcher of his time. The plates are very uneven in merit both as compositions and in technique—and it is pretty certain that Turner did not etch several of them. Some, it is said, are signed W. S. W., one of his engravers. Even in Turner's case the word " etch " is very vague and it is impossible to say whether it really means drawing or biting or both. Ruskin's etchings after Turner in his manner, are some of them most accomplished. Others are so perfectly bitten that it is evident they are the work of engravers—others are very clumsy—but many are drawn with the most vital lines and bitten with consummate art. Though Ruskin, Rawlinson, Thornbury, Hamerton, Finberg have written volumes about the intellectual, moral, and commercial aspects of the *Liber* there is scarce a line of reliable technical information about these etchings.

Turner's mezzotints, the few he did, there are about a dozen, were fine—that is in the early proofs, trials when the plates were, he—or the public—thought, half finished; for nearly all finished mezzotints, to me, look played out, scraped and burnished and grey, till there is no life left in them. Turner and his engravers tinkered at these plates —till the confusion over states has become to artists incredible. No one but Turner knew anything about them and his records, comments, and marks are unintelligible. Even Lucas' prints after Constable's Landscapes suffer in this way, but all this is the fault of the mezzotinter, who is rarely an original creative artist. Mezzotint, however, is most deceptive, most tedious. The design one has scraped on the rocked plate looks beautifully, and prints abominably, all black and smudgy, all wanting endless work before it is right—and if the artist gets mad and goes for the plate, he digs white or black holes in it and ruins it. Turner's prints were printed mostly in a hot red brown, a clumsy attempt to imitate—apparently with cheap ink—his sepia originals—or other originals. Mezzotint, beautiful as it is, is scarce an art for artists. The copies, for example, of artists' rapid sketches are only produced by long hours of labour and drudgery by the plodding mezzotinter. Soft ground, aquatint, sandpaper ground, or the roulette are far easier to work, to manage. Few artists have found it easy to scrape or to print original mezzotints. Whistler tried once to prove a plate by Josey and made an awful mess of it.

Claude and Canaletto are the direct opposites to Turner. All three were great artists, but only one was a great etcher—Turner. Claude's designs, sepia drawings, pen drawings, are magnificent. *The Liber Veritatis* was never intended for mezzo-tinting—it was but a record of his paintings for reference—Earlom's engravings were not made until years after Claude's death. In line, his etchings are poor and empty or crowded and niggled. Canaletto is still worse, that is, if the etchings attributed to him were by him. The Venetian plates were intended to be worked on by others in line. But Canaletto's and Claude's lines, unlike those of Turner, have little feeling. The original designs become quite unimportant as etchings. And the same is true of Piranesi; his compositions are fine, but he never, even in the *Carceri*,—his best work,—depends on the vital line, and technically all these men with especially one of their descendants, Samuel Palmer, should be avoided by etchers. Piranesi's prints make a good frieze, or line a stairway well, but they are not good to set before students; he had not even the grandiose feeling; his perspective is as poor as his industry is great. Of course he is far better than the hacks of to-day, but he is not a great etcher by any means.

There are certain big painters who have been little etchers—men who had no real feeling for line, whose feeling was for colour and tone, and who only could express themselves by these methods.

No better examples are to be found than Claude and Canaletto, both great painters, great draughtsmen. Claude's designs, his wash and pen drawings, are unrivalled, though many have tried to imitate or surpass him; but when Claude etched, he lost his freedom of working, of expression. He could put down an effect with a sweep of his pen, or with his brush make a splendid sky or a gloomy foreground; he tried and failed to get the same effects with a multitude of meaningless lines on copper. Line—as line—meant nothing to him when he etched. Besides which his etchings are compositions; the same towns, ports, palaces, ships, and people that one finds in his paintings, reappear in his prints. In the paintings, and more so in the drawings, we delight in these compositions; in the etchings they are tiresome, proving that he only copied himself. Some of the apparently unfinished plates are better; but he was not among the great etchers, nor was Canaletto. There is in his work—if it is his work, for this I doubt—the same stodginess and elaboration, the same trying for tone, for elaborate mechanical skies, for worked out foregrounds. But Canaletto was a painter, his drawings are usually tiresome, and those in that great collection, the Correr Museum, in Venice, I do not believe are his work at all, but mere architectural schemes set up by pupils mostly, slightly touched by him for the professional etcher and engraver. The *Thirty-Eight Views of Venice* by Visentini, ruled, laboured, uninteresting, save as showing most clearly to the student Canaletto's methods of composition and perspective (and in these matters he is supreme), are uninspiring. There are a few plates carried out with more freedom than the thirty-eight views, but they look like pen drawings and have no spontaneous, only laborious, qualities in them.

There are any number of French, Dutch, Flemish, and Italian painters who once in a while make a good plate, but there is no supreme etcher among them. But if one will study the best etchings by the best men, when a fine work by an unknown etcher is found the student will recognize it, though this is more than Hamerton and those who have followed him have been able to do. The average critic-collector-curator can tell you all about the three lines in a corner of this plate, the scratch at the bottom of that, the wonderful paper the other is printed on; but whether the design, the drawing, or printing is good is beyond them and does not matter. The cataloguing of trials and of states and of numbers alone does.

NOTE. In the *History of the Liber Studiorum of J. M. W. Turner*, by A. J. Finberg, published while this book was being revised, the author states that Turner only made five—I think it is—of the etchings for the *Liber*, but which they are I do not know, and about the same number of the mezzotints have, for a long while, been known to have been engraved by him, in fact Turner in most cases gives the name of the engraver of the mezzotint in the lettered state of the plate, and also in this state the words "drawn and etched by J. M. W. Turner, Esq. R. A." are engraved and printed on it. Finberg therefore proves Turner, his hero, the man to whose work he has given the important years of his life, a liar, a fraud, a swindler—and Finberg does this perfectly naïvely, not seeing or understanding what he has done. Ruskin, Rawlinson who made the three first catalogues, and Stopford Brooke, who described the *Liber*, are silent in the matter, but Brooke says Turner etched the plates, so Finberg says virtually—"They are only etchings"—the critic again—what does it matter whether the R. A., like Herkomer, tried to delude the public or not? But it does matter, and for two reasons: first, because Turner had no business to take the credit for making etchings he did not make—and second, if he did not make them, who did? and why did Turner say he did? I think Finberg is correct even if he has, an an etcher, killed his hero. For Turner, in letters and notes to his engravers, tells them how to make and correct them —the plates—and that he will touch up the etchings, proving that he, Turner, was conniving at a fraud on collectors, for they are signed, as I say, "drawn and etched by J. M. W. T. Esquire, R. A." The irony of it. My reason for believing that Turner did not do the etchings is because they have been reversed in copying the drawings—the original sepia drawings—or rather the pen lines in them by Turner, and to reverse them must have been a long and tedious affair. But, on the other hand, the pen lines in the drawing and the copied etched lines in the prints are magnificent in their vital directness, simplicity and force, though this Finberg neither sees nor understands, and such lines could not have been invented by any one save Turner, but they could be copied, more or less, by a skillful engraver engaged in a swindle, or an innocent deception, and if Finberg is correct the affair is a swindle. But if Turner did not make these etchings, who did? for all the best of them are by the same hand I am certain. Here is another problem, for the authorities, and if Mr. Finberg goes a little further he may discover that Turner did not paint his oils or water colours, but that they were done by a syndicate, and Turner was only the Esquire, R. A. salesman.

I thought, after seeing Finberg's statements, that Turner might have made the etchings first, and done the sepia drawings over the prints but this is not so, for I have seen the drawings in the National and Tate Galleries—and we now have Turner's written evidence that he did not do the etchings, only lied to the public about them. But who ever made them they are all made in the same manner and are interesting and valuable works of art, the greater number of them, and I believe most were drawn, or copied and etched by the same hand. Whether Turner swindled the public or not don't matter so much, the etchings do, and most are very fine.

NOTE TO THIRD EDITION: Hamerton in "*Etching and Etchers*" says positively that Turner made the Etchings for the *Liber Studiorum*.

J. M. W. TURNER: ST. CATHARINE'S HILL. BITTEN LINE
ETCHED BY TURNER. MEZZOTINTED BY J. C. EASLING

In several instances Turner not only made the etching under the mezzotint, but printed proofs from the etched plates. This is one of the finest; every single line in it is most expressive and most decorative. The biting too is extremely well done. Yet all this is hidden in the finished plate which is covered with the mezzotint ground. The etching is used to strengthen the drawing and also as a guide to the engraver when at work.

These *Liber Studiorum* mezzotints were all made, except a few by Turner, by professional mezzotinters, and are of varying merit. They were copied but very freely from Turner's sepia, or monochrome studies in the National Gallery, London. Turner, though he did little of the work, took a great interest in it, and endlessly revised and corrected the proofs and generally made the engravers' lives a burden. Like many other marvels of engraving it was a complete financial fiasco—so great that it was not even completed during Turner's life time and only finished by Sir Frank Short who has made several new plates from the drawings, most admirably. Not only in this plate are the graceful trees to be admired and their lines delighted in, but in this etching, as in Whistler's *Bridge*, the lines of the road, the hedge, and the ground carry the eye right up to the abbey, unobtrusively but surely. It is rather comic however to compare Turner's figures and animals with Rembrandt's or Whistler's. I have added a reproduction of the finished mezzotint which shows Turner's completed design—an engraving of his sepia drawing from which the prints were made. There is an undoubted charm in the added colour—but to me the pure etching—the pure line—is just as expressive and it renders truly the subject with the fewest and most vital lines, the end and aim of etching. It is most interesting to compare the original drawing with the etching, and that with the engraving in mezzotint made on it, whether by Turner or another engraver, in almost every case Turner added or made the engraver add the more subtle effects in skies and water specially, though some of the unfinished trial proofs—untouched—are the finest of all. If access cannot be had to the originals A. J. Finberg's *History of the Liber Studiorum*, may be consulted. Finberg states Turner did not make the etchings but who ever made this etching made most of the rest in the *Liber*, and they are fine works.

St Catharine's Hill   near Guilford

OF SEYMOUR HADEN

JUST as to-day it is the thing for imitators to prig from Meryon's Paris, so a few years ago they prigged from Rembrandt's landscapes. Now to imitate Rembrandt's mistakes and mannerisms is easy and no one did so better than the late Sir Seymour Haden. But the Surgeon Etcher had something to say for himself, and when he etched plates like the *Sunset in Ireland, Grim Spain, Kilgarn Castle*, or the drawing of the ship in the *Breaking Up of the Agamemnon*, or when he copied Turner's *Calais Pier*, he proved himself an etcher; in the latter he rivals Rembrandt. But most of the time he was struggling away with nature on one hand and Rembrandt's proofs on the other. He tried for and got all Rembrandt's tricks—little of Rembrandt's art. Haden was the first of the modern plodders, the first to make etching pay, the first to hire someone to do his work for him—Goulding the printer—the first, and still, I imagine, far the most successful business etcher of modern times. Mr. Keppel said —and he should know—Haden sold ten thousand copies of *The Breaking Up of the Agamemnon*. Apropos, I remember one story he told me in his own house. How he went down the Thames to Greenwich, one day, to a whitebait dinner with the members of the Royal Academy Club possibly, and he saw the subject, *The Breaking Up of the Agamemnon*, and just went and sat on a pile, and pulled the plate out of his dress coat-tail pocket, and etched the ship and forgot the dinner, and then came back the next day at sunset and put in the background. "And what sized plates do you carry in your ordinary coat-tail pockets, Mr. Haden?" said a guest. After that the subject was changed.

The drawing (however it was done) of the hull of the old ship is marvellous. What a cheeky incompetent Hamerton was when he had the audacity to copy it, to prove something or other, somewhere or other, and completely lost the drawing. Haden's translation—which is what it is—of Turner's *Calais Pier* is masterly, the swing and movement done with the fewest lines, amazing; and it is a huge plate. But plates like *Shere Mill Pond* are cloying in their prettiness, while the dark masses of trees are messes. Haden's work of this sort is not to be compared to Lalanne's. Lalanne is graceful, Haden clumsy. Yet in two or three of the dry points, *Sunset in Ireland*, the best by far, where he is quite himself, he is exquisite, in feeling, in line, and in colour; this is one of the most beautiful dry point landscapes ever made, far better than any by Rembrandt, far better than any of Whistler's; but in this case Haden was doing something for himself. I forget if it was this plate he is said to have thrown away in a stable in disgust and resurrected years after.

Haden's weakness and commercialism and artlessness are proved generally however by his steeling all his plates, and then turning them over to Goulding to print— print as much alike as he could, so that Haden only had to sign them; and he, Haden is responsible for starting or carrying out this shop idea of printing which has debauched British and American etching. Haden had a press and Goulding to run it after the plates were steel-faced in a sort of conservatory behind his dining-room, where I saw it in Hertford Street—and I have also seen him at work in his study at the top of the house where I believe he did the fine *Out of the Study Window*.

The most poetical dry point landscape that exists. These are strong words—and so are those I have used about the other plates in the book—but I have selected the best etchings—those which are universally acknowledged to be the best, and the ones which should be known to all lovers of prints, and prized by print lovers, and therefore they demand the highest praise. No one has better rendered the heavy dense foliage of the summer woods, or so well contrasted it, with the printed sky reflected in the slow moving water, or better put the design on the plate. This plate was evidently done straight from nature, probably at one sitting, with the dry point. Work as true as this can not be faked. Haden once in a while was a very great artist, yet I believe it was this plate which he was so disgusted with that he threw it away in a stable, only like Rossetti, to resurrect it years after and find in it a great work, as Rossetti found his poems to be when he resurrected them.

F. SEYMOUR HADEN: BREAKING UP
OF THE AGAMEMNON. BITTEN LINE

No finer etching in pure line was ever made by a British artist, in it Haden surpassed himself, and the reason was that having studied and absorbed Rembrandt and Whistler he, in this plate, carried on tradition and did something for himself.

The plate is fine because every line in it means something, expresses something. Every line is bitten with the thought in Haden's mind of how he wanted it to print. The balance of light and shade also is remarkable and with a very few lines and masses he makes the glow and glitter of the sunset and the long lines of the tide. In this plate too the lines are not only expressive, but one set leads to the Hospital and beyond to the setting sun, and another to the gaping hull of the ship and the hull is the finest thing in line that has ever been done in etching.

Haden told me he did the plate in two afternoons on the spot, but there are early proofs which were far from successful, and there must have been days in the studio before he got it right. He also made a mezzotint of the same subject but neither that nor any of his other attempts at mezzotint are to be compared to his work in line.

Among modern etchers Buhot was one of those rare artists who have something to say for themselves and say it in their own way.   Buhot made endless experiments in all sorts of methods and on many of his plates, as on this one, with its reminiscences of London.   These were done to please himself or to please collectors of remarque proofs, and they were rarely scraped off, or the plate cut down to the real design upon it.   I do not care so much for this plate—it is hard and photographic with a scrawly sky but it is characteristic.   Buhot was also a mighty hunter of old paper—possessing a large stock of it—and he made many experiments in tinting or soaking the paper in tea, coffee, and other colouring matters.   He also at times printed his plates in two or three colours, that is, he would ink the border with the sketches, in one colour or tone, and the main design in another.   He also used a little coloured stamp of an owl and the letters F B on either side it, when he was particularly pleased with a proof. I do not think he added to the merit of his etchings by these games, but despite them they are good and he occupies a distinct niche in modern art.

MAXIME LALANNE: RUE DES MARMOUSETS AND A CUSSET. BOTH BITTEN LINE

For a generation Maxime Lalanne typified Etching in France, he flourished while Meryon went mad, Lalanne succeeded while Buhot struggled. True Jacquemart and Bracquemond and Manet etched, but Lalanne was the etcher. He was patronized by royalty and petted by young ladies, and was commissioned to illustrate all the books, with landscape and architectural illustrations, which contained etchings during his lifetime. He was boomed by Hamerton and brought to England to illustrate the *Portfolio*. But besides—and despite all this—he and a few reproductive etchers of France, Waltner and Brunet Desbaines, were consummate craftsmen. Lalanne wrote the best technical book of its day. This was ably and well translated by S. R. Koehler, who did as much—and in the same way—for American etching as Hamerton did in England. Lalanne was a master of every method of making a copper plate. But Hamerton regards it of equal importance that " he was the first artist who ever received knighthood for his qualities as an Etcher." Hamerton rightly says "no one ever etched so gracefully," and his plates are graceful and gracious and display, every one of them, his love of beauty; and the line in most is vital, but most are too sweet, too drawing-booky. Still, as Hamerton says, he was "a master of his craft."

For simple, direct, straightforward work, built up on simple lines, showing the construction of a street scene, this *Rue des Marmousetes* is a marvel in every way, it is better than Meryon, and Lalanne was, in this plate, doing Meryon's subjects. I do not believe, however, that this was done from nature, any more than Meryon's plates. Instead of giving facts like this, which would be useful to students, Hamerton and the other authorities tell that a pastry cook who lived in the street, with the aid of a barber murdered a man who came to be shaved and made, says a French critic of art, "*des pâtés*"; and Hamerton adds, "the pies were highly appreciated by the public." The excellence of the study of architecture, the truth of the perspective, the roughness of the pavé, is seen and felt, but the pies are the important matter. Lalanne drew trees beautifully with beautiful lines, a secret that he shared with Claude and Turner and Corot. Years ago I wrote the following about him, and I wrote rightly:

"To my mind, at least, Lalanne was one of the most exquisite and refined illustrators of architecture who ever lived. His ability to express a great building, a vast town, or a delicate little landscape has never been equalled, I think, by anybody but Whistler. To a certain extent he was mannered; so was Rembrandt; Whistler is the only man I know of who is not.

"Lalanne probably acquired his refinement of handling in the production of his innumerable delicate etchings. . . . His etching of Richmond and the Thames, which appeared in the *Portfolio*, is the most exquisite example of his work I have seen in any English periodical."

Some of his best work, but mostly in photogravure, was published in *Hollande à vol d'oiseau* by Henri Havard. As simple direct line the plates are well worth study in these days when sloppiness in attempts to disguise incompetence, calls itself cubism.

Lalanne's dry points too are very fine, and so are his soft ground prints. Everything he touched he made beautiful, only often he made it too pretty.

He loved Bordeaux, his native town, and returned to etch it again and again, always under some new effect, though he frequently worked from the same spot. But whether he treated a little village, a great landscape, or a lovely river he always got beauty, and that was obtained by the use of the most beautiful lines bitten and printed in a perfect fashion.

The small *Cusset* proves exactly what I have said about this.

FELIX BRACQUEMOND: EDMOND DE GONCOURT, EARLY STATE

Bracquemond was one of the most accomplished technicians of modern times. His portraits are amazing—and the Goncourt is the most amazing of all, worthy to be ranked with those of Dürer or Nanteuil but it is etched, theirs engraved, there is the same sureness of line, the same character, and in some, it is evident how much he studied Dürer and the other engravers. Though Meryon called him a real etcher, most of his work is not spontaneous but worked out through many states, real states, not dealer collector baits—but there are certain studies of water fowl which might be studied with advantage by

BRACQUEMOND: EDMOND DE GONCOURT, FINISHED STATE

some of those who today supply the demand for that sort of commodity in etching—and notably a study of a crow nailed to a door which proves how much he was indebted to Japanese prints which he with Whistler made known to Europe and even to the Japanese themselves. There are several states of this plate, and the first and last are reproduced, showing the way he developed it—and it must be remembered that in every case the ground had to be removed before each printing—the plate regrounded and rebitten —as described in the chapter on regrounding, another proof of Bracquemond's mastery of his medium.

195

WILLIAM STRANG: THE SWINEHERD

Strang was the most varied etcher who ever lived and if he had lived before Rembrandt he might have been a greater artist than the greater Dutchman. Strang's trouble was that though he had endless messages to give the world he never had his own way of giving them. He started under Legros—who I do not think has enough character to be included here—and when Legros showed Strang, Holroyd—and maybe Short—what had been done in the past, the two first did not try to carry on basing themselves on the masters—but like Morris they harked back, they did not carry on. Strang was a little master of the past, not as he might have been, for he could etch, a great master in the present and possibly in the future. *The Swineherd* has no modernity no observation of things around him in it, but it is extraordinarily well done. It was always thus with Strang, he did the things around him, the Salvation

WILLIAM STRANG: KIPLING

Army but it was not the Salvation Army of his time but the Round Heads of the Civil War—marching not to Hyde Park but Worcester. Look at the man's coat and his staff and the pig pen, they were things he got out of books and prints—not what he saw—he changed his style with the years and after he had finished with the past, he took up the cheapest, easiest, slovenliest French work, ending by imitating Forain's tricks not his drawing, but Forain and Bauer who influenced Strang at the end can't etch as well as Zorn. His portraits are his best etchings—this one of Kipling is amusing but his study of Emery Walker and some other of his contemporaries were far better—but this one is Strang himself, and if he had only been himself he would have been a bigger and a better artist—and he could have been.

197

AUGUSTE LEPÈRE: L'INVENTOIRE

Lepère was an artist who could express himself in any medium—and a serious artist—not an incompetent duffer who funked things because he could not do them as is the fashion today for the benefit of the artist and the bewilderment of the art lover who always swallow the rubbish and reject the jewel thrown at them, and more docilely here than elsewhere. I do not think Lepère was a great etcher —but he was very interesting and could say and do what he wanted, and that is very much, in his own way and this plate *L'Inventoire* proves it, and both for architects and uplifters as well as collectors it is worth study for the careful rendering of the Cathedral of Amiens almost in outline, made to tell by the dark mass of figures full of character in the foreground. It is all built up but well built up—not faked and therefore worth study.

THE MATERIALS NECESSARY FOR
AND THE METHODS OF
MAKING AN ETCHING

OF THE MATERIALS NECESSARY   CHAPTER XVI
FOR MAKING AN ETCHING

A LIST of materials, utensils, and appliances for Etching may be found useful, and is here given. All these could be obtained before the war, some now never can be got. Also today many of the materials, including copper are nothing like so good as formerly.

Copper, Zinc, Aluminium, Steel or Iron plates. Good copper can be obtained from photo-engravers.
: These may be obtained from any plate maker or dealer in artists' materials.

Celluoid, Holophone Films.
: Roberson & Co., London.

Needles and Points
: Dealer in Artists' Materials.

If the artist desires to have needles made, he should go to a surgical instrument maker, but he must show a sample or specimen to be followed. Even then most makers are very careless and their work is poor. The best by far are made by the French.

Dry Points, Diamond Points, Roulettes, Mezzotint Tools, Burnishers, Scrapers.
: Dealer in Printers' or Artists' Materials.

Etching Ground.
: Ditto.

The best ground made to-day, the best time, temperature, and acid-resisting ground, is that of F. Weber & Co., Philadelphia, Pa., United States.

Liquid Etching Ground.
: Ditto.

Roberson's, 99 Long Acre, London.
Weber, Philadelphia.

Etching Varnish used in Germany. Made of lacquer.

Stopping out Varnish.
: Ditto.

All prepared stopping out varnishes I know of are unsatisfactory.

Acids, nitric or nitrous, or Dutch Mordant.
: To be obtained of Druggists or Chemists.

Perchloride of Iron.

Hydrochloric Acid.
: Eimer and Amend, 23d St. & 3d Avenue, New York are most excellent and reliable for chemicals.

Purchase in glass-stoppered bottles. The acids should be guaranteed to be chemically pure.

A supply of bottles with glass stoppers.
: Ditto.

Turpentine.
: Ditto.

Beware of cheap trash.
American most reliable.

Alcohol.
: Ditto.

Spirits of Wine or Methylated Spirit.
: Ditto.

Denatured alcohol is good and cheap.

Kerosene.
: Ditto.

Polish—"Globe," or other polishes to clean plates; to be used with caution.
: Must be obtained from Makers or Grocers.

Liable to be bad and corrode the plates, or anything they touch. German Globe was far the best.

Whiting, in block, not powder.
: Chemists or Colour Makers.

Muriatic acid for cleaning plates.
: Ditto.

Two-hand Vises with wooden handles.

Hardware Dealer.

Scrapers, and Burnishers. Burins, Mezzotint Tools.

Sellers & Co. or Printers' Materials Makers or Artists' Materials Dealers.

Baths of Porcelain or rubber.

Photo Materials Dealers or Artists' Colourmen, Dealers in Lamps, etc.

Wax Tapers—a bundle.

Two Etching Rollers for grounding and re-grounding plates.

F. Weber & Co., Philadelphia, Pa., United States.

L'Amour, Rue de la Harpe, Paris.

A Roller for inking plates.

Etching Materials Dealer. Made in New York.

There are two sorts: the composition or rubber roller used mainly by wood engravers for proving. And the new flannel-covered ink roller which is far better than the dabber.

Charcoal, for cleaning and rubbing down plates.

Printers' Materials Dealers.

Flowers of Sulphur for tints.

Chemists.

Emery and Sand Papers and Tissues of various textures for making grounds,—and tints.

Hardware Stores.

Aquatint Materials.

Printers' Materials.

Feathers, small, for removing acid bubbles.

Chicken Yard or Pigeon House.

A Glass Funnel for acid.

Chemical Materials Maker.

Whetstone for sharpening points.

Hardware Dealer.

A copper Plate Press, and complete outfit for printing.

Messrs. John Haddon & Sons, Salisbury Square, London; or Messrs. Kraus, Leipzig; Lee Sturges, Chicago; or W. Kimber, Tankerton Street Works, Cromer St., London, W. C.

The small presses made and sold by various firms, though excellently made, and very portable, are of no use for large plates for two reasons:

1st, they are not large enough; and 2d, they are not powerful enough. And therefore one cannot either print a decent sized plate on them or pull a proof which shows real strength or true state of lines. See below.

The press to get is a mangle-geared or double-geared machine: the former has been designed for printing etchings.

These geared presses work more easily and smoothly than the old star presses, even those with an inverted wheel and gearing, and despite their greater cost should be purchased, and the larger the better.

Nothing less than a fifteen-inch roller should be bought.

Second-hand presses, perfectly good, can frequently be picked up at a lower figure, and when in good order are frequently to be preferred to new ones.

The Model Specialty Co. has at last made a really good small-geared press worked with a handle which has been tested for a year in my class and proved most satisfactory.

Model Specialty Co., 401 E. 19th St., New York.

Anvil, Hammer.

Printers' Materials.

Calipers for correcting, finding imperfections in plates.

Ditto.

OF THE MATERIALS NECESSARY FOR MAKING AN ETCHING

The materials necessary for printing are the following, none of which are supplied with the press, though wrenches for adjusting it are included usually.

Zinc Bed Plate.
  Slightly smaller than the bed of the press. Some printers use two.

Blankets.
  Cut slightly smaller than bed of the press.
  At least eight pieces of blanketing should be purchased in order to have enough for a change without waiting for one set of four to be dried or washed.
  A set of hard, tough French blankets are useful.

Fronting.
  Four pieces cut of the same size as the blankets.

Copper Plate Ink.
  The best French or Frankfort Black should alone be used. Get it ground and mixed with medium oil, and have it put in pound or half-pound oil colour tubes and not in tins. A couple of tubes of burnt umber also. If inks are put in tubes they will keep any length of time; in cans they soon become hard and worthless, even if kept with water on the top. Avoid all other colours.
Also get some black and umber in powder. It may be necessary to add colour to the ink at times.
  Beware of most "best copper plate ink"; it is often poor stuff, with brown or blue added—utterly worthless.

Oil, thin, thick, and medium.
  For mixing with the ink.
  Don't get a dabber.

Marble Muller.
  For mixing ink.

Large and Small Palette Knives. For mixing and cleaning.

Ink Slab.
  On which the ink is spread and taken up from by the roller.

Ten Yards coarse brown Canvas.

Ten Yards coarse white Canvas.

Ten Yards soft white Muslin or Taffeta Silk.

Cheese cloth.

For wiping plates. Have the various qualities cut into uniform half-yard or square sections.

Heater. Electric heater is far the best.

Sterno Stove and cans of canned heat.
  To heat plates, be careful with it.

Printers' Materials.

Ditto.

Ditto.

Ditto.

Haddon & Sons, London.
Kimber, London.
Weber & Co., Philadelphia. Weber's have lately made the best ink I have been able to get in America, the only ink worth anything made here that I know.

Printers' Materials.

Ditto.

Ditto.

Ditto.

Kimber, London.

Macy's, New York.
Kimber, London.

Edison Electric Co.
Druggist.

Jigger.   Printers' Materials.
  To wipe them on.
Oil Can.   Ditto.
  To lubricate press.
A Screen of tissue paper or oiled silk or muslin,   Carpenter.
    placed on a stretcher the size of the lower
    part of the window, over the work-table.
Printing Papers.   Wherever they can be found.
Blotting and Backing Papers.   Stationers.

These are all the tools and materials that are necessary for the making of an etching.

I usually ground my plates in the studio, if going from home to work, and see that they are right, and carry them wrapped in Canton flannel; and take with me ground, liquid ground, and the wooden-handled vice and needles. Everything else can be bought at any chemist's anywhere. If plates have to be re-grounded, the grounding can be done with an alcohol lamp or on a stove, or with sterno. One can also get acid and turpentine anywhere.

THERE are many kinds of copper plates made from many kinds of copper. The English plates, which may or may not be of English copper, are hammered and polished by hand. They are, in their usual form, thicker and heavier than any other plates. The edges are bevelled and the corners rounded or cut at an angle. They are beautiful to look at and abominable to work on. They are frequently found, when one commences to draw upon them, to be full of variations in the density of the metal, full of invisible spots and streaks harder or softer than the general composition of the plate; consequently the needle digs into the soft places, and slides over the hard, in a most unpleasant fashion. And when they are bitten this unevenness of the metal produces unevenness in the bitten lines. Even if etchers, as some are said to, hammer and polish their plates, these variations (unless the plates were drawn and scratched all over) could not be detected, and if this were done the plates would have to be hammered and polished all over again. The etcher in these matters must depend on the maker unless he owns a copper mine, and smelting works. In fact, some bad etchers might make good coppersmiths. For it is at the works that the unevenness in composition occurs, other metals, or other kinds of metal, or alloys, being added. Then the hammering and hardening and polishing of the plates by hand is always uneven, and adds to their unreliability. The polishing by hand is a slow process, with sand and water, emery, and finally charcoal, and it is also costly. As a result the English plates are the most expensive—and the most unreliable.

American plates are rolled, like sheet steel, from the beginning to the end, and polished by machinery. They are far more even; they are far lighter; they are far more reliable; and they are far cheaper; there are no bevelled edges on which one cannot work, which have to be carefully wiped in printing; there are no rounded corners —but the corners of American plates are too sharp, and unless they are filed and polished, are liable to tear the paper; in fact, the edges should be felt all round, as, frequently, the plates being cut by a machine, are rough and will cut the paper in printing. I have now used American plates for years and found them most reliable. They can be obtained at any artists' or printers' materials dealers, and they can be cut to any size and polished—in a few hours; the British plates take days to make ready, for they never are ready of the size one wants.

American plates cannot be ground down and used repeatedly, as they are too thin, in the usual gauge, though they may be obtained of any thickness or gauge, and then, if thick, be ground down for a new surface;* but they may as well be scrapped as old copper, for as a new plate costs just about as much as repolishing an old one, there is

* After the etching made on them has been printed; lately, however, some of the American makers of copper plates have been adding brass or some other metal or alloy with disastrous results, in most uneven biting and tarnishing after. American zinc plates are now frequently badly polished having lines over them which leave a tone of scratches. It is best to get copper plates—sheets of pure copper from a photo engraver—and have them cut to the size wanted by him.

scarce any economy in having them ground down. Grinding down is grinding and polishing and scraping the bitten lines out of the copper; that is, grinding the face of the plate down to the bottom of the lines and so getting a new clean face to work on. I have tried French, German, and Italian plates: they all seem to possess all the imperfections of the English ones.

Steel and iron may be used; also marble and lithographic stone; only, save steel to a certain extent, no etchers do use these metals or stones.

Zinc is the only other metal much employed; there are two reasons: the first because it is cheap, and the second because it is light.

Aluminium also has been tried. If it could be bitten with certainty, or used for dry point, it would supersede copper, as both the colour and lightness are altogether in its favour.

The Germans, who make very large plates, use galvanized zinc; it has a coppered surface, works well, cutting easily, and is very cheap. It is specially employed for dry point. I lately saw—but was, owing to the war, unable to get—similar light plates— with a copper deposit on tin. These were as light as a sheet of paper. I believe they are no longer made.

The question of colour of the metal is of small moment; the etcher soon gets accustomed to seeing his lines which are to print black in glittering metal, though if he could see them in black, as he can on zinc, he would be surer of what he is about than when he is working on copper; but the great advantage of zinc, and especially aluminium, is lightness, therefore portability. The etcher who is an artist makes his etching directly on the copper or zinc; the duffer, or manufacturer, or swindler, traces it or photographs it. The artist working out of doors can carry half a dozen zinc, or a dozen aluminium plates almost as easily as one copper, and the cost of zinc is almost in the same ratio. I do not know the cost of aluminium as compared with copper.

Messrs. Roberson make a sort of celluloid (Holophone) plate which is of extreme lightness, for dry point. I have had little experience with it. For some reason these plates have not, I think, been much used by artists. Only small editions can be— I understand—printed from them, they wear quickly.

Steel is used largely for commercial work, but most artists find it, in colour and substance, most unsympathetic, as are steel-faced copper plates.*

Iron I know nothing about, or whether anyone since Dürer has used it.

Lithographers use stone extensively, as described in the Volume on Lithography.

---

* Steel facing must be done by depositing a thin steel surface of steel on a copper plate, if a large edition is to be printed—to protect the etched work—or an electrotype of the original plate can be made. The steel facing may be as easily removed as deposited by dissolving it in a bath.

THERE are many makes of etching ground, a varnish which is applied to the face of the plate to prevent the acid from biting it, and through which lines may be drawn or scratched, and where the surface is laid bare the acid acts. (See *Of Grounding Plates*.) I have tried English, French, German, and home-made grounds, and discarded them all for a ground made by F. Weber & Co., 1125 Chestnut Street, Philadelphia. I have no detailed knowledge of the composition of the various grounds save my own, and that was too bad to give; but generally they are composed of wax, pitch, resin, asphaltum, or some such materials, melted and mixed in certain proportions—materials which when mixed and applied to the face of the plate can be easily drawn through yet will resist acid. Grounds are far better made by manufacturers, more uniform than any artist can make them.

What is wanted in an etching ground, a covering, protecting varnish, is:

First, that it may be easily, thinly, and uniformly applied to the face of the plate.

Second, that it will adhere firmly to the plate.

Third, that it may be drawn or scratched through to the surface of the plate with a point, with perfect freedom, in any direction, without cracking up, or peeling off.

Fourth, that it will absorb smoke.

Fifth, that it will last for any time and be so tough and adhere so strongly that the plate may be carried without risk of rubbing the ground off, either before or after it is drawn upon.

Sixth, and the most important, that it will resist acid.

The grounds in general use are made up into solid black balls. But there are white grounds, so made as to show the lines dark in the white coating of wax. I have never tried a white ground but once, and found it like candle grease to work on, a poor protection against the acid; it ploughed up before or under the needle, and the sole advantage of seeing the lines dark is of no importance; the etcher soon accustoms himself to their glitter on the black surface.

There are also liquid grounds which I have never used, that may be poured on the plate, and then by tilting it, spread all over it in the fashion that photographers prepare wet plates with collodion, but they are most useful for stopping out.

Soft grounds are ordinary varnish grounds to which grease or tallow has been added in certain proportions by melting them together.

Aquatint grounds are made nowadays in several ways. Either a box with a fan inside it is used; in this box powdered resin is placed. If the box is violently shaken or the fan worked, the interior will be filled with flying particles of resin, after which if a door in the side of the box is opened, and a slightly warmed copper plate placed in it, and the resin dust allowed to settle on the surface of the plate, to which it will adhere in tiny grains, when it is cool it may be drawn upon and bitten, as will be explained.

Or resin in solution in alcohol may be poured on the face of the plate and allowed to dry by slightly heating it. The resin in drying will crack into tiny particles which will protect the copper, where the dried resin lies, and this surface may be drawn on and bitten, the acid biting the spaces between the particles of resin.*

A German method used in the Leipzig Academy to ground plates for line work, is to dissolve lacquer—"*lacque.*" I was promised the recipe for this, but alas! never got it. We got the War instead. Pour the lacquer—it was quite liquid—on the plate, and let the superfluous ground run off at one corner; then place the plate so covered over a spirit lamp or on a very hot heater; the ground dried evenly, quickly, and very hard and black, and needed no smoking. I was given a bottle of it, but it had to be left behind in Germany on the outbreak of the war. Later I left everything in England.

* A somewhat similar method is used by photo engravers. But a far better method invented by H. D. Welsh is to take powdered resin, put it in a thin, fine meshed piece of silk, fold the silk into a ball. The resin will fall to the bottom, like a pouncing bag; dab this on the plate, either evenly or more in places which are to be lights and less where there are to be darks. The resin will come through the meshes of the silk, the plate should then be heated and when it is cool the resin will be found adhering to it. Or the bag of resin may be hit with a stick or pencil holding it in the air and not touching the plate, which should then be heated.

Or another fashion is to dissolve the resin or asphaltum in alcohol; dip a toothbrush in the mixture and spatter it on the plate by rubbing a pencil or stick over the hairs of the brush.

In most aquatints the outline or main masses of the subject are usually first etched in line on the copper. To get pure whites it is best to draw their forms on the bare copper before the resin is put on the plate—this is the most sure method. One of my pupils, Mr. Fagg, invented an excellent fashion of doing this. He drew his whites solidly on the ungrounded plate with Higgins' waterproof ink, and some of the lighter tones with a half dry brush which left open spaces in them; he then dusted the aquatint on, and heated the plate—when it was bitten and the ground removed the high lights were perfectly sharp to the smallest dots—while the lighter tones had the greatest possible variety in them. This is the best method I know of, for obtaining clear, sharp, white lights by aquatint. I have, however, not been successful with it. Instead, I drew with lithographic chalk on the bare copper all the lights, and then put on the aquatint, and bit; this worked excellently.

THE American etching roller for grounding plates is unknown, or at any rate unemployed, in Europe, but a few etchers use the rubber or composition roller, which wood engravers use to prove their blocks.

This latter is a roller, six inches more or less, of composition with an axle attached at the ends to a handle. The American roller is made of solid rubber much thicker and shorter; it runs on bearings, is adjustable, and has a couple of prongs projecting from it to prevent the hot ground on it touching anything; on these prongs it rests; the handle is well made; the whole extremely well designed. It is made by Weber of Philadelphia. I have shown it to British etchers who have gazed at it listlessly and turned to their dabbers—"An ingeneous ienstroomint" was one comment.

The American printing roller is made of flannel with projecting handles at each end; these, unlike the litho roller, run on bearings, as a free wheel. When the flannel becomes hard with ink, a layer can be cut off and a new soft face obtained. These are really the most ingenious instruments I know of, and naturally are unknown in Europe.

The dabber is a round pad of flannel built up on a cardboard and horse-hair basis tied together at the top into a handle; this is dabbed in the printing ink and takes that up, and then the face of the plate is pounded with it. The dabber destroys quickly all delicate work—it has been in use for ages, because until the present, no printer has had the brains to invent a better tool. The roller is infinitely better and easier to work.

ETCHING needles are made of all forms, shapes, and sizes, from the heavy bar of steel to the delicate diamond point, from the finest single needle to the multiple comb arrangement.

Each artist must choose for himself the point or needle he likes. Haden is said, though he said many things, and many things have been said of him, to have used a heavy steel bar. Others have used rat-tail files ground to a point ; others wooden pencils with a needle within. I was shown as a perfect instrument, which I once only tried, a sewing needle stuck in a penholder wound round with thread, and as the winding was being done, the thread was covered with melted sealing wax. One could hold it well enough, but it was impossible, owing to the bulged mass of thread and wax, to see the drawing. Whistler used small, beautifully balanced, double ended points needles with a twisted corkscrew middle to grip them, which were made for him carefully by a Paris surgical instrument maker. It is impossible to get such tools anywhere outside Paris.* The makers either have not the brains or the patience to make them. The heavier, clumsier copies they do make, however, suit me, and they can be bought at any colour makers or dealers in etching materials, but though nothing like them, they are known as Whistler needles.

The question of needles, however, is a personal matter, and what the artist should use is a sharp-pointed tool which suits him with which to scratch the plate. The point must not be too sharp, or it will dig into the copper and stick fast or jump ; or if too dull, it will not remove the ground. It must be just right ; it must be carefully sharpened ; and to get it and keep it right requires much experience. It is sharpened on a whetstone with oil.

There are also multiple needles—three or four sewing needles fastened side by side in a metal holder, very flexible. They are much used, I believe, by reproductive etchers, as with them brush marks can be copied and other tricks performed.

Some artists draw through the etching ground with diamond points, but they are mostly used for dry point. Dry point needles are much heavier than ordinary etching needles as they must dig into the metal ; any heavy pointed instrument will do ; a very good one was invented by William Strang, which will make in three directions a deep, firm, clear cut.† The trouble I have found with dry point is to get this strong, clear-cut, deep line. However, it is all a matter of skill, and that comes by practice—but the intelligent practice and perseverance of a lifetime.

Some of the text-books say, but I have never known it done, that, to save biting, different sized points—wide, narrow, and blunt—can be used ; but to use small needles for fine lines and large ones for big is not to etch but to make things that look like, and are like, reproductions of pen drawings. The darks must be deep as well as broad, and the acid alone does this. One needle of the sort the etcher likes is all that he wants, though he will probably lose that and should therefore have a number. These may be carried in a leather instrument case. Italian leather cigar cases are excellent.

The sharpening of needles and scrapers is an art,—the tools merely a small whetstone and oil.

* Good points can be made from dental tools.

† Safety razor blades may be used. They make deep lasting lines. Another of my pupils Mr. Ziegler's discoveries, they are set in a handle.

SCRAPERS—triangular cutting knives—are used to cut down the surface of the plate when lines are too deep, or to remove burr, and to make mezzotints, these last, flat knives, burnishers, oval-shaped knives, are rubbed over the surface to remove scratches, whether in the copper, or made by the scraper, and to take out lights.   Roulettes of various sizes and shapes, small wheels in handles, are employed to get tones or tints with, by rolling them heavily over the surface of the copper, into which the sharp points of their little wheels or points dig holes.   Sand and emery papers and rough cloth can also be used as well as mezzotint tools to roughen the surface of the plate, and so produce a tint.   There are also pear-shaped mezzotint revolving tools set in handles, others are flat like a roller, which are very useful for making tints.   Also flowers of sulphur may be painted on the plate with olive oil, which will stain the copper and print as a tint.   In fact, anything that roughens, scratches, or digs holes in the polished plate, or stains it, will print—one difficulty is to prevent scratches and stains appearing where they are not wanted in the prints.

NITRIC acid is mostly used to bite copper plates. There is only one thing against it : as soon as it begins to act on the copper it begins to spread below the surface, instead of biting straight down into the metal. It begins to bite out in an inverted ∧-shaped manner for some chemical reason which I do not know—I only know it is a fact, and anyone who wants to find out the reason can ask a chemist.

Hence, if a number of fine lines are placed close together, the etcher may find before he has finished biting his plate, that parts of the design have been undermined by the acid, and caved in, and will not print. Otherwise nitric acid is excellent; but care must be taken to obtain it chemically pure. It should be purchased from a reliable chemist, or any sort of diluted trash may be foisted on you. As it is a poison, a medical certificate in many countries is necessary to buy it. The great trouble is to get it pure.

Nitrous acid bites straight down into the copper and the lines do not widen out below. The only thing I have against it is that it makes a line too clean and sharp; it is not accidental enough; a final wash of nitric, however, will correct this, or should. It is useless to make positive statements about biting etchings. The man who can do just what he wants in etching is not an etcher, but a duffer or manufacturer—no etcher ever really knows what he is doing till he pulls a proof from his plate, and then he has the time of his life. Most people who manufacture etchings by yards or dozens don't know anything about etching. A map or visiting card etcher or photo-engraver can bite perfectly; an artist is in a funk every time the acid touches his plate.

Some photo-engravers bite a dozen plates at once. Some turn them face down in the bath to prevent sediment gathering in the lines. Some painters throw them in a bath and go play golf or take a nap. The etcher nearly goes mad with excitement, worry, fumes, and burns.

There are any number of other acids with which copper, zinc, and other metals may be bitten—hydrochloric, Dutch Mordant, perchloride of iron, etc., but either these bite very slowly, or else they discolour the plate so that the lines in a short time cannot be seen, or do not give off fumes or bubbles, or make deposits in the lines, it is impossible to see if they are biting, and all the lines become black and dead, and there is no visible action. I know that these mordants are used and are reliable. It is said that Rembrandt used the Dutch Mordant. But most modern etchers do not, though they may have a bottle of it about.

Nitrous acid does not tarnish the lines; as it bites, it gives off bubbles, and as soon as you see them you know the biting has begun. It is visible, vital, and human in its action, and an etching which does not possess these qualities is of no artistic value, though for the moment valued at hundreds of pounds by connoisseurs and collectors.

Because Rembrandt got wonderful results with abominable materials, like Dutch Mordant if he used it, is no reason to imitate his difficulties—which is easy—but it is very difficult to improve on his successes.

Always insist on getting and using chemically pure nitric acid known as C. P. The commercial stuff is worthless.

I have lately tried as a mordant perchloride of iron. It may be used pure, but if so though it bites rapidly, it is so dark that you cannot see the lines when poured on the plate and it also like Dutch Mordant turns them black. But if a few drops of it are added to a nitric acid bath it seems to make the acid "take hold" of the copper quicker and make it bite more straightly down into the metal.

I have also tried the Dutch Mordant again, as prepared by Mr. Ernest Haskell— I do not know the formula but bought it mixed by Eimer Amend. It bites much quicker than any I have tried, does not discolour the lines, bites straight down, as nitrous and perchloride of iron do, but I do not think it gives much life to the line, it is too sure and calm. It gives off a green grey sediment which can be brushed off, the nitric fumes and bubbles are much more lively—and dangerous—but I have found a happy medium as with the perchloride of iron—I mix a few drops of nitric acid with it, and get good results. Mr. Haskell tells me the Dutch Mordant does not deteriorate with time—It is used pure —undiluted.

I also find that in cold weather slightly heating the plate after it is put in the acid bath will often start biting.

THE person who does not print his own plates or cannot is not an etcher, but a shop-keeper and manufacturer, a lazy, incompetent loafer.

The bigger the press one can set up the better, because the pressure is more uniform, and while it is impossible to print a large plate on a small press, a small one will work better on a large press. The toy presses invented by Hamerton to carry about and screw on a table are worthless, though some of them are excellently made. They do not give the real state of a plate, the real strength of the lines, if one wants to see them. Consequently when used, owing to want of power, the artist may re-etch his plate, when it is quite right, and ruin it. Proofs and prints should always be made on the same press and by the same person—the etcher who made the drawing and bit it.

The old-fashioned star press is now being superseded by the geared press, and not only is this much easier to work, but the pressure is far more uniform, and the results are far better; there was a delight in hanging on the old star wheel, but there is a certainty about the fly wheel which compensates for it.

The copper plate press consists of two metal cylinders placed in an iron frame one above the other, the lower much larger in diameter, and therefore heavier; both have axles running through them and resting on the sides of the frame; one end of the axle of the upper cylinder is prolonged so that either a geared wheel or handles of a star shape are attached to it, directly or geared up. Between the cylinders is a flat metal bed or "plank"; the upper cylinder is adjustable and is screwed down on to the top of the plank, the bottom of which touches the lower cylinder; and these screws give the pressure, cards placed under them add elasticity. If the wheel or handle is now turned, the plank will, under great pressure, pass between the two cylinders, which by turning the wheel also revolve and carry the plank through exactly like a wringer or mangle, and squeeze the ink on the etched plate (placed on the top of the plank) out of the lines on to the paper, or rather the paper into the lines, and make the print.
The plank is now made of steel, but it was formerly of wood, hence its name.
This is the whole principle of the action of the copper plate press.

The best American Press is made by Mr. Lee Sturges of Chicago; it is really a copy of Sir Frank Short's English press, and though not too carefully finished, it stands endless wear as I have proved, after two years' work in my classes. One special feature of Mr. Sturges' press is a small press at the bottom of the frame for drying paper and pressing proofs; beside which it steadies the press and keeps the weight at the bottom.

A very good small geared press is made in New York by the Model Specialty Co. This I have tried myself and so have other etchers and my pupils with excellent results at the Art Students' League where one has been in use for a year. Mr. Gorr also, the manager of the Company, arranges for repairs to presses and does excellent work in this way.

WITH ink the print is made and without the very best ink only a very poor print can be made—nor can a good print be pulled without the best. The best inks are lamp—*encre de bougie*—and Frankfort black—they are all made from the soot of lamps—or fires. The ink may be had in powder or mixed with oil. If a reliable ink maker can be found—and there are such— who will make a pure solid black—and make it always of the same colour and consistency—use that ink. The ink maker prepares and grinds quantities at a time, and it should therefore be of the same colour and consistency. The printer will then know what he is using. The average "best black" is trash—weak mixed with blues or reds or greens—or any filth—not pure black or pure burnt umber, the only colours to use. This may cost $1.00 a pound—good ink costs $4.00—yet ink makers prefer to sell the cheaper. The painter can depend on the colour maker to always give him the same quality of colours—but the etcher cannot always depend on the ink maker—or what the maker gives him.

The professional printer buys his ink in powder and mixes it himself—with oil— rubs it down with a muller on his ink slab and with all his experience never gets the same colour and consistency twice running in his mixture—twice in a day unless he mixes enough.

The ink maker usually supplies the prepared ink in cans—tins. On opening them the ink may be right—but after they have been opened once and a little taken out, that remaining must be covered with water—and then the ink at once changes—either the water does not completely cover it, or penetrates it; in either case it is spoiled, gets hard, or gets water in it.

There is only one way to be sure of your ink: when you have got a sample that is right have a quantity put in strong oil colour tubes with large mouths—you will know what you have got—and can use it safely—and it will last for a year or more—but even then the ink makers will put it in weak thin tubes with small mouths and when the tubes are squeezed they burst or the ink comes out the wrong end. This is the way of ink makers—but it is a fact.

To make ink, to burn it, grind it, mix it, is an art, so is colour making, but as I say no painter grinds and mixes his colours—no printer does either. The painter trusts his colour maker—the etcher reviles his ink maker; one process is as simple as the other, but the printing ink maker involves the etcher in endless difficulties and despairs. The method, however, of having the best ink made in large quantities—mixed and ground uniformly and kept in air-tight tubes—is the only sure and practical one for etcher printers. Only use pure burnt umber, this is the only brown which mixes well with black without turning it green—the only brown which is not hot or sooty. Oil colours may be used, but they have not enough strength or body to be satisfactory. The etcher must have the best tools and then know how to use them. That is the only way.

PAPER is as important as any other factor in the making of etchings. The only paper on which etchings can be really properly printed must be one hundred years old. Doubtless a little of the paper being made to-day is good—or will be good for printing in a hundred years. But the paper which has lasted for a hundred years is good, though not all of it. The tone of time, if the paper itself is good, is everything. The best old papers are Dutch, Italian, French. English paper is scarce ever good, German I know nothing about, and though there were American mills, I never have found any of their products, that is, only a few sheets, some of which were good. The etchings in this book are, as may be seen, printed on the same paper as the letter press, and well printed; but this machine-made paper has none of the beauty of the hand-made.

The qualities necessary for good printing paper are—that it can be easily and uniformly damped; that it is not brittle, or it will tear or crack; that it should take the ink and retain it on the surface without spreading or sinking in; and last, but most important, that its colour is good.

Some papers, excellent for mezzotints and aquatints, are of no use for etchings or engravings. The softer and more absorbent papers are more suitable for the former, the less absorbent better for the latter.

Some artists like Japanese and India papers; others, including myself, dislike them; though occasionally beautiful old Japanese paper may be found, most of the modern so-called Japanese is machine- or bad hand-made trash; the mere fact that a thing is hand-made is no guarantee of excellence, rather it may be a proof of hide-bound stupidity.

All good printing paper is hand-made, from cotton and linen rags, which are cut up and ground and then boiled and stirred to a pulp. The pulp is cleaned and not bleached, though in most old hand-made papers, there are foreign substances. Some colouring matter, at times, is added, as there are rose, blue, and greenish papers, and some of a beautiful ivory tone, though this is mostly due to age. The old paper was more or less sized—the less for printing on the better—but damping or soaking will remove the size. At times, however, there is so much size in it that if left damp long, the sheets may stick together or adhere to the plate, when being printed on.

The size was put in to make the paper repel water and ink. The pulp was run or ladled into a mould, the bottom of which was covered with wire gauze or threads. The water ran out through the gauze and the pulp was caught and retained on it, in a thin layer; in the wire gauze were designed figures of fools' caps, unicorns, crosses, grapes, mountains, which impressed themselves into the pulp, making it thinner in those parts as it dried and became a sheet of paper. These marks gave the name to the size of the paper, the different marks being used for the different sizes of paper,—Foolscap, Raisin, Gesu, etc.,—and later national and city arms were added in royal or municipal paper. Thus one may find Papal Foolscap, Venetian or Tuscan Gesu; or the Stemma of monasteries, where there were illuminators or scribes, appeared, and finally the marks of the paper makers themselves. Sometimes these water marks are as beautiful as the paper. They however became more and more elaborate and aggressive; in many modern makes, the paper is rendered worthless for printing on as they stand out and completely ruin any design, by appearing in white when prints are made on it. These water marks are not only useful to identify the make of paper, but they give the time—approximately—and place where it was made, and though there are some sixteen thousand of them known, they can with a little knowledge be classified by countries and periods. Some papers, especially English, bear the date—Whatman's always—some of the older papers also; and though it is easy to detect frauds in prints by the date, it is almost equally easy by the maker's marks. Still, some modern firms now use old water marks—a disgraceful proceeding.

Tones are sometimes added by etchers to papers by placing them in trays or baths filled with liquid tea, coffee, snuff, tobacco, or other colouring matter, and leaving them for some time to soak and absorb the colour; but they seldom do this uniformly and it frequently rots the paper and generally makes it smell badly. Such tricks are most unreliable. Sometimes the colour comes off in printing, leaving spots, or the paper so treated may crack.

The hunt for old paper is as fascinating as for any other prey, and all etchers who are artists get all the paper they can find. The greater number, however, being mere hack manufacturers, neither care nor know anything about the subject, especially the fact that, if the artist knows how to print, the better the paper the better will be the proof.

In the Leipzig 1914 Book and Graphic Arts Exhibition there was an old German paper mill and printing shop in operation, a water mill, and on this paper was being made by hand.

The rags and papers were ground up in huge revolving tubs; the pulp was conveyed to another tub, into which one workman dipped a ribbed, water-marked, fine-meshed sieve or tray, let the superfluous pulp and water drain out and handed the tray, with a flat layer of pulp on it, to another man who turned the layer of pulp out on to a piece of flannel or cloth; then he covered the pulp with another piece of cloth, and continued to do this, making a pile of pulp, cloth, sandwiches. Afterwards, the pile was placed under pressure, but I did not see this, and the water squeezed out, and the sheets hung up to dry, and the paper was ready for sizing and use. But the paper that I saw made was coarse and rough, and not very good.

Vellum, silk, satin, and other abominations have been employed for catching collectors, but no artist would use such stuff.

Gone forever are the mills along the little streams of north Italy, and the little streams of Philadelphia. Gone is the old paper of France and Germany and Belgium, gone for war work—gone to end a war that need never have cursed the world (Jan. 1, 1919).

I N all etching manuals one is told how Rembrandt grounded his plates, Bosse tells
how they were bitten; no doubt he used the best and simplest methods known
at the time, though no one to-day knows certainly what they were. But we have
at our command better and simpler ones; the only trouble about grounding plates
now is that there is no trouble—the work is too well and too easily done by those who
know how; but the average etcher, the average teacher of etching, knows nothing of
the present-day tools and methods. Even when using these new tools, however, unless
care and precautions are taken, failures, partial or complete, will be the result. And
sometimes with all possible attention to details failures happen, and this risk of failure
is one of the charms of the art to real etchers.

The present, the best, and the surest method of grounding a copper plate is as
follows:

Take the plate and clean the face of it with turpentine, being careful to dry it
thoroughly with a soft rag—the least drop of turpentine on it will spoil the ground.
Rub it with whiting in powder on a clean rag, till it shines like a mirror. Clean the
whiting off with another—best a silk rag. In Germany a strong acid bath was used;
the plate was dropped in this, by wires, for a moment, and came out glittering. (I do
not know what the acid was—I probably never will know.)

Take a vise with a wooden handle; put a small piece of cardboard between the
jaws, bending it over the face and the back of the plate; and place a corner of the
plate between the folded piece of cardboard. Screw up the vise tight; the paper is
used to prevent the teeth of the vise from scratching the plate. It is better to prepare
two plates, if one proposes to etch them at the same time. Never have too few plates
or tools; remember the advice of the Florentine merchant to his son: "Never stint
thyself in thy work or with thy tools"; one had better spend on them and save on the
results. Put the plates with the vises attached to them (have two vises) on the Heater
(which will be described in the Printing Chapter), turn on the gas, full head, and let
them get so hot—it is the etching way—that if you spit on one corner of the plate, the
saliva will dance about on it; when this happens the plate is hot enough. But there is
another way: take the ball of etching ground—there is no necessity to tie it up in a
silk bag, but be careful it does not scratch the plate—and rub it all round the edges
of the plate; as soon as the plate is hot enough the ground will melt and leave a border
of ground all round it, the rest of the plate remaining clean.

Then take the etching roller (the only good ones are made by Weber & Co., of
Chestnut Street, Philadelphia), and with it, by rolling from edge to edge of the plate,
using the melted ground, at the edges, as a supply, one can lay in a few seconds a perfectly flat, even, thin, translucent ground; the longer one rolls the thinner the ground
becomes; the ground leaves the plate and adheres to the roller; if that becomes over-
charged, roll the excess of ground off on the second plate standing on the heater. There
is only one thing to remember—not to let the plate get too hot, or the ground will either
be boiled or burnt. In the first case, bubbles will appear in the ground, and the biting

will be foul, that is, full of holes, though sometimes these produce, when in the right place, interesting tones or tints, but foul ground, which causes foul biting, is usually a nuisance. In the second case, if the ground is burnt, it will turn dull or smell strongly of the varnish, it will not adhere to the plate, will crack and peel off under the needle, and the acid will attack the burnt surface, destroying the design drawn on it.

In either case, remove at once the plate from the Heater, to the Jigger (see Printing Chapter), slide it over, and turn down the gas in the Heater. Continue rolling, and as the plate cools, the burnt spots or bubbles will disappear, as the fresh ground from the roller is rolled over them. If the holes or burnt spots still show, put some more ground round the edges of the plate and roll again; if too cold, and the ground will not melt, slide the plate back again on to the Heater, turn up the gas, and heat it again. When the ground seems on all over the plate evenly, hold the plate towards the light at various angles, on a level with your eye, to see that no portion has not been covered with the ground; if there are ungrounded spaces, they will glitter and must be covered with the roller. If the ground still looks burnt, let the plate cool; if very hot the ground can be rubbed off with a rag; or wash off the ground with turpentine when cold, clean it with whiting, and begin again. Lay the hot grounded plate again on the Heater; never use gas rings or spirit lamps, if you can help it, as advised by authorities; they either do not heat the plate uniformly or too much.[1] If the heat from the Heater is too great, lower the gas. When heated, as the plate heats one can see the ground change colour,—become brilliant. When it is completely changed, which will be in a few seconds, lift it off with the vise; take four wax tapers, twist them together, light them at the flame of the Heater, hold the plate high in air, grounded side down, over the lighted tapers by the vise still attached to the plate, so that the flame just touches the ground on the surface of the plate, and pass the tapers back and forth rapidly over the entire plate several times; but on no account must they touch the ground, or they will rub it off and spoil it; if the smoking has been properly done, the plate will be found to be of a uniform brilliant black all over, which becomes like dull ebony when cool.

If the plate cools before the smoking is finished, put it on the Heater again for a short time, till it is again hot. The same change in colour as it heats will be noticed; as it heats, it will become shining.

There is no necessity to make the plate entirely black with the smoke, and there is some danger of burning it; a brown tone of smoke will enable the artist to see his glittering lines in the copper, when he draws, and that is all he wants. If it is proposed to bite the plate in a bath, it is best, while it is hot, to cover the back, either with liquid etching ground or stopping out varnish, poured on and allowed to run about, or put on with a brush; when the plate has cooled the varnish will have adhered strongly. When applying the varnish rest the plate on a ledge, being careful the hot grounded face does

[1] There is a lamp made in America, a tin box containing alcohol and tallow mixed, with a stand on which the plate can be placed, which is good; it is called a Rock Alcohol or hand fuel lamp, also Sterno Stove and the fuel is called Canned Heat. The Sterno Stove must be used with great care, as if upset the fluid runs about blazing and is difficult to extinguish. But far the best and cleanest, safest is the Electric Heater; get a large one with three degrees of heat.

not touch anything. Then stand the plate on edge with its grounded face to the wall and leave it for at least twenty-four hours; for no matter how well the ground is put on, if the plate is not properly allowed to cool and the ground to harden, if packed up before the ground really hardens, or drawn on, it will crack or rub off. But if left alone for a day it may be carried anywhere and in any climate, and remain good for any length of time,—qualities possessed by no other method of grounding and no other etching ground that I know but Weber's. Still, many good and conservative etchers will not practise this method, and most know nothing about the system, and don't want to; and dab, hammer, and mess about, as they have been told, and would never dare to think or act for themselves, simply because Rembrandt and their teachers knew nothing about it.

As to carrying plates when grounded, wrap them in Canton flannel with the fluffy side next the plate. I have carried them fourteen thousand miles this way in my trunks and bit them after six months without any trouble from the ground. They can be carried in grooved wooden photographic cases, but this is a much more clumsy method; wrapping them up is best and lightest.

If a roller is not obtainable—though there is nothing to compare with it—the ground from the ball may be applied in the same way, or the ball of ground placed in a silk bag and rubbed about all over the heated plate, when it will melt, come through the silk mesh, and adhere in streaks or blobs to the plate. If now a dabber, an instrument made of a pad of horse-hair wound over a circular piece of cardboard and covered with silk, the ends of which are twisted and tied up as a handle, is used—a small flat form of ink dabber—and the plate dabbed all over, a more or less uniform surface will be obtained, but the plate nearly always gets cool in spots before it is finished, or gets burnt or has holes left in it. This process may have been good enough for Rembrandt, in his day, but if he were alive to-day he would no longer use it. When the dabbing—a slow process—is finished, the plate is again heated and smoked, as described, with tapers.

Always use the same roller for one sort of ground, never for hard and soft, or both will be ruined. The roller should occasionally be cleaned with turpentine.

Grounds may also be rolled on from one hot plate to another, as described for rolling off excess grounds.

The ground may also be dissolved in oil of lavender, made into a paste, which can be spread on another plate, a wood-engraver's proving roller, or the one described, used to roll the paste from one plate to the other, the grounded plate heated, when the oil of lavender will evaporate, then smoked; but why this stupid method should be employed it would be difficult to say, if it ever is employed.

Another way is to dissolve the ground in chloroform, pour the solution on the plate, tilt it about and let the excess run off at a corner; let it dry, then heat and smoke the plate, if you can.

By the German method the liquid ground—Lacquer, lacque—is poured on, and the excess poured off at a corner. The plate is then placed on the Heater or over a spirit lamp and the ground dries quickly, and is of such a dark colour that it does not need smoking.

Soft ground is made by mixing tallow half and half with the ordinary etching ground; both must be melted together. More tallow should be used for cold weather, less for warm; and the mixture put in a flat silk bag. It can be rolled or dabbed on to the plate in the ordinary fashion; for the soft ground the dabber works well. But special rollers or dabbers must be used for this soft ground only. The ground in the bag can be dabbed on fairly smoothly. It should then be smoked, but as it will always remain soft, it must not be touched, or allowed to touch anything.

Aquatint grounds are made in one of two ways. Either a tight box is used with a fan inside, which may be made to revolve by a handle which projects outside; the box also has a narrow door at the bottom to admit the plate; in the box powdered resin is placed and the fan revolved or the box shaken; the interior becomes filled with the particles of resin. The door is then opened, and the plate slightly heated with the polished side upward slid into the box, and the powdered particles of resin soon settle on it. The longer it remains the more resin will settle on it, and therefore the more ground. The plate is removed from the box after a few minutes, and again slightly heated, when the powdered resin melts and adheres to the plate.

The other method is to pour resin dissolved in spirits of wine on the plate; the alcohol in the spirits soon evaporates, and the resin dries in lines and ridges, which form the ground, and protect it from the acid bath.*

Sand paper grounds are made by taking an ordinarily grounded, smoked plate, putting it on the press, and laying on the grounded face a piece of sand, emery, or glass paper; the plate is then run through the press three or four times, but care must be taken to shift the paper every time the plate is run through the press, or the ground will be scratched into great holes. After passing through each time, the plate should be carefully looked at for big holes; it will be found that the ground has been all broken up by the sand paper into little holes, and through these holes the acid will bite as in the case of aquatint.

Grounds of various textures can be made in the same fashion by placing roughish canvas, silk, or any grained or ribbed material on the grounded plate and running it through the press; the pattern, grain, or threads will break up the ground.

Roulettes and mezzotint tools may also be used in this way.

* Beside Mr. Welsh's and other methods already described, a line of powdered resin may be placed on the edge of the plate and then blown over it with an eye dropper and heated. When cool it will be found to have adhered. Other grounds may be made by graining copper plates with lithographic sand, and then scratching lights on them, or ordinary sand may be sprinkled on the plate and in various density a clean iron or steel plate placed on that and run through the press which will scratch a varied tone on it. The ground may be also spattered on by dissolving the resin in alcohol, dipping a tooth brush in it and rubbing a stick across it—and the charged brush held over the plate and then heating it. Asphaltum may be used in the same way.

UNLESS the artist is an etcher, he never will become one, and if he is an etcher it is impossible and unnecessary to tell him what he knows better than any one can teach him.   Still there are theories and methods of drawing, that the design may bite, and print well, and these methods must and will be used by the etcher if he is an artist and not a grinder out of copper plates.   The artist makes his design straight away on the copper,—the fact that it will print reversed does not trouble him, if he is an etcher.   The more spontaneous and vital the lines, the better selected, the fewer these are, if they are good, the more quality the etching will possess. There is one authority who talks solemnly of the etcher "opening up the line."   If the authority's head were opened up it would be found full of misunderstanding.

In a complicated design it is better to mark a few points and spaces on the plate, with the needle.   It is not well, as some do, to paint the design on the smoked copper with Chinese white ; do not trace it with greasy red chalk ; as it is difficult to get these things off without spoiling the ground, and some grounds, in the acid bath, are affected by them, and chemical action occurs, the design drawn or traced, being bitten into the plate, though only slightly, but very unpleasantly.   If working from nature out of doors, the best thing is that the artist should train himself to work straight away with the etching needle on his grounded plate.   Doing so will make him careful in placing his subject on the plate, and thoughtful in the selection of his lines.   Until lately it was very difficult after covering a line or passage which was unsatisfactory, with stopping out varnish, to draw again upon it ; either the stopping out varnish was so thick the needle ploughed it up, or it dried so slowly that it was a long time before one could work on it ; or it destroyed the ground.   Anyway, the artist lost time and temper, and frequently spoiled the plate.   One of Rembrandt's or Bosse's or somebody's maxims was, "One hour with the needle, two days with the stopping out varnish."   But what they meant by this was the removal of unnecessary lines.

Now, however, all these difficulties are over.   If the artist wishes to make changes or corrections, all he has to do is to paint over the place with Roberson's Liquid Etching Ground with a brush dipped in it.   The finest lines may be covered, and the largest spaces filled with the varnish, which unites perfectly with the ground on the plate.   This liquid etching ground is now used by those who know it, instead of stopping out varnish, and it does not spread, and dries at once.   Weber's liquid ground is good.

The design made directly on the plate will of course print in reverse, but the amateur who is worried by that should confine himself to photographs,—no artist bothers about it.   Mechanical hacks reverse the subject in a mirror, or work from sketches, and so give themselves away.

If one is working from a design or sketch in the studio, the most satisfactory method is to make a drawing in compressed Russian charcoal—there is democracy but no charcoal now in Russia—this is much better than pencil or chalk—on paper.   Lay the sketch on the grounded plate, face down, run it through the press under slight pressure, when, on lifting the paper, it will be found that every line and tone of the charcoal drawing has been transferred to the plate and shows distinctly, and these lines may then be gone over with points, or other tools. The design can be seen until the lines are completely bitten in. And this method is far to be preferred to the messy transferring with smeary red chalk or other sticky materials, practised because of their respectable age, and because their users know no better. The subject is also reversed.*

In making the design on the plate, however, the artist must remember that this design is but a means toward the print, and though it must be a work of art in itself, it will never be seen by the public, or the collector, not even by the etcher—when printed.

The etcher must also remember that the lines must be so arranged and spaced as to allow bits of copper to remain between each when bitten, for if these do not remain, and the lines all run together (and in the biting the lines spread at times under the ground, if nitric acid is used or they are too close together) the spaces between the lines will be bitten away, and the surface will all be lowered, and instead of printing black as the subject looks on the plate, a dirty grey will be the result, as the flat bitten surface, though lower than the surface of the plate, will not hold ink, at least, not as much as the artist wished. Therefore he must think of every line and remember that the deeper it is to be bitten the further it must be from that alongside it.

Again the etcher must remember that though he may make the finest line imaginable with his point, he can also, by biting, turn it into the broadest, deepest, therefore strongest. So he must all the while think of what all the lines are going to look like when bitten in and printed from. For to be printed from is their purpose. Therefore fine printed lines can be drawn closely together; heavy, deep-printed ones must remain far apart, the wider and deeper the lines are to be bitten the further they must be placed apart to leave the necessary space between each, and this is one of the most important matters to remember in drawing on copper.

Some etchers use for different sized lines, different shaped and sized points, which at times enable them to get the broader lines more quickly, as more of the ground is removed, and the acid should attack the copper sooner; but such plates have little quality, and the work looks like a pen drawing. It is the amount of ink held by each line which gives quality, strength, depth, richness, to an etching; therefore the blackest lines must be deepest as well as broadest to hold the ink—which gives the color.

Most artists only use one point, which must be very carefully sharpened on a whetstone, not too sharp or it will dig into the copper; not too blunt or it will leave a film of ground, and the acid cannot penetrate this, even though the lines are visible. When, however, the etcher only uses one point, and when he commences to draw on copper, he will be somewhat perplexed by finding as he goes on working that his drawing is in light on dark, that his design is perfectly flat,—that there is no relief, no perspective in it; these things he must get in the biting; therefore it is absolutely necessary that every line is put down, not with a view to making a drawing on the plate, but to making lines which will print properly on paper after they have been bitten into the copper plate.

Another matter is that the lines show in glittering gold, not in black as they will print. And most deceptive is the fact that the glittering lines drawn in the black

* NOTE: I now make lithographic drawings from nature on paper and transfer them to the plate by running them through the press.

grounded plate seem far more numerous, and far closer together, than they really are, and after the plate has been bitten, the bitten design is usually beautiful—black in gold when the ground is removed, the black lines caused by shadows. Yet when the plate is bitten and the ground taken off, and a print pulled, frequently the result is thin and poor, and more lines have to be added, but it is luckily far more easy to add work to an etching, than to remove it.

But unless one can make a line which will bite and print—not an imitation of a pen line—one is not an etcher; few are, or ever will be, but many think they are, and more people think so too.

SOFT GROUND. LONDON OUT OF MY WINDOW. JOSEPH PENNELL

In making this plate I grounded it with the soft etching ground which is made by mixing tallow with ordinary ground, and this mixture was put up in a silk bag, then dabbed on the heated plate, and the ground laid with the roller in the usual way, and then slightly smoking it.   The ground never hardens because of the grease or tallow mixed with it.   I took a piece of canvas grained drawing paper, made by Roberson of London, folded it tightly over the plate—and round the edges at the back.   It might be stretched like paper for water color—but I never did this.   I then made the drawing with a hard No. 5 stick of Russian Compressed Charcoal (that is gone with many other things that made life worth living—probably the secret is lost too), and carried the drawing on the paper out completely.   There are only two things to remember in making the drawing: you cannot touch—you must not touch—the face of the plate with anything but the charcoal, or it will leave a mark.   Every line made on the face of the drawing paper—which must not be too thick—cuts right through the soft ground on the plate and when the drawing is finished and the paper lifted off, the ground adheres to the back of it, and the drawing is seen in glittering lines on the plate.* It is well during drawing to lift up a corner of the paper and see if the work is on the plate.†

The design on the plate is then bitten in the usual way—you can stop out but scarce make any additions as the effect of roulette or dry point lines is quite different and they swear at the others.

Tones and tints of ink may be left on the plate or it may be printed cleanly like a visiting card when it will look exactly like the charcoal drawing—or should—only sometimes it doesn't.

* While the soft ground removed from the plate will be found adhering to the back of the paper.

† That is if the lines the artist is making on the paper show in the grounded plate when he lifts the paper.

NO matter what acid is used for biting a plate, the acid mixture must be prepared at least a day before. If nitric or nitrous is employed, two large glass stoppered bottles should be obtained that will each hold a quart at least. Fill one of them with acid. Acid is sold by the pound or kilo. Care must be taken to obtain it from a reliable dealer, and that it is what is known as *chemically pure*. Measure one half the quantity from the bottle of acid into the empty one and pour on it, through a glass funnel, an equal quantity of water. Some people say the water should be put in first; I don't believe it makes any difference. Leave the bottle containing the mixture unstoppered; little action save a slight change of colour, a slight blue-green tone, will be seen to take place, both being colourless; but there is violent action; much heat is generated, and there are strong fumes given off which, if confined in the bottle, may burst it or blow out the stopper. And the heat is so great that if the mixture is at once poured on the plate it will melt the ground. It must therefore be left for some hours before using—a day or night is best.

A photographer's bath of porcelain is most useful, either as a bath or a sink into which the acid may drain.* The plate being now drawn on and the back having been covered with ground previously, place it on the corner of the bath, balancing it and getting it level by placing needles or sticks under it. When balanced on the edge of the bath the plate can be instantly tipped up and the acid poured off, as is often necessary, into the bath; it is much more difficult and takes longer to pick up the plate out of the bath and pour off the acid, so long that the design may be ruined. Another way is to put an upturned saucer in the bath and lay the plate on that.

Having got the plate level, pour out in the bottom of the bath some of the now cool, diluted acid and water; take a small chicken feather, dip it in the mixture in the bath and paint with it the lines it is first wished to bite, the lines which are to be darkest and deepest. It is the general belief that acid must be poured in quantities on the lines; as a matter of fact, after the acid has got to work, a drop will bite as strongly as a puddle. Frequently, however, it is some time before the acid begins, or appears to begin to bite.

In a few minutes bubbles should commence to rise from the lines of drawing if nitric or nitrous acid is used. These prove that the plate is biting. With Dutch Mordant and other similar mixtures, the rate of biting can only be told by drawing a point over the lines, when they can be felt, as soon as the biting commences, as there are no bubbles, no evidence of biting save that the lines turn black. It will be noted that the acid sometimes does not begin to act for some time; or there are no bubbles; but it may be biting all the while, and the plate should be taken up and washed and dried with blotting-paper, and looked at to see how, or if, it is really biting. When dried between blotters, hold it up level with the eye toward the light, the lines will be seen,—rather, if biting, the design will be visible. It will also be found that the biting commenced soonest where the lines are closest together, and sometimes a passage of this sort must be stopped out before other parts of the plate with few lines have begun to bite. As

* The rubber baths called trays are lighter and do not break so easily.

soon, then, as the bubbles appear, with the feather gently brush them away; otherwise they will remain on the lines and prevent the acid from working in them. If after some time there is no action, put the plate on the Heater, light the gas, and the heat will usually start it; be careful, however, that it does not get too hot and melt the ground. Continue with more acid on the feather to paint on the design, commencing with the foreground, painting it first; then, still leaving the acid on the foreground, paint the middle distance; then, leaving it still on those parts, paint in the extreme distance. If, for example, the foreground is allowed fifteen minutes before the acid is applied to the middle distance, that might require ten minutes, the foreground now will have been biting for twenty-five; if the extreme distance is now given five, the foreground will have been bitten half an hour, the middle distance fifteen minutes and the distance five, and the desired relief and perspective should be obtained. Some etchers make a record of biting, an etched guide on the plate, but as all plates bite differently, this is not of much value. The entire foreground should not be covered, but the acid continually painted about. This will give variety to the work, a variety obtainable in no other way. The work too will not have to be stopped out—unless it seems to be over-biting. Stopping out is stopping the biting when a part seems to have been bitten enough, and is done by removing the plate from the bath, washing it in water front and back, and carefully drying it between sheets of blotting paper; then taking on a camel's hair brush some of Roberson's liquid etching ground,—not the vile, sticky, slow drying stuff mostly sold as stopping out varnish,—and painting out the passages where it is desired to stop the biting; the finest lines in making corrections can be stopped out as the liquid ground dries almost immediately, does not run about, and can then be drawn over if necessary. By using this liquid ground, all the terrors and tediousness of stopping out are destroyed, and the rule I have quoted—"one day with point, two days stopping out"—abolished. But by this method of biting there frequently is no need to stop out; the acid may be brushed off the lines with the feather and the biting so stopped or taken up with a blotter. It is by no means so simple, however, as it seems, and the method is most uncertain. The needle should frequently be drawn across the lines to feel if they are biting; the other way to be sure they are is to take the plate out of the bath, wash dry, and look at it as described. If it is biting, the lines will cast shadows and show the design, but this is deceptive as the ground on the surface makes them look deeper than they are.

If one is not sure what is happening and cannot tell, remove the ground by painting a small spot with turpentine and lifting the dissolved ground with a blotter; if the lines are biting they will appear black in the shining spot of copper. Then clean the spot with water, and paint it over with liquid ground, and it may be drawn on almost at once, or the lines, which can be seen in the re-covered spot, opened again by going over them with a needle removing the varnish on top of them.

No great etcher, however, has ever mastered the art of biting; a photo etcher, a visiting-card etcher, an etching manufacturer, can bite one to a dozen plates at the same time perfectly. No artist ever, except by luck, though this is backed by science and experience and art, gets exactly what he wants; he usually gets a shock, when he sees a proof.

BITTEN LINE. SAINT PAUL'S OVER WATERLOO, THE TURN OF THE TIDE.
JOSEPH PENNELL

When the Thames tide turned the barges came up or down on it—drifting, or sailing when there was a breeze—never more will I watch them from my wondrous room—gone, all gone, through this worthless, useless war.   There it was I got endless subjects by day and by night.

The plate was grasped and held in a wooden-handled vise, heated on the printing heater—till it was hot enough to melt the ball of etching ground which I never cover with anything, but just rub it round the edges of the plate, till it forms a border about an inch wide of melted ground, then I roll this border by rolling the roller from top to bottom and side to side till I get a flat, uniform ground all over the plate.   Then heating the plate again, which is beginning to cool, I smoke it by passing under it, held high in air and face downward, four long wax tapers lighted, passing them back and forth near the plate but not touching it; the smoke sticks to the hot ground and when cool will not rub off.   The plate should be left at least a day to cool.

The drawing, after carefully considering the space and position it should occupy on the plate, was made straight on the copper, and completed, but it requires—just a little—thought and care and trouble and pains.   When finished it was bitten by putting it in a photographic tray, painting the design with acid.   I used *nitrous* in the darkest barges, put on the plate with a small soft chicken feather and then dragging the acid about over the lighter bridge and then over the city and finally the dome of St. Paul's.

That is the way biting is done, but the doing is another matter—when the plate seems bitten enough I wash the ground off with turpentine, and I polish it with Globe Polish—gone with Germany—and when polished the lines show dark in the glittering metal.

I then wash it with turpentine and the plate is ready to print.

OF BITING IN

The acid never in a studio bites in the same fashion on two days, or even half a day, though the acid comes from the same mixture in the same bottle. Sometimes it will commence, as I have said, furiously to bite immediately; then souse the plate with water at once; at other times in half an hour; then place it on the Heater; or on another part of the plate the acid won't bite at all. The causes are mainly changes in temperature and composition of copper or strength of acid. In summer generally, or in warm countries, plates may be bitten better and quicker than in dampness or winter. The proper temperature seems to be about 70 degrees Fahrenheit, but even with this uniform the atmospheric conditions dominate everything.

But in drawing on copper one may work in any sort of weather—pouring rain— though the hot sun on a plate will soften the ground.

As the acid is used, it turns green and becomes dirty, and at last it will not bite; throw it away, but not down the sink, or you may have to pay for new drain pipes. A method, an excellent—but not a very nice one is to spit on the plate, pour the acid on the saliva, and paint with a feather the mixture, the acid and saliva unite, and will not run off the plate and bite extremely well.*

The usual method of biting, and a far simpler and easier one, when the back of the plate is grounded, is to place the plate on the bottom of the bath, pour acid all over it, till it is completely covered, leave it a few seconds or minutes, take it out, wash it and dry it, and paint out the lightest parts with liquid etching ground; then immerse it again till the middle distance is bitten, say ten minutes longer, and stop that out, leaving the foreground to continue biting only maybe half an hour more. And finally, both by this method and the previous one, a few drops of pure acid, one at a time, may be dropped on the lines or parts which are to be the strongest bitten. A mug and some clean water must be at hand and poured immediately on the spot where the pure acid is, or ground and lines too will go. In fact, a supply of water at hand, for instant use, is absolutely necessary.

Another, the negative method, and this can with ease alone be employed in the studio, or by bringing the plate back to the studio, is to commence by drawing in the darks of the design, put the plate in the bath and bite them for some time; then draw the next lighter parts, put the plate in again, the darks biting still; and finally draw the lightest, or most distant parts; the whole should now be bitten. The advantages of this method, which requires very careful forethought and arrangement of the design, are that there is no stopping out and that lighter lines can be drawn over darker ones with perfect ease, and there is great variety to be obtained in the bitten lines in this way. The disadvantages are that it is not easy to carry acids and bath about, and that breathing acid fumes as one draws over the bath is most disagreeable.

Haden and Hamerton say they have worked from nature in this way in the bath; it is doubtful if anyone else ever attempted it, more than once anyway, as half an hour's breathing acid fumes while drawing with the head over the bath will demonstrate, on the throat of anyone foolish enough to try it, as it is most inconvenient and unpleasant;

* NOTE: See page 253.

and to work out of doors, the artist would have to carry a battery of utensils with him, and most probably could not see what he was doing. I tried it once and upset the bath on my legs. I ruined my trousers and bit a hole in my foot.

If the plate is biting in the bath of acid and has to be removed, either finger covers of rubber may be used, or what is better, an old needle, to raise the plate out of the bath. The artist, however, will probably grab the plate, burn his fingers, destroy his nails, and ruin his clothes; but if the plate is a success he won't mind.

When the plate is thought to be bitten enough, take it out of the bath, wash it and pour turpentine over a bit of it, rub the ground off and look at the lines; if they seem sufficiently bitten, pour the turpentine over it all; this will dissolve the ground, and that can be all rubbed off with a soft silk rag. If it does not all come off wash it with alcohol—and as a last resort melt it off. Then put on the plate some metal polish—Globe Polish made in Germany is the best, the English sort is no good—and polish the surface thoroughly.* The polish and dissolved ground will remain in the lines and if the plate is now wiped as in printing, the artist can see the actual state of the lines almost as they will print. Then, wash all the polish and varnish out of the lines carefully with turpentine, otherwise the mess will harden and prevent the ink from getting to the bottom of the lines, and then the prints will be weak. If this happens the dirt must be boiled out of the lines. Always wash the plates after working on, or printing from, with turpentine or kerosene. Some printers clean the turpentine off with sawdust in which they dip the plate, but soft rags are just as good. If the plate is tarnished clean it with salt and vinegar mixed.

In biting zinc plates, either much more water must be added to the acid (one part acid to ten of water), or the acid must be allowed only to remain on the plate for a tenth of the length of time. Otherwise the acid will tear the design to pieces, eating the zinc up, too, turning everything black. If Dutch mordant is used the etcher can only tell that the plate is biting by drawing with the point across the lines—the mordant bites slowly, stodgily and well corroding the work. It is a method for slow, stodgy people. Mr. Thomas, of the A. H. Thomas Company, has suggested to me another fashion of biting: that a large quantity of acid be mixed in a test tube and when the mixture bites rightly that the specific gravity be found, and the mixture always kept of the same strength—but unfortunately the temperature is always changing and the copper always is different and I am afraid this method would not work—as with almost every plate, and often when biting the same plate the strength of the acid must be varied—biting can not be standardized—if it could there would be more etchers, though not more good ones.

* NOTE: There are endless other metal polishes, be careful as they may contain corrosive acids, or substances difficult to get out of bitten lines. Plates may be slowly cleaned with salt and vinegar or ammonia, or rubbed with emery powder and water. If very much corroded or tarnished they may be rubbed with a bit of rag dipped in muriatic acid, which will remove all stains instantly, but may lower the surface of the plate. There was the mysterious acid I saw used in Germany which may have been muriatic; the plate was lowered in it by wires and on removing it in a minute it was clean and shining.

OF BITING IN

Difficulty is frequently found when the acid is painted on the plate to prevent it running about; if the portion to be etched is painted with a feather dipped in gum arabic and water, gum water used by lithographers, and the acid dropped on this solution, it will not run. The primitive way is to spit on the plate, and paint the saliva where it is wanted with a brush, and pour the acid over it, this also prevents it from running.

When holding up the plate to the light to see if it is biting remember the drawn lines and bitten ones in the ground and copper cast shadows and they are not so deep as they appear. If lines are not deep enough, the plate must be rebitten; heat the underbitten plate, melt some ground on a heated clean plate, put both side by side on the heater, roll the ground from the clean plate on to the bitten one; it should cover the face of the plate, leaving the bitten lines exposed; when cool they may again be bitten and stopped out, as in ordinary biting but it is a difficult process. There are special grounds and rollers made for regrounding. The surest way of all is to get a photo engraver to lay a rebiting ground; they do it perfectly, as they have tools for the purpose. Another method of the photo engravers is to burn the ground on the plate.—This last is the way grounds are laid in Germany.

SOMETIMES, in fact frequently, the artist is not sure how his plate is biting. If he will hold it up horizontally on a level with his eye, or a little below it, against the light, he will see the bitten lines in it as shadows, but this method is deceptive, as the ground through which the lines have been drawn also casts a shadow into the bitten lines and may therefore give the effect that the line is twice as deep as it is. Another fashion of testing the biting—or whether biting is taking place, especially if Dutch mordant is used, which not only bites slowly and throws off no bubbles but turns all the lines black—is to draw across them with a needle, and if they are bitten the needle will jump from line to line; or they may be scratched with the thumb nail, and so felt if there is any biting going on. The surest way, however, is to take some turpentine on a brush and wash off a small piece of the ground, when the lines may be seen, but as the dissolved ground fills them, they may even then look stronger than they are. To restore the spot of ground destroyed, paint it over with liquid ground and go over the lines which may be seen dark in it, opening them up with a needle. But the best way of all is to go ahead trusting a great deal to experience and a little to luck. Mechanical manufacturers of etchings never make mistakes, or take the ground off completely and pull a proof and then re-ground it again. Artists never do such things if they can help it.

IF the plate, when a proof, or proofs rather, are pulled, seems weak, it can easily be re-grounded with the roller,—in fact, the roller was first used for this purpose,—in one of several ways.

Take a clean plate, and either solid or liquid ground. If liquid ground, put it on by the first manner, described in the Grounding Chapter; * heat the plate to be re-grounded; by the second manner, leave it cold. Pass the roller in either case over a heated clean plate with ground on it—the bigger the roller the better—and when the roller is evenly charged with ground, pass it once evenly and rapidly over the under-bitten plate; the ground should leave the roller and adhere to the surface of the clean plate, and the lines already bitten should not be covered but show bright in the varnish. Do not smoke the plate, as the lines would then disappear; the finest lines will probably be covered with a film of varnish, but either they can be gone over with a point if they want strengthening, though the acid will most likely bite through the ground just laid in those parts where there are lines. Bite in the ordinary way—in fact the trouble is to keep the acid from biting unevenly; if it commences to work where it is not wanted those parts must be stopped out.

Other plates, though not underbitten, may not have enough work in them, but when grounded with the roller in this fashion, they may be drawn on with a point, but two things will very likely happen: the point will jump about unpleasantly over the already bitten lines, and these bitten lines themselves will soon begin to bite again, and are thus liable to ruin the design; it is much better and pleasanter to finish the plate with dry point or do another one. A photo-engraver can re-ground the plate.

As to taking out passages, if large, they must be hammered up from the back, by putting the plate on an anvil and finding the spot with calipers, and then hitting it up with a hammer from the back. When the spot to be lightened or removed is hammered up, the plate must be scraped and burnished and polished with charcoal.

If small, it can be scraped and burnished without hammering up.

It is better to have this (the hammering) done by a professional, or not do it at all unless the hole or bump is very bad; but if it is done by the etcher, a pair of calipers must be taken, and the exact spot, front and back, on the plate, found and marked; the plate then laid on an anvil, and with a blunt piece of steel, a steel punch, or a specially made hammer, the sunken or raised spot, either front or back, hammered up or down and then polished with scraper and then the burnisher, and then rubbed with charcoal dipped in oil. It is very delicate, nasty work. The moral is—see that the back of the plate (the most frequent cause of bumps) is clean. The least speck of dirt or ink on the back will cause pimples on the face, all of which will print as grey spots—and they always come in the places where they show most.

Etchers' charcoal is supplied in large sticks—and with much patience and muscle a brilliant surface—and a little lowering of the lines—may be had.

The finest emery paper will do the same—or make a tint too—if the etcher is not careful. Corrections in etching are an abomination; it is easier to start a new plate.

* See 253.

DRY point is drawing on the ungrounded plate with the point, though by this method, instead of letting the point play lightly over the grounded surface, the etcher must dig into the copper with the point; and not only this: the amount of colour he will get in printing depends on the angle at which he holds the point, which will either have to be heavier than an ordinary etching needle, generally, a steel bar,—or a diamond point set in a handle. A tool invented by Mr. Strang is useful for dry point, line work, and engraving.*

To see the work, the plate may either be smoked—but that makes a dirty mess as the lampblack is not fixed and smears everything—or, as the artist works, he can rub paint, ink, or copper polish in his lines and so see their effect. The whole theory and practice of dry point is that the more vertically one holds the point on the plate and the more lightly it is used, the finer will be the line produced; the less metal will be thrown up beside the line; and the more it is inclined from the perpendicular, and the more strongly it is dug into the metal, the broader and stronger will be the line, the bigger the ridge of metal that will be ploughed out and brought up like a furrow on one side—this is what holds the ink, and is called burr.

In the first instance the plate is only scratched; in the second it is not only dug into, but ploughed up, and a ridge or furrow of metal thrown up on one side of the line. It is this burr more than the digging which holds the colour and gives the richness to a dry point. In metal engraving the line made by the burin is sharp and clean; there is no burr; that is cut off by the tool. The burr, if it holds too much colour in dry point, can be cut off with the scraper.

Till the new roller for printing was invented, but a very few proofs could be obtained, as not only was the burr removed in printing, but the dabber smashed it in inking. I have seen the burr come off both on the dabber and the paper with the first proof, and a bit of burr on the dabber or a rag will scratch a plate terribly.

When the design is all scratched on the plate, wash off with turpentine the paint, grease, or whatever else has been rubbed in the lines to see them, and print it in the ordinary fashion. Only do not try to clean it too much or with the hand; otherwise the burr will go too.

Formerly half a dozen proofs were about the limit a dry point would yield without degenerating, or being re-worked. Now with the roller one can get probably a hundred. I note this has been recently done, but how it was done I do not know; anyway, all the preciousness of dry point—if that was of any value—is gone. Its financial value is still maintained, however.

Draw away with the point, cross-hatching or digging in; do not be afraid; if too black, the scraper will lighten the spot by removing the burr, or if too light, another set of lines will darken it. There is nothing to be afraid of as in biting. Often, too, designs in dry point have the burr scraped off and the lines alone are left to print like an engraving. But plates done in this way usually have a thin, raw, played out look.

* Safety razor blades are good.

When dry point is added to bitten work, however, the burr usually does have to be scraped off, or it will print too black. Do not do so, however, till the plate is being inked; after inking, then, if the lines are too black, that is, if there is too much colour, remove it by going carefully over the dry point lines with a scraper, and then with the finger rub some more ink on the spot.

Dry point work is quite unlike engraving. The dry point is held and used like a pencil, and gives its own beautiful quality. The burin or graver is held in the palm of the hand, and pushed away from the artist, dug into the copper; it is not intended to throw up burr—that is cut clean off, or should be—and the lines are sharp and clear. But metal engraving, which requires great skill of hand, is not to be considered here. Dry point is almost always added to bitten plates, in very delicate passages, or to strengthen and repair lines that are broken or weak. The dry point can be drawn over the bitten lines and, if too strong, the burr removed.

DRY POINT. LONDON FROM MY WINDOW. JOSEPH PENNELL

The dry point is a simple heavy point made of steel and the design scratched into copper with it. The lighter the pressure and the more vertically the point is held over the plate the lighter and more delicate will be the lines made. If it is depressed at an angle and dug into the plate a furrow of metal will be thrown up and this holds the ink rolled or dabbed on the plate and the film of ink thus retained added to that in the lines gives the bloom and richness to the dry point line. Comparatively few, sometimes very few, proofs can be obtained as the burr, the ridge thrown up by the point breaks off and the scratched lines wear down quickly, but now with the roller many more good proofs can be obtained.

This was mostly drawn straight on the copper from my studio window. This plate—and all the others were steel faced before printing.

Dry point is often, in fact usually as the artist pulls his proofs, added to the plate to make it richer, or the scraper is employed to take down passages which are too heavy. The dry point line can be drawn right over the bitten one, and if too strong reduced with the scraper. Often too the burr is removed with a scraper when the dry point lines will harmonize and blend with the bitten ones.

ROULETTE. ST. PAUL'S.

IOSEPH PENNELL

This plate was made with a roulette—or different-sized roulettes entirely—that is, the drawing was made with the little wheel with serrated edges which dug into the copper plate as it was rolled over it, and the scratches thus made produced the design which was then inked and printed.
The roulette is worked exactly like a dry point—only the tools are wheels with serrated edges instead of points.

THE sand paper method gives a proof very similar in feeling and appearance to a mezzotint, but it is made in an entirely different manner.

The plate should be grounded and smoked in the ordinary way and allowed to cool.

Take a sheet of fine sand or emery paper; cut it to a size a little larger than the plate; put the plate in the press, grounded side up, and the sand paper on top of it; cover the whole with a large sheet of backing paper and run it through the press, under light pressure. It must be larger than the plate or the edge of the paper will make a line on the plate. Then turn the sand paper about and run through again, and, always turning, repeat this three or four times. A fresh sheet of sand paper will probably be needed as the grains of sand come off the paper and adhere to the plate. When the plate has a golden mottled appearance it means that the ground has all been broken up into little holes. But the right amount of breaking up, the right number of times to run the plate through the press, is difficult to tell; it depends on the ground and the subject. And the sand paper can be cut unto various shapes following the contour of the design, or the foreground may be run through less than the distance as it wants more protection from the acid.

As it is almost impossible to make any corrections by this method, and the greatest certainty is required, it is well to trace, or rather place the drawing on the plate; after the sand paper ground has been made, by making a drawing of the size of the plate on a larger sheet of paper, with Russian compressed charcoal, lay it face down on the plate, turning the edges of the paper over the back of the plate to keep the design from shifting, run it through the press once, under light pressure; the charcoal should transfer perfectly, and the design can be seen on the plate till it is finished. Mezzotint subjects can be transferred in the same fashion; the design will be reversed and print in the right orientation if that is any merit.*

When the subject is transferred to the plate, if there are to be any whites in it they must be stopped out at once, before biting as this is altogether a method of painting. To get the whites, take a camel's hair brush and charge it with liquid ground—not too much or it may run, and paint out the white spot, where it is wanted and seen, in the transfer on the plate; let the ground dry and then put the plate in the bath. A tint will now be bitten all over it save in the stopped out part, and there will even be a little there, caused by the scratching of the grains of sand. Next stop out the lightest tone, again bite, and continue in this way till the extreme dark is reached, and then the design should be painted and bitten into the plate, made into a printing surface; but it is not so easy as it seems, for the ground being broken before biting into holes, when the plate is put in the bath—I have never tried painting the acid on with a feather—the ground has an immediate tendency to go to pieces altogether; and if this, or rather wherever this happens, a vile grey black hole appears—the least bit too much biting causes it—and if too little bitten and the ground is removed, it is very difficult to rebite; fresh emery or sand paper will not harmonize with the work bitten in. The best way is to cor-

* Lead pencil and litho chalk can be used.

rect or strengthen with roulettes or mezzotint tools. The whites, too, will have to be burnished most likely, as the dots or scratches will appear even on the unbitten parts; and care should be taken to thoroughly clean the plate, with a soft rag, and remove all grains of sand or emery, or, when it is being printed, the printing rags will take up the grains of sand and scratch the plate horribly. And when the ground is removed there may be no apparent work on the plate at all; do not be disheartened till you have inked and wiped and printed the plate, though invisible before, the design may be there and print perfectly. I have had this happen in this very print in this book—when bitten there was nothing to be seen on the plate. The grounding of an aquatint is described in the chapter on grounding a plate. The biting of an aquatint is done in exactly the same way, only as the dots are not pressed into the copper but deposited on it, the whites do not have to be burnished out—the surface is not indented. But the ground is much more delicate and sensitive.*

But the sand paper method is the more certain; the sand paper ground is stronger and yields more impressions, it is more deeply bitten. However, those who used aquatint at the beginning of the last century, seemed to have no trouble with it, but I have found it most difficult. I am afraid many of their methods and manners died with those brilliant technicians.

Silk, cloth, and other textiles can be pulled through the press in the same way on the grounded plate, and will break up the ground into dots or patterns which may be bitten just as the sand paper ground.

It is very risky to draw the design with a point instead of transferring it, as the line of the drawn design will be broken by the dots, or the dots will be enlarged by the lines and dirty holes will be the result. The works made in this manner are printed paintings and should show no lines.

The surface of the different spaces or tones is flatter, more uniform than mezzotint; but this can be got over by working in gradations with roulettes or mezzotint tools, or burnishing and scraping—which are far better methods than re-biting. The printing is exactly the same as with a line etching and presents none of the difficulties and delays of mezzotint.

Again, I can only say it is a very interesting but a very unreliable method. But so is all etching.

Other methods that may be useful are to take a plate, draw on it with litho chalk— dust resin on—heat slightly and bite, when cool wash it—the chalk dissolves leaving the design to be bitten. Or draw your design in oil colour mixed with siccative, transfer by roller to the place, dust ground of resin, bite slightly, wash, when oil paint will come off.

* NOTE: If pure whites are wanted in aquatint, they should be painted out with liquid ground before the aquatint ground is laid—using the already etched design as a guide. This method gives the finest white lines and also prevents hard edges, and is probably the method of the eighteenth century acquatinters. But the best way of getting whites is described p. 206.

SAND PAPER GROUND. ST. PAUL'S IN WAR TIME, THE SEARCH LIGHTS
JOSEPH PENNELL

The sand paper ground is in a way similar to aquatint—in execution and similar also in a way to mezzotint in effect. Though, really it technically more closely resembles aquatint, as the general tone is bitten in, is not rocked on the surface.

The method is as follows: the plate is grounded and smoked in the ordinary fashion, allowed to cool, a sheet of sand or emery paper is placed face downward on it and run through the press—then taken up and the ground will be found filled with little holes made by the grains of sand—it should then be shifted to prevent the same holes growing bigger and run through again and this repeated, until there seem to be enough holes in the ground; the design is then drawn on the plate; all the parts wished white stopped out, and then the plate bitten all over; in the next biting the grays stopped and so on, till the final biting should produce the blacks, but it is not as simple as it sounds for the holes have a tendency to break up the ground and undermine it, and then the acid bites the copper into dirty blotches which are very unpleasant and hard to remove. But when successful the effect is most pleasing—and from the solidity of the biting—a large number of proofs may be made without the plate wearing. The plate may also be covered with a tone made by the sand blast and then scraped exactly like a mezzotint. But the tone being made by a machine is mechanical, and has the same mechanical effect as when the air brush and other tools are used in drawing or painting.

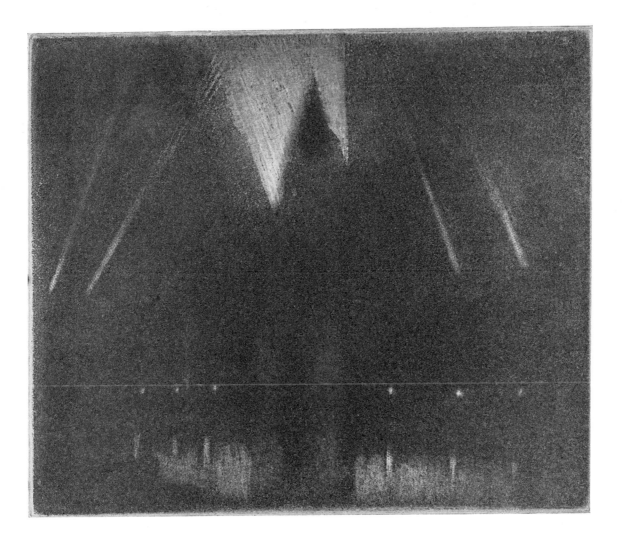

PENNELL: SONG OF THE SEARCH
LIGHTS.   LONDON IN WAR TIME

AQUATINT, RESIN GROUND. LONDON IN WAR TIME.

SONG OF THE SEARCH LIGHTS
IOSEPH PENNELL

This ground was laid with resin as described in the text and then bitten in the same fashion as the sand paper method. Aquatint has been wonderfully handled in the past, and apparently it was easy to manage, but the secret of using it successfully must be lost, as I have never found or encountered such a delicate, easily destroyed surface or one so difficult to bite.

The lines at the side of the rays were drawn with a point, they were not intended to print, but they did and it was impossible to get rid of them, without destroying the aquatint.

AQUATINT, DUST GROUND.   THE SHOT TOWER.   IOSEPH PENNELL

This ground was laid with resin and then bitten in the same fashion as the sand paper method.   Aquatint has been wonderfully handled in the past and apparently it is easy to manage, but the secret of using it successfully must be lost as I have never found or encountered such a delicate, easily destroyed surface or one so difficult to bite.

MEZZOTINTING is the most fascinating and maddening method of making a print that ever was invented. There are two ways of working : in the old fashion, which is far the simplest, and I imagine for artists the best (at any rate it is for me), the design is simply etched in outline—figure subjects, I believe, are not etched—on the plate. There is no etching in my plates in this book. The artist then takes roulettes, mezzotint rockers and any similar tools, and roughens the surface of the plate where he wishes to obtain his darks, draws the design with them in tone ; he gets his strong blacks by further going over the plate in many directions with a mezzotint rocker in his hand. If the work is too dark he lightens it with a flat scraper like a tiny double-edged sword blade. Formerly some sort of tool was used which made a series of lines ; now the rocker and roulettes make dots, with dry point burr on them ; and this burr, as in dry point, is what holds the ink and prints. If the plate is gone over sufficiently in a sufficient number of directions, it will print with a beautiful rich velvety full black. If too strong it can be reduced with a scraper ; if the plate is worked in this way it should produce fuller, richer, and purer colour than by any other method, as the tones are full, strong, rich—not scraped and brushed.

But it is not that generally employed, but one which is quite the reverse. Usually the plate is entirely covered with this dry point burr obtained by going all over it some twenty or more times in twenty or more directions with a tool like a chisel furnished with a rounded serrated cutting edge, made up of a row of little teeth, a rocker, which is rocked back and forth over it. This is most tedious work, though if the artist does it he can vary his tones ; but this is usually done by assistants or professionals, who use the tool set in a long pole, and rock that, and the grounding is quite expensive. Attempts have also been made to get the black ground with the sand blast, or by rolling rough marbles under pressure over it. I do not know if they have been very successful ; I believe not, as the burr is said not to hold. It might, however, be steel-faced.

Once the plate is covered with the ground of dots and burr, the engraver proceeds after he has transferred his design to the plate. If he has etched the design in previously, he can vaguely see it, and by means of the scraper to draw with, bring out the design by removing the burr—working from dark to light in *"la manière noire"*—the burr is cut away easily and the design appears, drawn by the scraper, glowing from the copper. The artist is delighted, inks the plate, pulls an impression, and gets a dirty, smudgy smear only a ghost of his glittering design. He finds at once that he must use different ink, different wiping, and different colour, different paper ; he cleans his plate ; if it is his first mezzotint he had better take it to a professional printer and see it printed, but even then he will be disappointed, if not disheartened or disgusted with the result. The apparent richness and luminous bits of light which he has seen in trials of unfinished mezzotints, he will find are frequently accidents ; he will find that though the design shows in the copper, it will not without endless labour of scraping and scraping print save in weak black and worn out greys ; and the more he scrapes and prints, the weaker and greyer it gets ; and then, a little slip of the scraper and there is a white patch or a black scratch. To get these right with roulettes or more scraping is heart-breaking, and the more and longer he works the more he learns that there is nothing spontaneous—vital—about this way of making mezzotints, that the beautiful early trials are accidents, that the wonderful Lucas reproductions of Constable's sketches are the results of endless labour, that most mezzotints are done by professional copyists, and pantographic, photographic hacks—people with patience greater than that of Job, though they may not know how to draw. In fact, in a nutshell, this beautiful (that is, beautiful in its unfinished state) art has never been and probably never will be practised by any artist of eminence to any extent for original work, because—beautiful as are its results—the methods of producing them are so slow, complicated, so deceptive, so difficult. Otherwise artists would not only have mezzotinted their own pictures, but created original works by this method themselves. They have not; the finest mezzotints are almost altogether the work of professional mezzotinters, estimable and plodding copyists, but rarely creative artists. Mezzotint up to the present has never to any extent been used for original, spontaneous creative work by artists.

There are a few who use it, and delight in it, and are successful in working at it—but they are very few.

DRAWN MEZZOTINT: ORIGINAL MANNER. THE SHOT TOWER AND THE BRIDGE. IOSEPH PENNELL

I have described this method in the text and there is every reason why it should be employed. It is simply to draw the design with mezzotint tools on the plate making the design in the dots which the tools leave on the plate, going over it more and more in every direction to increase the darks instead of covering the whole plate with the mezzotint ground and then scraping the design out in light from the darks. The original method is simpler and quicker—therefore it is little used.

MEZZOTINT : SCRAPED MANNER. WREN'S CITY PHOTOGRAVURE FROM THE ORIGINAL PLATE.   IOSEPH PENNELL

I did not rock, lay this ground myself—it was done by a professional mezzotinter—a patient plodding brained German, a pupil of Frank Short—killed or interned probably.   The method is simply to fasten the copper plate to a table and then with a mezzotint rocker attached to a long pole with a joint which permits the whole affair to rock, go over the entire plate many times in many directions till it is entirely roughened up and if inked will print perfectly black.

I then made in Russian charcoal a sketch of the subject on a thin sheet of paper and laying it face downward on the plate in the press passed it through and the drawing came off, was transferred to the copper and gave a guide to follow.   I commenced on the glittery water with muscle, and a scraper, cutting down the dots and then drew the design with the scraper—it was good to look upon— rubbing ink on the plate to see what I was doing—and then I put it on the press and pulled it—thinking I had done something which should rival and surpass the mezzotinters of the past, and got the dirtiest, scratchiest mess I ever saw.   So I appealed to Frank Short and he told me that all the Lucas copies, all his own work was the result of slavish drudgery—and I found this out.   Had it not been for this damnable war I would have found out how to work—I have maybe—but since the time of Prince Rupert mezzotint has become the means of expression of the methodic plodder.   I know something can be done with it.   This plate was my first attempt—and I am not ashamed of it—of trying to render, as well as I could Wren's realized dream, so I scraped and scraped and scraped my drawing, working with the scraper from dark to light, and I have done what I could.

I HAVE said little or nothing about this form of publishing etchings, because it is merely a method of printing; though it has grown both into a uselessly elaborate way of getting a simple but inartistic result and it has become also a commercial commodity.

The person who demands colour and the artist who supplies it in print are totally incapable of appreciating or understanding an etching.

Pure good colour never can be obtained by printing from sunken lines or tones in a metal plate, for the simple reason that the colour is squeezed and crushed and squashed and completely changed. Black and brown, and in brown only burnt umber alone, can be used to print from. No other colours whatever are any good. Turner's attempts to imitate sepia or bistre in the *Liber* are awful.

Colour can only be properly applied to wood blocks and lithographs (see *Lithography and Lithographers*), which are surface blocks to which no pressure is applied scarcely to remove it—to print it—the colour is not in any way pressed or crushed, and retains its quality.

In lithography and letter press printing in colours the same conditions prevail, but even here the methods of the wood block colour printers must be followed if good colour and not mud is wanted.

Etchings and other intaglio plates may be printed in colour in many ways—have been for years—one only worse than the other. As Whistler once said, good black ink on good white paper was good enough for Rembrandt and good enough for him.

The simplest, best (or least objectionable) as well as the oldest method of printing etchings in colour is for the artist to mix up his colours, that is, the colours he wishes to print with, using oil colours, on a palette or ink slab, and apply them to the plate with stumps, wiping off the surface colour with clean rags; it is a difficult operation, when there are a number of colours, to keep them pure, and the best results are obtained from the simplest plates. Some of these plates require a day or more to ink, and various dodges are resorted to, to keep the colours moist. Paintings have been reproduced in this fashion, which before being printed are quite like the original, that is, as like as a good copy, but when run through the press are quite unlike it.

The colour also may be painted on, or wiped on, before or after the plate is run through the press. The use of the single plate, however, requires a great deal of brains and care as well as patience, and is therefore not so much practised as the method of using several plates; this is simply that of misapplying the methods of the colour wood block printers and lithographers.

An etched key block is usually made and several plates for the various colours are made in line, or aquatint, or some other tone process—often photogravure—transferred from plate to plate and printed one after the other, one colour from each plate. I have heard of as many as fifty-six printings, and the fifty-sixth, and printed result, was fifty-six times worse than the first print—a triumph of misdirected energy—and the frame of this masterpiece, if I remember aright, was also etched or painted or printed.

Some few plates done in imitation of red chalk drawings, or drawings with a touch of red chalk in them, I have seen which are not bad, especially photogravures from the drawings of the old masters.

As for the coloured etchings which mostly are made in France, Germany, and Austria, they are the result of some sort of photogravure, or hack line work, in the hands of very clever photo-engravers, and printers, but the artist has nothing to do with making them, in fact he is usually not allowed to see them being made.*

If the artist must make coloured etchings, he should make them like a Japanese colour print—in mosaic—that is the properly mixed colors should be arranged and printed side by side and not superimposed. The colors should be mixed by the artist and not obtained by printing one on the other—but it is a waste of time as it is impossible to get good, or the best results from copper in colour.†

Nor shall I say anything about Photogravure, wonderful as some of its productions are, for it is a combination of photography and mechanical engraving, though in the best results there is much engraving and etching by very able men. The most interesting work was probably done by M. Amand Duran whose copies of Rembrandt and Dürer printed on old paper were so good that the most serious "authorities" were deceived by them, till they found out that M. Duran always signed the plates, not being a swindler. It is to be wished some "real etchers" were as honest and would tell how their "plates" were made.

Endless swindles have been perpetrated in this way not only by so-called artists, but by engravers, printers, and especially by publishers. The late Herbert Railton was much exploited in this fashion; I have been told by him that he never made an etching in his life, but any number of his pen drawings, and some of mine I find—without my knowledge—have been published and sold as such.

* On one occasion I went to a maker, or seller of coloured etchings in Paris. He said he knew nothing of the method, but he knew the maker of them would refuse to tell me how they were done. I then went to Fritz-Thaulow whose work was reproduced most extensively and popularly in Paris and sold all over the world. And he said, "*Me—Mon Cher*, all I know is I sign the prints and I get a checque."

† Some of the best colour etchings—are really coloured wood blocks made in the Japanese fashion —with a copper key block—instead of wood—others have lithographed tones applied to them or the inks are rolled or gummed up and those parts wanted dark, washed off, etched and printed.

THERE are several ways of using copper and other surfaces to print from, which have come to be classed with etching, though they have no relation to it. The most popular is the Monotype. This is simply a painting made in monochrome or colour on the face or back of a copper or other plate. The work is done in oil colours or ink, the subject being painted with brushes or rags. Or a flat tone of ink or colour can be rolled on the plate, and the design made by wiping or pulling the colour off with rags and brushes, or it may be made with turpentine like a water colour. The whole is but a development of wiping tones on or off an etched plate in printing, without any drawing or biting on it.

The most important matter is not to put, or leave too much colour on the plate, or use too much oil or turpentine, otherwise when run through the press, there is a chance of the whole subject being squeezed together in a mass, or even squirted out from under the cylinder, all over the blankets, even over the artist.

The method has been employed for years, but until lately only as an amusing game, in studios where there happened to be a copper plate press, when a number of men would make sketches of an evening on plates, and when finished print them. But in these last times it has fallen into the hands of the serious ones, and solemn, pompous, ponderous productions are turned out for the edification of the outsider, though what earthly merit there is in a printed squashed oil painting, it would be hard to discover, and if the work is really of importance and has taken some time to do,—I believe there arc methods of keeping the colour wet—why the artist should risk losing his labour by running it through a printing press is unknown. The press does give the work by pressure a delightful rich, soft, velvety quality, but this is accidental.

Herkomer, with that everlasting itch he possessed for doing the wrong thing, saw a fortune in it, and with that amazing cleverness for inventing something which someone had invented long before, dusted black lead, or something of the sort, on the face of the monotype, and then deposited a copper surface on it. He patented this only to discover that he had patented electrotyping, and though he formed a company and hired out plates and chemicals and did a number of prints himself, and gave demonstrations, the process died or disappeared, owing to too much booming, before he did. Whether seriously or not it was known as the Herke-type. He also invented (was it after reading Senefelder who describes it) the mezzotint or scraped manner in lithography, which every lithographer had been using for a hundred years. As for this monotype method of Herkomer, Spongetype I think it was called, the mere turning of the soft drawing into a hard metal printing surface destroyed all its accidental charm, but Herkomer had a habit of getting hold of the wrong end of things if he thought they would pay, just as he tried to prove that faked photogravures were "just as good" as real etchings. He only succeeded in injuring his reputation as an etcher and an honest man, but he has had some followers in this fashion.

Some really interesting results, however, have been obtained. One is to take a sheet of glass, set it up against the light, draw or paint the design on it, with brushes, fingers, rags, lay a sheet of paper on it, and with a burnisher or roller rub it off on the paper; the results are at times amusing.

There are numerous relief methods of making metal plates; the design is either drawn in some acid-resisting ink or chalk, or painted on the plate, and the untouched parts etched away, thus making a relief plate. This is what Blake did in the *Songs of Innocence* and other books.

Or the drawing may be transferred in lithographic ink to the plate, slightly bitten, and then more ink rolled on, the lines slightly heated, when the ink will flow down their sides and protect them, and the biting continued till the lines stand up sufficiently to print from. This was the basis of the invention of "process," photo-engraving.

There are endless other dodges of this sort which may be practised or invented, but real etching still retains its fascination for real etchers.

AS soon as the plate is bitten, it is the custom of most modern etchers to hurry, by special appointment, to the printer, who is a most important personage and to be treated with the greatest respect, to get a proof pulled by him in order to see "what is in the plate." So great a person is he that he calls his workroom a studio, while his signature as printer may be worth more than the artist's and he will add, or take away, in his proofs, anything the artist wishes, or cannot do. If the proof is right, the plate may be left with the printer—it is often sent —and the only further concern of the artist is to sell it, or to sign the prints from it, which he did not print, and pocket the cash, for money is the aim and end of most modern etching.

Now the rare—rarest—etcher, who is an artist, does not care a cent what "is in the plate." It is what he can get out of it, on his own press, not what a professional printer can get out of it, that he wants. At times when the etcher is doubtful as to his lines—the strength or depth of them—he may take the plate to a professional to see what the printer can get from it on his big press by his professional methods. There may be times when the etcher is compelled to seek the aid of a professional printer— in such a case it is only to be hoped he can find a competent workman, rather than a conceited poseur.

The young etcher is taught in the schools that he should get his plate, after end-less work, into such a state that it is fool proof, that the printer can grind out just as many prints as are wanted, if it is steel faced, just as alike as possible. In the whole affair the artist is an unfortunate necessity. The student is told that because Rem-brandt did not use tone, but wiped cleanly, he, the coming commercial genius, should do that, this, and all the rest of it; though some of the printers, to account for their work, say he did use tone, retroussage, and all their other tricks. No one to-day knows what Rembrandt's proofs really looked like, whether he left a tone on the plate or not, for in the centuries that have passed the ink has dried up and dried out and in. It is said in some cases, as I have stated, that it has become powder and dust; there is no doubt however that almost all his dry points are poor, weak and grey in colour now— utterly unlike what they were when he printed them; and even supposing he did print in this fashion, as they now appear it was bad, it can be improved on and should not be imitated no matter how easy that is. Whistler's printing was far better; and the artist who does not print in his own way but imitates someone else is not an artist. Carry on tradition, but do not succumb to it.

This is the modern spirit in which etching is taught, and etchings are manufactured. But as Hamerton said in *Etching and Etchers*, there have not been thirty great etchers born in the world, and in the intervening fifty years there have not been as many as the fingers of one hand added to his list, though there are dozens of etching societies, hundreds of teachers, thousands of students, and once in a while a real etching is produced, and generally ignored, by the dealers, collectors, and critics on the hunt for it.

The artist should try to get out of his plate what he tried to put into it. If, however, there is nothing in the lines when clean wiped, and he hires a printer to hide this fact in a cloud of ink, he is an incompetent and a fraud. How he gets his print is his own business if he does the work himself. He may wipe it like a visiting-card, or smother it in ink, so long as he gets what he wants.

Incidentally if it will not print as a visiting-card, if the line when seen cleanly printed is not good, the etching is bad, no matter how much it is faked by the printer; but a good plate always can be helped by good printing.

An etching is a purely individual statement, but most etchers have no individuality —only a craving to prig or steal from someone else—especially if he is commercially successful, with as little trouble and as much remuneration as possible for themselves.

There has been as much development and improvement in printing etchings since Rembrandt's time—rather since Whistler worked—as in biting them.

The proper way to print an etching is as follows—though the method is unknown to most professors and practitioners, and was unknown to Whistler.

Purchase the best ink you can get (Frankfort or French Black and Burnt Umber —you want no other colours) in oil colour tubes with large mouths. Look out, though you won't know it till a proof is pulled, that the ink is not slimy and weak or adulterated with blue or red, or half ground full of hard grains of colour which will tear the design to pieces. The conservative British ink makers, or ink dealers (you cannot get decent ink in America), will supply you only with small-mouthed tubes, and the ink comes out the wrong end when they are squeezed. This is not really conservatism, but sharpness, as half the ink is wasted and the other half gets hard. The professional printer grinds his ink and thins it with oil, every day, and never gets the same tone. The artist who knows where to get ink of a uniform reliable quality buys it in tubes and is sure that all his ink is the same, unless he has been swindled by the maker. He tells the maker to let him have it mixed either with thin, medium, or thick oil, and if not right, he adds more oil or more colour, that is, ink in powder. If your ink is right it is well to buy a lot of it—as the next time the ink is ground it may turn out quite different.

In grinding and mixing ink himself the etcher frequently gets tiny grains or bits of dirt which make scratches; good ink, if properly ground and mixed, never has any grit or lumps in it, any more than paint, and artists no longer grind their colours.

Press out the ink on a marble Ink Slab, which with the heater and jigger must be purchased and arranged on a table in this fashion. On the right is the ink slab, the ink should be squeezed out of the tube, when in tubes, at the left-hand top [1] of the slab in a pile, and pulled away with the roller as wanted. At the right-hand top corner put some oil which should be mixed with the ink with a big palette knife as it is wanted. Get the ink ready first when printing.

If dry ink is used, put it in a little pile high up on the slab, make a hole in the centre with your finger or the palette knife, leaving a wall of ink all round, pour the

---

[1] I am left handed and so it might be better to put it at the right-hand corner and reverse the other directions.

oil gradually in the hole, first with the palette knife and then with the muller gradually drag ink and oil away, grinding them together with the muller on the slab till the mass is of the consistency of butter.

Next the ink slab is the Jigger, a wooden box open in front. Whiting and the ink rags are kept in it. On the top of this the plate is wiped. Next to it is the iron heater, the same size and height as the jigger. The Heater is an iron box, open at the bottom, standing on four legs; inside it is a ring of gas pipe, pierced on the top with holes. There is a tap outside in front with a forced draught, and to this is attached a flexible tube; the steel-ringed ones are the best, rubber rots and breaks; the other end of the tube is fastened to a gas jet. It is absolutely necessary to have gas and water at hand.*

It is best to place these things in the manner I have mentioned because, if the heater is alongside the ink, that will get heated, and poor proofs may result, as the warmer the ink is made, the thinner and weaker it becomes.

Further on to the left should be convenient shelves within reach, without moving, for acids, varnishes, etc., and drawers in the table or case on which the Slab, Jigger, and Heater stand, for rollers, tools, etc. Everything within reach.

Before commencing to print the Press must be adjusted. On the moving bed which slides between the upper and lower cylinders, put a piece of smooth zinc, rather smaller than the bed of the press; this eases the pressure. Then the upper cylinder must be covered with blankets; two "facers" (smooth ones) and four "backs" (the heavy fluffy sort). Put the facers on the bed of the press one after the other, quite flat, and the four blankets on top of them arranged like steps, so the cylinder can mount them more easily.

Take the copper plate before it is inked, lay it on the top of the sheet of zinc on the bed of the press, face upward, place six sheets of blotting paper on the top of the plate; some printers also put a sheet under the plate; on them put flat, the bed of the press being pulled out as far as necessary to take them, one after the other, as I have said, two of the "facer" blankets; on these the four "backs"; pull them slightly under the upper roller by turning the wheel toward you, till they grip, throw them over the upper cylinder, and put the plate as near in the centre of the bed as possible, and place it with the greatest length parallel with the upper cylinder, so that it will go through quicker; then lay a sheet of paper on the face of the plate, lay the blotters on that, pull down the blankets on top of all, smoothing them by pulling them with your open hand tightly towards you, if the blankets are not smooth, they will be cut and the proof ruined; run your hands over them, and if you feel a crease, lift them and smooth it out, and then turn the wheel and pull the edges of the plate under the roller; if it will not go, the press must be turned backward till the plate comes out and the screws at the sides loosened to lessen the pressure, if it runs too easily they must be tightened, but the adjustment of the press can only be learned with practice. All these things are to be judged by experience, in printing the etcher printer feels the grip the press has on the plate, and he only tries a bit of it, and then removes the paper and looks at the plate mark made in it. He must be very careful of the adjustment, unless all his plates are

* NOTE: The electric heater which can be attached to an ordinary light is far better—get the largest possible, square not round, with three degrees of heat.

of the same thickness, otherwise he will buckle and bend them, and the press during printing often wants adjustment, as the blankets with the pressure become thinner. If he is not certain of the pressure, he may run the uninked plate through the press and he will, on holding the plate up towards the light, on a level with his eye, see the lines of the design embossed in the blank paper—a blind proof.

The plate is now ready to print from, the paper having been previously damped, —best, as I have said, at least a day before.

As to making the printing paper ready, some paper may be damped just before beginning to print—other sorts require days—the method is the same in both cases. Never for trial proofs use any paper except that on which you propose to print the edition; using cheap paper for trials is vile economy, as different sorts of papers frequently give quite different results in the prints.

To damp the paper, take some sheets of ordinary dry paper; lay them on a sheet of glass or zinc or a big flat tile. Take a sheet of the printing paper and with a bowl of water beside you, dip a sponge in the bowl draining off the excess of water; go over the whole sheet; lay another on top of it and repeat the process. Damp as many sheets as you want to print and put some dry paper on top, then another zinc or sheet of glass, and a weight on that. If the paper requires several days' wetting to get properly damped through—it must be damp all through or it will not take the ink—turn it every day, and if it begins to dry, wet it again with the sponge, but be careful that it does not mildew or rot—it will give off a vile smell, or yellow streaks or spots will appear, if this is beginning; then it must be allowed to dry, or it will rot or stick together. If you wish it to dry, spread it out, don't leave it in the pile—it will mildew. Some sorts of paper, bank note, for example, must be placed between sheets of damp muslin—or cloth under pressure to thoroughly wet them—otherwise streaks will appear.*

Japanese paper can be damped in one of two ways either just before printing or some days before; in either case it must be done very carefully, else the sponge will pull fibres and fluff out of it, and those parts will print white, and it cannot be brushed, and it is most important that the water touches every bit of it. If left for some days it gets bloated and swells up and feels like vellum but won't print unless it is placed between sheets of blotting paper and run through the press, or a letter copying press, when the water it has absorbed is squeezed out and it is in excellent condition for printing, but it makes an awful mess of the press and blankets which are soaked; after passing through the press it may be left under pressure for a while. Or it may be damped in the usual way—a few sheets at a time when one is ready to print.

Some printers pass all the sheets of paper held loosely in their hands through a bath of water or pass them under a tap, but the sponge method is the best; the printer sees what he is doing. Before commencing to print turn the pile of wet paper upside down; the bottom sheets are flattest and dampest. All paper before printing must be gone over with a soft brush to remove drops of water, or dust, and to make it flat and smooth.

* Hard paper may be softened too by making very wet and putting under heavy pressure for a day.

The ink roller is the first thing needful. Formerly—until within the last few years—a dabber made of tightly rolled or built up cloth or flannel was used; this was held in the hand, dabbed in the ink on the ink slab, and then pounded on the plate, and the ink forced into the lines. The ink went in all right, but the lines went out. Fine work scarcely lasted any time; lines were blunted; after a certain number of proofs were pulled, the edges of the lines became rounded and lost their sharpness; and dry point vanished. But even since Whistler's death all has been changed. First came the rubber or composition roller—really a wood engraver's proving roller, the rubber or composition cylinder,—with which the ink was rolled on the plate; but in the last two or three years, the principle of the lithographic ink roller with improvements has been adapted to etching printing.

The lithograph roller handles do not turn and finger covers must be used. The etching roller works on bearings and the handles do not revolve; instead of the pad or vertical dabber, made of flannel, the new roller is covered with it. Roll the roller backward and forward over the ink on the slab till it is covered with it, then roll it on the plate—rolling the ink off on the face of the roller. The plate can either be inked with a uniform flat tone, or with the most subtle gradation, in a tenth of the time and ten times more certainty then with the dabber, while the lines of the design in, or on the plate are not injured at all, as when the ink is pounded on them with the dabber. Yet if this new invention is shown to some authority, he will at once find fault with it or try to; but in the time of Rembrandt the authority would not have been an etcher but an engineer or a pedler. The roller is only made as yet in New York and I do not know the maker's name. When the surface of the roller becomes saturated with ink and gets hard, a layer can be cut off just as is done with a dabber, and a new soft surface obtained.

As to inking the plate with the roller, the best way is to have the gas under the heater lighted and the surface of it warm—not so hot that you cannot bear your hand on it. This is easy enough to regulate with gas. If gas is not available, an oil lamp made for the purpose may be placed in the heater. If the ink is too weak, add more colour to it; if too stiff, thin it with oil; but add very little oil—a few drops at a time; the pure black is usually too cold in colour; see that the ink maker does not put blue in it; add some umber,—most proofs want umber added. If the ink leaves the roller easily and covers the plate, do not put it on the heater but keep it on the jigger; if it does not come off, slide the plate on to the heater. The heat, or want of it, is as important as the oil. If the work on the plate is very strongly bitten, and the lines are deep or broad or both, the surest way to fill them, with ink, when commencing printing, is, when the plate is covered with ink, to rub still more ink into the lines with a paper stump, or fingers charged with ink, and then, when filled, roll the inked surface flat again before wiping.

Take a piece of wiping canvas, fold it about a foot square—some use it much larger—again fold it loosely into a smaller square pad that covers the palm of the hand; this takes practice, passing it from one hand to the other; and when flat place it in the palm, and with a pulling motion that can only be acquired with difficulty and a lot of skill, remove the ink from the surface of the plate, painting it off from the dark to the lights. The professional printers I have seen at work never do this. They rub it off anyway as soon as possible— only being careful not to pull the ink out of the lines—and this is the most difficult thing to do in printing. If it comes off easily it is all right, if not slide the plate on the heater and the ink will be softened and come off. But go on wiping and wiping and wiping, neither taking all the ink off of the surface, nor any of it, out of the lines, and this is at first impossible to avoid. Gradually the ink on the surface of the plate grows less and less, gradually spots and streaks disappear, and though at times they look all right on the plate they must be got rid of—they look all wrong on the paper. At last a golden glow spreads over the plate. Then it is wiped.

As to the printing canvas, it is of several qualities; try them all and use those you like; a very rough coarse canvas and a fine muslin or taffeta rag, are all one usually wants, however. When the canvas is new or fresh it is liable to scratch the plate slightly, but these scratches are very superficial and quickly disappear. If the unused canvas is washed and dried it will become soft and not scratch; or it may be rolled up and twisted about—the printer has endless tricks; nor will it scratch as soon as it is charged with ink. Paper and ordinary rags may often be employed to wipe with. If the ink comes off easily, that is, slowly but uniformly, from the plate, the plate need not be heated, which softens the ink, unless the artist likes; all this is a personal matter.

The first rag used to wipe with may be clean, to get the superfluous ink off; but when the ink is nearly off a dirty rag will clean it best—a warm rag saturated with ink (it is difficult to manage and impossible to explain)—and the plate will probably have to be put on the heater, but when the golden glow has come the plate is nearly ready to print. This getting ready, wiping, may take five minutes, or an hour.

Finally, the tone on the plate must be reduced still more by caressing it with the palm of the hand slightly inked, though by this time the artist's hand is usually inky enough, and then rubbing the palm on a lump of whiting kept in the jigger. To clean the plate with the hand is an art in itself, and the hundredth attempt to do it will result most likely in streaks or wiping the ink out of the lines. Some plates do not want wiping with the hand.

When finally cleaned with the dirty rag, or a clean one, or the hand,—every plate requires different treatment and experiments,—it is almost ready to print. Professional printers before printing clean the edges of the plate which they regard with reverence; artists don't, the ink on the edge adds to the effect; but not only must the back of the plate be clean, but care must be taken that no ink or dirt gets on the back; otherwise, a bump or pimple will at once appear in the face and print, and this can only be hammered out.—Carefully look at and feel the backs of plates before printing.

But it will be frequently found when the plate is wiped, it is too dry—wanting in richness and fulness; the professional printer obtains this by heating the plate again and going over the parts he wishes to strengthen with a very soft silk rag folded loosely, with a trembling sort of motion of his arm and hand, which, when one can do the trick, causes the ink to a certain extent to come out of the lines and spread on either side of them. This is called "retroussage." Whistler used to call it "the printer's pot of treacle." It is a wretched artless makeshift to be avoided, like the printer.

A far better way is to continue wiping with a heavily ink-charged warm rag till one gets the required tone, or sharpness, for with a dirty, ink-saturated, warm rag, and a warm plate (only it must not get so warm as to smear), one can wipe ink on to the plate as easily as wipe it off; that is, after years of practise and under the right conditions. Therefore it is well to keep old dirty rags, heating them before using, by placing them on the heater, for the final wiping. Do not wash them, as washing only half cleans them and wholly takes all the texture out of them. Use them till they become a hard mass and then burn them—otherwise they are liable to burn your place down by spontaneous combustion—anyway don't put them away in drawers.

If highlights are wanted they can be got by drawing them with a match, stick, or stump. When the wiping is finished, if too bright, tone them down with a rag.

Do not think, however, that everything goes smoothly in printing. You may get a good proof with the first attempt and not be able to get another, if the temperature should change or something else happen, that day. Printing is a sensitive art and all printers know this; the best offices now are kept by steam heat or cool air, at the same temperature all the year round. The artist can scarce do this in his studio, and suffers in consequence; day after day he cannot work decently, and then suddenly everything goes perfectly—or doesn't go at all.

When the plate is wiped, put it face upward on the sheet of zinc in the adjusted press —many etchers put a clean sheet of common white paper under it; get a sheet of the damped paper from the pile beside the press, lay it down on the plate; the paper should be just a little larger than the plate, with more space at the bottom than top; look at it first carefully to see if there is any dust, or drops of water on the paper, if so brush them off; a soft blacking brush is good. Lay the paper carefully on the inked plate; put the blotting papers on it; pull down the blankets, seeing by pulling them towards you that they are flat, if not smooth them out, then pull the plate through the press; on a star press pull as steadily as possible; a geared one runs steadily.

When the proof is through the press you can tell this by the feel of the pressure, though the cylinder should not jump off the plate; lift the blankets, throw them over the cylinder, take up the blotters altogether. The print will stick to the bottom one, and the print adhering to the bottom blotter should be laid flat on a board.

One matter to remember is that the first two or three proofs scarce ever show the full strength of the lines in the plate; the ink does not get in them; but after three or four trials they should be filled with it, and for some time give excellent proofs.

When the plate has passed through the press, the proof will be found, or should be, adhering to the bottom sheet of blotting paper, when the blankets are lifted, this last one of the six sheets of blotters, placed as backing, on top of it. Lift the sheet of blotting paper, lay it on the floor or a table, with the proof still adhering to it. Place the other proofs as pulled beside it. If there is any sign of their curling up—which there should not be—put one on top of the other, which will stop that. The blotting paper not only adds elasticity in the press, but it also dries the damp paper, squeezes the moisture out of it as it passes through the press. And at the same time the proof sticks to the blotter perfectly flat, and remains flat, as it dries, and requires no subsequent hanging on clothes lines, hot air drying, or pressure to flatten it, which smashes the lines. In this way the proof dries naturally and flatly, and I never met a printer who used the method or knew about it. I have taught one to use it.

One other matter—pull steadily, never jerk the press; you will feel the plate being nipped by the cylinders, you will feel it coming off them; pull easily and slowly and steadily, or you will break the press. The geared press with a flywheel will do this steady pulling for you.

When the day's work is finished, if the proofs seem fairly dry, they may be stripped off the blotters and placed between dry fresh ones; then they will not cockle. If not dry, and the drying of the paper may take a couple of days, leave them alone—the ink won't dry for weeks. If they stick to the blotter be careful, or you will crease or crack them when you strip them off.

If there are folds in the print, or too sharp a plate mark, the pressure on the press must be reduced, otherwise the blankets will be cut, the proofs cut, the plate buckled and the press broken. In learning to print, all these things will happen most likely. At any rate, they have happened to me.

After pulling a proof add a fresh sheet of blotting paper to the five—on the top; look at them carefully to see that there are no creases in them save the plate mark; otherwise they will show in the proof as white lines. Also in printing in this way it is necessary to frequently change all the blotters and sometimes all the blankets as the dampness of the paper is squeezed out on them much more than when ordinary plate paper is used as backing, though this should be changed every time. In a good proof the lines are all embossed by the ink pulled out of them which should stand up on the surface. If the hand is passed over the print, the lines can be felt in relief—one way of distinguishing between an etching and a photogravure. After finishing printing a plate, wash it with turpentine or kerosene, seeing that all the lines are free of ink; otherwise it will harden in them and have to be boiled out. Everything must be thoroughly cleaned with turpentine or the ink will dry and clog everything. The printer's hands can be best cleaned with hot water and powdered Hudson's soap.

With these few directions and great practice one should eventually learn to print. But print in your own way; try for the result you want and not someone else's. Never try slavishly to make all your proofs alike when pulled from the same plate; if you get a good result, follow that, but you will not be a decent printer till you can repeat it; and if an etcher, you will see in each proof you pull some new thing, and you will strive for that, whether you burnish or add dry point, or change the way of printing. Every proof should be a distinct and individual work of art. If you do not care for printing, you are not an etcher. If the printing does not appeal to you as much as the drawing or biting, you are not an etcher, though you may be a very successful maker of copper plates.

OF PRINTING

Learn the craft of printing thoroughly (and you can only learn printing in a printing office with a good professional printer), and once you have learnt it, go ahead in your own way and do something of your own; otherwise you will never do anything.

Whistler usually trimmed his proofs down to the edges. Mr. Menpes said he laid strips of glass on the edges so he could see—using them as a straight edge, and cut the margin with a razor—certainly a good plan; but I have seen him frequently trim the edges with a pair of scissors and never saw him use glass.

The reason he trimmed his proofs was because either he wished to save the old paper, or because the plate had cut the proof and it had to be trimmed; undoubtedly a trimmed proof looks better than an untrimmed one, but if a mount cut close up to the edge of the proof is used it will look better still.

The disadvantage—with many etchings it would be an advantage—of trimming proofs is that with handling they are bound to be damaged; the paper around them protects them, and if it is torn or soiled or frayed it does not matter, but if the paper is trimmed up to the print, in the course of time the print will be ruined, as when unmounted, if the prints are handled, the edges will disappear from this handling. It is rare to see an old proof with margin untrimmed. They have usually been cut, or torn, or worn away.

If a large edition of a plate is wanted it must be steel-faced—that is, a coating of steel must be deposited on it—electroplated; when this surface begins to wear out the worn one can be removed and a new one can be added. In this way, or by making electrotypes of the original, any number of prints can be made from a plate. Most electrotypes are very poor, but I have tried some by Emery Walker of London which are perfect.

Seymour Haden is said, as soon as he got his plates right, to have had them steel faced, but his plates were all, or almost all, printed for him by Goulding; I do not know if Haden could print. There is however no such unpleasant, unsympathetic, slippery surface to print from as steel.

Whistler's Thames series were very early steel faced, after a few fine proofs had been pulled by Delâtre and himself; and after they were steel faced large numbers of prints were pulled from them. I suggested to the late Frederick Keppel that he should purchase the plates (this was during Whistler's lifetime and I told him of it) from the Fine Art Society, who owned them, remove the steel facing; this was done, and Goulding got a number of remarkable prints, for they were in wonderfully good condition, preserved by the protecting steel face,—not however to be compared with Whistler's rare early printing, for he had not Whistler's advice or a proof of his to go by. Goulding could imitate and follow an artist's proof; but he could not invent, he could not prove; he was not an artist, and he was a most conceited person.

As to the number of impressions that may be taken from a copper or zinc bitten plate, they vary with each. Generally speaking, the stronger the biting the longer the plate will print, but the sharpness and brilliancy frequently go after a few proofs are pulled, and the edges of the lines become rounded. If steel faced, any number of impressions may be made, as the facing can be renewed. The artist however limits his editions.

Dry points unsteeled cannot be printed in any number; the best will only yield a few proofs; but at the present time editions of a hundred are being hawked about in the name of Charity. Charity which suffers long. Either then these plates are steel faced and then thousands could be printed just as easily—and they have no commercial value—or there is some discovery about printing dry points and preserving them that I know nothing about. Though I believe with my American roller I could get a large number off any plate. Anyway all the genuine dry point quality is lost.

When, however, an edition of a plate, as for this book is published, it is impossible, or not worth while for the artist to print it himself, he rarely would have the time, and he rarely would be able to print a large number of impressions all alike. He must then depend on a reliable printer and in the firm of Peters Brothers, I have found such printers in the country, genuine craftsmen, who love their craft, and do their work intelligently and well. They allowed me to work with them, to get the proofs as I wanted them, and then carried out my wishes, and so added to the completeness of the book.

The plates for a large edition, as in this book, must also be steel faced—at times electrotypes are made and printed from—when the steel facing wears it can be taken off and a new face added. It is a coating of steel, deposited by electro plating on the surface of the copper, it may also be added to dry points. Steel faced plates, however, are not pleasant to print from, being slimy and slippery, but they add enormously to the numbers of prints that can be pulled. Though with the new inking rollers, I have printed near one hundred proofs from an unsteeled dry point. The greatest advances in printing are the inking roller and the electric heater, both American labour saving inventions, but unlike most things of that sort, really valuable improvements.

OF TRIALS
AND STATES

STATES, if not an invention of the Devil, certainly are the spawn of the Dealers. Yet trials and states are a joy to the artless collector, the ignorant cataloguer, the canny shopman, and directors are as bad.

Now these subjects should be carefully considered, as they never have been. As to trials; while the artist is biting his plate, or making a dry point, or mezzotinting, he may either get frightened at the way in which he thinks it is, or is not biting; or in the case of a dry point or mezzotint, want to see what he is doing. He will then pull a trial, and this alone is a genuine trial proof of the plate. But nowadays, trials cover a multitude of commissions. First, the earliest, the first proof from what the artist hopes is the finished plate, is known as a trial, and this may be accepted as such, and is genuine. But if the artist is satisfied—which he rarely is—he either follows this trial himself, trying to improve on it, or turns it over to the printer to follow. As a matter of fact, even if the plate is properly bitten, drawn or scraped, and printed, it, the first trial proof, has rarely ink enough in the lines, and it is almost certain it will be necessary to pull three or four proofs or impressions before it is properly inked and properly wiped; but when this is done and not till then it is "*bon à tirer*," that is, ready to be printed from, as an edition. It has become the custom in published etchings, frequently to deliberately pull a number of such "proofs" and to call them "trial proofs." They are nothing but swindles. Others are described as "artist's proofs,"—why not printer's proofs? Footling scribbles, too, are added to the margin by the commercial etcher—in the case of reproductive etchings by the reproducer—and these are described as "remarque proofs," and sold for a superior figure. And in other published plates there are proofs on Jap, on Vellum, on Van Gelder. And now when the plate is worn out it is made into a photogravure and printed in color, or stolen because of the rotten law of American copyright which permits it. These are popular baits, and there are "proofs before letters," "open letter proofs," "lettered editions," and I know not how many other traps are set for the innocent collector. I have even seen rubbings sold from accidental offsets—*i.e.* the print has been left on the press and used as a backing when it will come off on a clean sheet of paper in the right orientation. Sometimes this is done deliberately and the trash is dealt in as a valuable property; while in lithography the swindling is worse; the printer cleans the stone on an ordinary piece of tissue paper and throws it away; apparently in the case of Whistler, these half-inked tissues were rescued from the waste paper box and sold by an eminent dealer to an ignorant collector, as "rare China paper proofs."

The only genuine trial proofs are those made by the artist during his work, and the first two or three proofs, a better name, pulled when the plate is finished. No others are either trials or proofs; they are impressions, though each may vary.

The matter of states has been equally prostituted, and equally great swindles perpetrated. Rembrandt deliberately perpetrated states and is responsible—though indirectly—for much dishonesty. He took out large parts of the design—of some of his plates—and etched entirely new compositions on them. Now a state really means that after an artist has been printing for a longer or shorter time a plate, he becomes dissatisfied with it, and he thinks he can improve it, or the plate becomes worn or some accident happens to it. So he changes it or again works at it. At any rate, a state means, that when a certain number of impressions have been pulled, then a radical and definite change is made in the work, and a trial of the worked-over plate made, and if satisfactory, a number of impressions pulled, thus constituting a second or further state; and sometimes by conscientious artists this may be done four or five times. An unscrupulous, mechanical, shop-keeping, pedling etcher does it, as often as he thinks the public, the critics, and the cataloguers, will stand it, or it can be, simply to make money, by compelling collectors to collect all "states" of as many of his machines as he can get them to speculate in.

The cataloguer then comes along, and finding an accidental scratch, a bit of burr, on a weak part, or three lines somewhere, none of them on the same proof, at the same time, or a change in colour of ink, he utters a whoop and writes an article in The Know All Von Judea or La Gazettina of Moderne Kunst, and proves, as Whistler once said of one of the editors of one of the greatest of these authorities, that "he knows far more about my work than I do, and also that he knows nothing at all about it." Haden describes a state as when "a distinct interval of time must always be supposed to have elapsed during which the spirit of the work has been allowed to cool and undergo a change, and it is not every addition—of a line—to a plate that constitutes a state, but—a complete change."

Now I know nothing of the production of proofs and states by any etchers save Whistler and myself.

As to Whistler, I have stood beside him as he pulled his proofs—not that exactly for Whistler's description of that person was, "the man who stands beside the printing press has the chance of making a good collection,"—but I have had the inestimable privilege of being taught printing by him, while at his invitation I helped him. Some others have had the chance, but not the brains to profit by their opportunities.

In Whistler's Paris plates, all underbitten, because the ground came off, as the first trial proof was pulled, in almost every case he found them weak and: "Well," he sighed, "it's not right, I don't like it; still, it's the first, and somebody will." And he wrote first proof on the back or margin of the fresh damp proof, before he threw it down between a folded sheet of dry blotting paper, on the floor.

But in the few plates that came reasonably right, this is what happened. He looked carefully—so carefully and lovingly—at the impressions, and then he would take his little needle and caressingly strengthen a line, add a fold to a gown, or colour to a shadow in the plate. This might only mean a dot, a dash, or a line; it might only mean a black was made grey, with a touch of scraper or burnisher, a weak line made fair, with point—he really himself could not have told quite what he did—and between each pull of the plate, something usually was done, so that in some of the two Venetian series, there are not, as the wise men have said, ten states, and as they have catalogued, but about one hundred, for there was work on each proof. They have never yet had the brains to compare the first proof with the last, and learn how much they have yet to see, and to learn; how little they have seen; but seeing they cannot perceive, and hearing they cannot understand. Such is the cataloguer and the compiler.

In these authorities' cataloguing of dry point, their incredible ignorance and stupidity is even more amazing and amusing. Now when dry point is added to an etched plate to strengthen it, every etcher, every printer—but no cataloguer—knows that it is impossible for the artist to say what effect the dry point, "the burr," will have on, or among, the bitten lines; he adds it to the bitten plate in those parts where it seems weak or bare. The plodding toiler re-grounds the plate and painfully, laboriously, patches it up with a day's labor with the point, and re-bites it. The artist coaxes the plate with a needle or diamond point, he inks it and then commences to wipe it. Immediately he sees a black blob; the dry point is too strong; he takes his scraper and scrapes the burr and the ink off together before he prints the plate, after dabbing ink with his finger on the part he has scraped, finishes wiping it, and pulls it through the press; that bit is pale, wiped out; the cataloguer comes along: "eleventh state, dry point almost gone." It was the first. The artist adds a little more dry point; it is not strong enough; and this second state is described as the ninth.

Finally, after several more workings by the artist with the point, we have, according to the cataloguer, the magnificent first state, which is really the last. It is in this way art history, art criticism, states, proofs, and catalogues are made by the artless.

In fact in some plates no one but the artist knows which was the first state—and he has forgotten!

There is one other matter that might be referred to here—the signing of proofs—no artist will print an excessive number, nor will he sign any but the best, he should sign them either when printed—or when he sells them—never exhibit them unsigned—but if he wait until they are sold he may wait a lifetime—I remember seeing Whistler signing some of his early proofs just before his death—and he signed them with the latest butterfly, adding confusion to the confounded. This method of signing may be seen in early proofs of the Avery Collection in the New York Public Library.

In fact, the collection of prints is becoming more and more a matter of rarities and states managed like stamp collecting while the prices of many artist's works have been so ridiculously boomed that they are out of the reach of the ordinary individual. But collections may still be made by the intelligent if they have judgment and avoid the popular who are always with us—waiting for a fall.

THE publication of the print is the root of most modern etching, and like money the root of the evil of bad prints which flourishes, or did flourish, till the War. The labourer is worthy of his hire, but in etching he mostly is not worth hiring. It is quite true that Dürer sent out his Frau to his stall in the marketplace, to sell his prints, and travelled in and drummed them during his journey to the Netherlands, remitting orders to be filled, that he took from emperors and business men by the way, to the house in Nuremberg. Rembrandt too worked for Clement de Jonghe, who was not only amongst the first, but is still amongst the small band of intelligent, appreciative dealers.

But there is no question that Dürer did his prints for his own pleasure, and so did Rembrandt more or less, but the pecuniary success of these masters instilled into their pupils the hope of gain—before the love of art. And after Rembrandt came a slump.

And until Whistler and Meryon appeared, the love of etching for etching's sake disappeared off the face of the earth. Meryon certainly etched in his way for the love of Paris. Haden as a most profitable amusement. Whistler because by etching alone he could say certain things he wanted to say. But for years that was really all he got out of it.

There were always a few people who cared for his prints. The French Set of Twelve, published in 1859, was sold and advertised for years at two guineas; but prices were gradually and slowly increased. The Thames Series were at one time published for a pound apiece. The first twelve Venice Plates were a failure at fifty pounds. There were a hundred proofs printed, for years few wanted them at four guineas each; and the Second Set of twenty-six of which fifty each were printed, (thirty-five of some) at the same price—the commercial can work out the figures—and Whistler never could get any more sets published. Meryon had sold his proofs for a few sous, but he did not print them, until he was cornered and boomed in the Stock Exchange fashion. Haden alone flourished. Then America was tapped by Cadart, a French dealer who brought a collection to New York and exhibited it. Clubs were formed all over the world. Then there began to appear books, portfolios, magazines illustrated with etchings made to order; and large machines, original or reproductive, real or faked, with remarques and other baits to the amateur, vellum proofs and satin pulls, and I do not know what all—all over their surfaces, fronts and back. They were an appalling success, and the artist etchers were suppressed. Then came the huge architectural offences, and the poor artist could not get the chance to publish anything or even sell anything, while of these machines, the proofs could not be printed fast enough to supply the market. The dealers made fortunes, the printers made fortunes—even the people who turned out the plates made fortunes. All the while Whistler was working, Buhot was working. Haden went on making a fortune. It was a happy time all round for all but the artists. Hamerton has described it; others exploited it.[1]

[1] Two artistic attempts were made in England by Hamerton and Seeley in the *Portfolio* to issue good etchings and here by S. R. Koehler in the *American Art Review*, and in his book *Etching*. The *Review* came to an end in two years, and the book on *Etching*, containing much valuable information on prints and collecting, is scarce known.

And then came another slump.   Great work had been done but no one wanted it, and the only thing that was wanted was the huge plate, "the offence."

Disgusted, even bankrupt, Whistler smashed his plates.   Meryon was dead. Haden sailed on triumphantly.   But there was scarce a painter who did not etch—the world was flooded with etchings.   Then—I do not see how or why—people got tired of etching, and the bubble burst.   All but the few who really cared stopped etching.

And for years the etcher hid his plates and lived somehow by something else.

Still the big plate continued to appear in France, Germany, England, and America.

But things got worse and worse, till—the new etchers appeared and they came on one after the other, mostly the product of Societies of Etchers and Engravers, and to these geniuses the same old methods were applied with new ones—the same old tricks, only more wonderful; geniuses were not only invented, but hallmarked, catalogued, canonized; prints were subscribed before made and cornered before printed. You could pick up a Rembrandt any day: you were scarcely allowed a peep at these precious precocities.   Whistler was knocked from his niche, so it was said.

One new trick was a Guild of Print Sellers, who formed a ring, and tried to compel artists to join, with a threat of neither showing nor even selling etchers' work if they did not join this trust.   It was made in Germany, swallowed in England, approved in America by some dealers.

The artist was frightened, and whole societies, including the Painter Etchers, joined; but the scheme was, if not the invention, the support of, or supported by a number of German Jews, and they disappeared at the commencement of the War.   Some got caught in Germany, a few volunteered—on which side was not stated—others removed their shop signs in England and America, and this scheme for encouraging print selling has not since been much in evidence.

As to the number of proofs an artist should pull: that depends on two matters, how many the plate will yield and how many the Etcher within that number wishes to pull— or how many are ordered—generally speaking no more than one hundred—many plates won't yield that—and frequently collectors would not have a print if they knew so many had been pulled.   It is a good thing, as some do, to number proofs.   All these genuine proofs of course should be pulled from the bare copper.

The etching bubble will soon burst—even now, the dealer boomed and inflated are coming to their senses or collectors are—and dealers too.   Prices of prints have soared to such a height that the chosen and boomed are frightened for the crash is coming, and swell studios will be vacant and swell artists forlorn.

ETCHINGS and other prints should be placed in sunk, cut-out mounts, the back of which should be of white paper—mounting boards; and the prints should only be fastened down at the top corners by folded bits of adhesive paper. If there are cockles in them they should be properly pressed—but not till long after they are dried,—and if printed in the way described in this book, they will require very little pressing. It is best to get a mounter and print cutter to do this if necessary. Before being mounted they should be placed on sheets of drawing paper, to judge their colour, which, if the paper they are printed on is thin, will greatly improve their appearance. If the mount is fastened at the top and hinged, it can be lifted up and the margins of the print examined; while the print may be raised up, and the paper looked at from the back. The real, the true collector loves to handle, to fondle his prints, to caress them, as well as to look at them.

Now as to looking at prints, they should be held sideways to the light; this will cause the embossed lines to cast a shadow, and this gives the true effect to the etched lines, in fact adds to their effect. And the collector should get all the effect he can, all the effect the artist tried for, out of his prints.

The shape of the mount is as important as the colour. All etchings should be so mounted (that is, if they are of reasonable size) that the mounts may be all upright. A definite size of mount must be chosen, roughly six inches taller than the tallest upright print, five inches wider than the broadest one. There are positive and fixed proportions for mounting a print, as for printing a book, and equally fixed rules, scarce any of which are known to or observed by mount cutters, collectors, printers, or etchers, even by museums or galleries. If uniform sizes were adopted, print shows could be arranged with half the present delay, trouble, and expense.

First, all prints must be mounted of the same height measured from the top, and that height should be two inches. The sides should both be at least half an inch wider— better an inch wider; there should then be at least four inches of mount at the bottom. The mounts all the same size, the openings only cut to fit the prints; therefore they will always fit the same sized frame, box, or portfolio.

As to the colour of the mounts: never use dead white, or any strongly coloured paper; none but creamy yellowish tints. Any others always make the prints look mean. Gold mounts are vile for etchings. A simple yellow-toned paper or board—very slightly yellow, really ivory-toned—is best of all. At any rate the mount must be lower in tone than the paper of the print which will concentrate the effect on that.

There are many things to-day to be guarded against in collecting etchings, amongst them outrageous frauds. The worst was perpetrated some years ago by an etcher who made a series of pen drawings, had them reproduced by a photo-engraver, and after more or less tinkering at them with a point, sold them as etchings. The swindle was detected, and the Etcher is almost forgotten.

It is quite easy in most cases to detect these frauds by simply passing the fingers lightly over the print. The sham etching has no relief on the paper and the fingers glide over the surface without feeling any resistance. On a genuine etching the lines can be distinctly felt. The colour, too, of the lines is different in the fake; it is mostly flat and grey. And the quality of the lines also, unless they have been gone over with a point or burin, is mean, because there is no depth to them,—they hold no ink.

Many swindles and fakes and photographic deceptions have been perpetrated in late years, but the genuine etcher will not condescend to such tricks, and the genuine photo-engraver usually signs his name on the plate; though he often conceals it for the purpose of deceiving—as a joke—the elect, or so that the print may not be injured or disfigured.

But briefly, the person who cannot tell a reproduction from an original, a commercial print from an artist's proof, had better not collect, catalogue, or curate, certainly not without consulting someone who can tell him what he is getting, what he is looking at, when he sees it.

To artists who have their plates printed for them, there is always a danger of more prints being pulled than were ordered, and in a few cases of these not being handed to the artist or destroyed. It is the custom of printers that the master printer may, if he likes, ask the etcher to sign for him, to dedicate to him a proof, and most printers who care, have fine collections of signed proofs, with often most interesting personal records by the artist and printer written on them. But it is a very different matter, when, after that printer's death, or his abandonment of business, in a burst of conscientious generosity, a whole mass of artists' prints, sometimes unsigned, appear. In this case the artist should seize them. If they are signed, and this has happened, and the artist can detect his forged signature, he should destroy them. But the moral is, the etcher should print his own plates. The master printers are mostly honest, but strange things have been known to happen when the artist leaves his plates about printing offices. I cannot repeat too often, as Whistler said, "the man who stands beside the printing press has a chance to make a very good collection."

Some most excellent printers have played most extraordinary games. There was one, who, when he had pulled a proof, with the etcher standing beside him, would look at it, groan, crush it, and twist it in his hands, and with a sigh throw it in the waste paper box. It was months after that the artist in a print shop came across his finest proof, which had been carefully flattened and pressed, and he was invited to sign it; sometimes he did, and sometimes he seized it. But that printer is no more.

Solander cases, tight fitting cases, are the best for preserving prints. The mounts must therefore be uniform—and there are museum sizes—but rarely do two museums keep to the same size. A little elementary interchange of brains on this subject amongst curators would be a good thing. But if the artist or collector will have his prints all put in the same sized mounts, and all upright in these mounts, as I have said, he will save himself much trouble and big frame bills, and can look at his collection with pleasure, or send it easily to an exhibition.

The cases also should be kept in chests of drawers, each drawer labelled with its contents, and a catalogue made. Or the prints may be kept in these shallow drawers in brown paper covers with the titles written on them. These or the cases should only be taken out one at a time, looked at and then put away. I state all these rules, but, save in the case of uniform mounting, I am afraid I practise little of my preaching, and waste hours in consequence, putting things to rights after my prints have been looked over. Still, the methods I suggest are the right ones.

The framing of etchings is also an art, and etchers have no knowledge of the subject mostly, any more than of mounting. White enamelled, or a creamy white, wood is best. Whistler used to paint over the white enamel straight narrow parallel lines in rose, purple, or blue, sometimes, but rarely, adding a butterfly. Now the advantage and the use and the beauty of the scheme is this: if the frames are all of the same size,—as his were and mine are—if hung in a private house they look uniform and quiet; in a public exhibition the hangers can hang them in a group; and not only this: being hung in a group they attract attention and prove that the artist had some idea not only of making people look at his work, but of decoration.

The average etcher frames his prints in any old thing of any size that is kicking round the studio; it is therefore impossible to make a group; that is, however, the last thing the average hanger thinks of.

Some prints look best in dull black. The gorgeous frames of the average print are a cloak for the bad work within them.

And if the Committee of an Exhibition makes any suggestion, it is to use narrow mounts and frames in natural wood—the most unnatural, inartistic, and vulgar method, their only ideal is to stick as much as possible on the wall, when, as everyone knows, a foot of good white mount in a decent frame thoughtfully and spaciously hung is worth a yard of bad etching badly mounted, badly framed, badly hung; but the latter is the respectable business method of the respectable commercial etcher.

In the Salon and Royal Academy gold frames are required, but no one visits those sepulchres to see good etching. The right rule is to frame prints uniformly in a way that displays them.—The way I have described.

THERE is as much art in presenting a work of art as there is in producing it. And there are as few people capable of showing a work of art as of making it. Yet the world contains more galleries than one can see to-day, and more bad results in selection and arrangement are displayed on the walls than ever before in the arrangement of a Print Room.

To-day every town must have a gallery—and every gallery its print room. And these must be made and furnished while you wait. There must be Raphaels, Friths, Titians, Bouguereaus, Lippo Lippis, Hobbemas, Michael Angelos, Rembrandts, Turners, Marises, Corots—to say nothing of the local home-made genius and Whistler— and the directors get them while they wait—and they don't have to wait long—and the print rooms are made up in the same fashion.

The public gallery is the outcome of the private collection. Often it remains in the original rooms, never intended for the exhibition of works of art at all. The collector of the works frequently knew nothing of art, but he knew what he liked; he knew nothing of hanging and arrangement, but he knew just how and where he wanted his collection placed and proper presentment had nothing to do with it. The present-day collector and hanger follows tradition in this matter, as the wayfarer and tourist may see, no matter how fast he hurries through a collection armed with Baedeker and Berenson to do his thinking and seeing for him. Though galleries are the "grave-yards of dead art" there is no reason why they should be sad, dreary, tiresome, pompous, gaudy, pretentious —but of a certainty they are—and from most modern Print Rooms, Galleries, and Exhibitions one comes away tired, bored, fatigued; even the most hardened of us, now that art is upon the world—or was—but in time of war a little brains would enable us to prepare for peace even in the arrangement of galleries if anything is left of any of them. Most of the European Galleries too are cursed with legacies and the American millionnaire also has descended on ours. In Europe now the Galleries only accept what they want. Here the collector or owner threatens, demands, and dumps.

Can this all be changed? Guide Books, artless but artful authorities, perambulating lecturers, circulating shows, students and hacks making messes of masterpieces, competitions for the best picture of the year, the judgment of babes and sucklings, will not do it—nor most of the other methods of dragging people to galleries. But the proper lighting, arrangement and hanging of the rooms will make them bright, attractive, and gay, will make visitors come to Exhibitions in them, temporary or permanent, and when they come, look at the works shown with pleasure, instead of wandering aimlessly or conductedly about—a duty to be done. I am referring to all sorts of Exhibitions. There are any number of ways of arranging art shows—there is only one right way. We all know the academic method, and artists who are mostly artless and cowards or toadies are responsible for it. As many works as possible are accepted, and the walls are papered with them from floor to ceiling, the hanging committee saying they must hang everything selected, and the selecting committee accepting everything they can. This idea of two committees to do the work of one is ridiculous—if mainly American; the only workable committee is composed of three artists, a painter, sculptor and graver; and if two of these should fall ill, the result will be far better. No collectors with taste, patrons with cash, or curators with unpractical ideas should be allowed to select or hang, but the entire management should be in the hands of a committee of artists, preferably exhibitors. The average curator follows the academic method, forgetting his cellars and garrets, where certain of his treasures—and most of the things sent in—should repose.

As for the collector when he starts hanging there is no stopping him. I have known some who have not only covered their walls, but their doors, others who use bath-tubs and dark entries, and of one his housekeeper said, "I know in which bureau drawer the new Crivelli is, but I don't know where his old shirts are now."

Another method is to select a work owned by an important collector or popular painter, especially if on the committee, give it the place of honour, and surround it with the worst rubbish accepted. The picture in the place of honour will look quite well sometimes; the owner or painter is delighted, and so are all those hung near it—till they find out that they would not have been hung otherwise.

There are many more schemes but they all have had one result, the formation for reform, of independent societies and secessions managed by artists for artists. These frequently have gone to the other extreme, and the results are evident all over the continent of Europe, though they have culminated in Austria where one frequently has to hunt for the art amid the riot of architecture and decoration.

I do not propose to say anything either about Arts and Crafts Exhibitions—in Germany and Austria they were well arranged at times—the endeavour being made to show the exhibits as they will appear in the places they are intended for. In England these shows are hung like a bargain sale, or else so elaborately that it takes endless time and money to arrange them. They please their customers—they are nothing but shops—but few artists, and to be a decorator one must be an artist, though this was never understood by William Morris and is unknown to most of his successors. The French have lost all sense of decoration and arrangement, though the British Decorative Art Exhibition in Paris, 1914, arranged by the Arts and Crafts Exhibition Society, was wonderfully well done—a model both to the French and British.

To make a proper exhibition of art there must be a proper gallery, a building, rooms, or a room built to show works of art in and not to show off the cleverness of architects and decorators or the costumes of the visitors. The spectator should think of nothing but the exhibits when in the gallery, only see the works on the walls; there should be no evidence how they were shown—they should just be seen.

Very few such galleries have been built; frequently an accidental or unintentional building is better and answers the requirements perfectly. The best galleries I have ever seen were built up inside a skating rink. I do not advocate skating rinks, but this was an occasion on which "art happened," and so did the rink, and it happened under the direction of Whistler, who is entirely responsible for the proper arrangement and hanging of modern exhibitions, though this fact is not known. Yet much that is improper in their arrangement is improperly attributed to him.

OF THE ARRANGEMENT OF A PRINT ROOM

The question of lighting is most important of all.

Whether the roof—skylight—is flat, curved, or peaked does not so much matter, save structurally. What is wanted is that a flat tone of light should fall on the flat wall just where and when it is wanted, and nowhere else. That the light should be uniform—unbroken—not cut up by reflections or shadows from girders or corners.

Where the light is wanted is alone on the walls of the room, where the works are to be shown.   If the gallery is devoted to sculpture the light should be as near as possible that without the gallery, the light of nature. The skylights should either be of plain glass or whitish glass. I have seen the most fierce and weird effects with tinted glass made by an ingenious architect with decorative ideas, or with the shadows of girders— by one who had no ideas—or brains.

What I have now to say concerns the exhibition of prints, but the statements refer to the proper showing of paintings as well, though most painters do not believe it.

Let us say the roof of the gallery—the skylight—is flat.   There must be a piece of ceiling, whether flat or curved does not matter—all round it, which must extend out so far as to cast a shadow, or rather prevent any light falling on the wall above a definitely chosen fixed line, higher than which no work may extend.   The position of this line of shadow, and the width of the ceiling which makes it, must be ascertained in this way. The line of dado—picture rail—line space—must be first fixed—for prints higher than for paintings—then prints tried on the walls—never more than two placed one above the other—at such a height and so spaced that the spectator, at the proper distance, can look at them restfully without stooping or standing on tiptoe.   When this top line is found, the ceiling must be made to extend so far into the room that the shadow will meet it. Trials can be made with a bit of canvas.   It must be evident, though the matter is scarce ever considered, that if above the prints there is a vast space of brightly lighted and usually gaudily painted wall, that and not the prints or drawings will be the first thing to catch the eye, belittle the prints and worry the spectator.   The Turner Rooms in the National Gallery of British Art (Tate Gallery) are a lamentable example of this. You cannot get the gaudy glitter of the overpowering, empty, useless wall space above the works out of your eyes.   This was passed by a painter director.   And in the Vienna Gallery everything, even the decorations of Munkacsy, is killed.   In the new British Museum Print Exhibition Gallery large labels glare at you, and kill the prints under them—those which are not killed by huge shadow boxes.

The width of this piece of ceiling must vary in different rooms, or they must be built of varying height, with a definite idea that different sized as well as different sorts of works are to be shown in them.   The height of the wall however is most important, a gallery which is too low is as bad as one too high.   In the Leipzig, 1914, Exhibition all the rooms were too low, and I felt as though I was going to bump my head all the time, except in the very lowest, which I had something to do with arranging, and there did not, for the roof could not be seen, we put up a Velarium, and the Velarium makes the exhibition and will be described.

In the rooms in which paintings alone are to be shown, the shadow ceiling line must be fixed six or eight feet above the dado at least, as the paintings can of course be allowed to run far higher up the walls than prints. In print rooms far more careful experiments must be made. But as I have said, only space for two "landscape shaped" prints one above the other should be allowed and one upright—unless they are very small. The space on which the prints are to be shown should not exceed sixty inches between the dado and the upper line of shadow, and as I will explain it is a good thing to have a definite change of colour as well as a shadow above. Just within this shadow there should be a flat moulding strong enough to hang prints from, but this should be removable as it may have to be shifted a few inches up or down; in fact a chalk line can be made around the walls and the moulding put up after the prints are hung, only very heavy ones being hung from it. A piece of tape placed all round the room produces an excellent effect— tying the prints together. In the new British Museum Print Rooms and at the Grolier Club prints are shown in glazed cases on the wall. The cramped effect obtained and the shadows are horrible, and as the cases are divided it is most difficult to arrange the prints. Most print exhibitions are either hung from the bottom line, that is, lower edge of the frames is made of the same height from the dado. This is the painter's way; or a middle line is chosen which is level and the prints are arrayed in a jagged saw edge above and below it. This is the print room fashion. But the only right way is to commence from the top, make the top line level all round the room and hang down from it. As to the actual hanging, unless the work is preposterously large, when it is usually preposterously bad, and can be re- jected, it can be hung by screw eyes and hooks from the walls. This is the simplest, quickest, and most practical method. In hanging the British Section at the Leipzig Exhibition, the screws were all placed in the frames before they left London. As soon as their places were settled on the wall, in Leipzig, the screw eyes were chalked, the hooks driven in on the chalk marks and the work was done. And there was no evi- dence of how the drawings and prints were fastened to the wall. The Austrians, in the same Exhibition, made one huge frame all round the room in black wood, covered the walls with gold canvas and killed the prints utterly. And not only this, the roof sprang a leak, and the immaculate and undivided frame had to be hacked to pieces to get the prints down; in the English Section they were lifted down without trouble and rehung as easily. German and French prints were screwed or nailed up and glittering pieces of metal hit you in the eye. The best way of all is to have a double ended nail, with a punch, one end is driven into the frame, the other into the wall; there is no measuring, chalking, or loafing, the work is done in a minute.

Two other matters to be carefully considered in building, especially in print rooms, are corners and doors. Now no matter how carefully the system of lighting is worked out, shadows will creep into the corners; there will be a lower tone on one wall than the other which it joins; there will be waste space or crowding caused by the corners. What is the remedy? Don't have corners—cut them off—and make the room into an octagon and put the doors in the corners. This is the solution, and it has been most excellently carried out in the Scottish Academy at Edinburgh. The consequence is all the long wall spaces are unbroken and there are no corners, for the octagonal system is carried out all around in those spaces where there are no doors. Small groups of works may be most effectively arranged on the piece which joins the two side walls or sculpture may be placed in these spaces.

I have spoken of the roof and corners and doors first; they are most important, they are up anyway before the walls are ready to hang the works on. The space on which the works are to be hung must be of wood, into which at any point the hangers may be able to drive nails and screws. This is for prints of course. No framework, shadow or glass boxes, steel sliding bars, battens or other ingenious abominations should be tolerated, for they are intolerable, but the simplest, cheapest woodwork which, when it is riddled with nail holes, can easily be taken down, should be the material on which the prints are hung. The rest of the gallery may be of lapis lazuli, gold and frankincense if you like—I should save the money to buy prints—but the space where the prints hang should be soft wood. I am told by the Director of the Edinburgh College of Art that he is now using that thin wood, in his Exhibition Rooms, which comes from Norway in rolls, for hanging on, as it costs next to nothing, can be put up easily like paper, coloured as he wants and pulled down, cut up and used by his pupils to paint on if he does not like it or wants a change.

Owing to this carelessness and artlessness on the part of so-called artists in framing, it is often almost impossible to make a decent group of their works—quite impossible, if they cannot be fastened to any part of the wall space without thought of battens or wires. The average hanger, however, never thinks of such things; he hangs as much as he can jam on the walls and that is the end of it. I once in Venice had to hire carpenters to build a wall while the hangers waited, as the background was concrete.

And there is a new gallery in America with concrete walls where everything must be hung on wires.

Having then got the walls, and the ceiling, corners, and dado right the walls must now be covered.

As to the wall coverings on which the works are to be shown, the wealth of a gallery is usually gauged by its gorgeousness. I know of one in London where the decorations are so precious that nothing may be driven in them; consequently the whole place is disfigured by hanging masses of wires, and it takes ten times as long to hang. And people are easily bored by the same gaudiness, gorgeousness, and glitter and demand something more gaudy, gorgeous, glittering. A gallery is not like a hotel with new guests to be overpowered by old splendour, but virtually the same people visit the gallery over and over and they want a new sensation. Not that it should be sensational but a change. This is also felt by all artists. It is awful to have to hang the same old marble-mounted, nail-pierced red or green draped walls year after year, I know, for I have had to do it. It never seems to occur to most gallery directors that a change would be advisable, till it is absolutely necessary, through time and use to substitute new gorgeousness for old; nor does it ever occur to them that each show, each room in it, demands a different background, different hangings. The Directors sweep the walls, wash the floors and tell the artists that is all they can afford—take the gallery or leave it. They even remove the dust which gives character and colour to the wall hangings. And it never occurs to them that the walls can be covered at little more expense with new stuff, in a different fashion, than it costs to clean them.

For prints and drawings there is nothing like a white or ivory wall for hanging on. Nor for hanging colour on either, but painters funk it, forgetting that there is rarely any white in their work but always red or green to be overcome, which will kill the works hung, while a gold wall may and sometimes does wipe out the frame, just as it sometimes helps black and white. The stuff that is wanted is white muslin or cheese cloth of the cheapest sort. The background behind it may be red or yellow or black, and the tone will come through and bind the room together.

Now it is generally admitted that the dado should be dark—but it is rarely made black—of a blue or green black, and the floor darker, the hanging space white and above that the walls and ceilings dark again. It sounds funereal but it is glittering, as all the light is concentrated on the exhibits. Round all the hanging space run a quarter-inch triangular gold fillet, and you will have the delightfullest coloured gallery you have ever seen, when it is finished. (This I did in the Anglo-American Exhibition, London, 1914.) All this sounds perfectly easy and simple and fool-proof—but it is not. In the Ghent International Exhibition, 1913, France started out to make a hit, and put up a bonnet-box wall-paper in some rooms, and in others a canary yellow background that swallowed up all the gold frames and yellow paint in the pictures. Such an artless combination never was seen. The only decorated gallery at the Graphic Arts Section of the Leipzig, 1914, which was, besides the Austrian, thought out and then carried out was the British, which was designed by Mr. Morley Fletcher and myself on the invitation of the British Government, an invitation I accepted as there was no official American Section, in the most interesting exhibition of the Graphic arts ever held.

The scheme was grey and green, very light grey walls—I could not get them white— darker dado and space above, grey-black mouldings, all distemper put on with a whitewash brush, and we wanted black floor matting but did not get it. Still, it was the quietest, most restful, and most concentrated group of galleries in the Exhibition and we had exactly the same men, colours, and stuffs to work with as the other nations. A British architect and decorator near ruined the place with his furniture, however.

The stuffs were the cheapest, the colour distemper and the floors matting—the German carpenters, painters and decorators the cleverest and most intelligent I have ever seen, and I have had experiences almost everywhere in hanging large exhibitions.

One other matter is the angle or slope at which the prints are hung. They must slant forward, or there will be reflections in the glasses. This by ordinary methods of hanging cannot be done, but the nails or screws high up in the back do it automatically.

But there is nothing scarcely in what I have written that is not already known, if not practised. Where is the new thing? Even it is not new, but it is not used—in picture galleries—it is the invention of the Greeks and Romans, and The Velarium, after the works on the walls, is the most important part of the gallery, and it is unused—and unknown.

The few artists who care, always try to get a quiet concentrated light, but they do not know how to get it. Architects know nothing about it. But a few times has it been got, then only by Whistler; and when imitated always wrongly.

The Velarium is a screen of the same stuff—or of the same colour—the stuff may have to be a little thinner or denser—the colour too a little lighter or darker—as the wall covering, which is cut out of this material of the size of the skylight—about—and hung, a foot or so, below it. A screen is often placed below the skylight at times, usually right against it, stretching all across the gallery; it then has exactly the effect of movable shades, which are also used. But the method of Whistler is quite different. The screen is bounded either by a cord, sewn in its edges all round, or by a light bamboo or thin strip of wood, or a wire. To this edge is also sewn a valance of the same material as the wall covering which hangs down a foot or so, and removes the hard sharp edges and angles, and tones in with the wall. The cords with which it is hung should work in pulleys or be adjustable, so that the velarium may be raised and lowered. All artificial lights too must be arranged above the velarium and so be hidden.

It is used for one purpose only, to concentrate the light on the works on the walls. The hangers should, once it is ready, take their place under it and have it raised up till the shadow it casts falls just below, or rather commences just at the bottom of the lowest picture frame, or maybe the dado, while the shadow above is cast from the ceiling just above the top line of prints. It will thus be seen that the entire gallery, save the space of wall where the works are hung, is in shadow. They alone are in light, and this is perfect lighting. The cords must be adjustable, so that with the changing sunlight of the seasons it may be raised or lowered,—then the shadows are always the same. All artificial lights must be above the velarium under the skylight—and they must also be arranged to raise and lower—they should be at the corners, otherwise they will cast spots, if the stuff is thin, on the floor. The shadows will not be strong on the wall; they commence gradually; but the actual size of the velarium, whether slightly larger or smaller than the skylight, can only be determined by experiment. It may be too that there will have to be a second screen around and outside it, to further concentrate the light. But what is wanted is that the light falls on the prints alone. Of course nothing can be shown in the centre of the gallery, though on one occasion I cut a hole in the centre of the velarium, and placed Rodin's *Main de Dieu* under it; that looked splendidly, but the walls were ruined. Ladies do not like the velarium, as it is not adapted to show off their gowns. Still, one would think people went to galleries to look at pictures, but it is not so—they go to gossip, see each other, drink tea, and endure music[1]—the pictures are an unfortunate necessity. If you put up a velarium they must look at the pictures only—it makes them look, for they see nothing else. The only place where you can see a velarium nowadays is in the summer time, in the streets of Southern France

---

[1] I do not object to tea or music and advocate a café, a real one, but these attractions which increase receipts must be in separate rooms not among the prints.

and Spain—the velarium of the Sierpes of Seville is wonderful, but you never see it in the gallery of that city.

The spectators do look at the pictures in such a gallery as I have described and nothing else—they do not understand why—all they think of are the works on the walls. The velarium even makes them quiet, but they come out saying how fine, how charming the show was. A proof of this was in the London Memorial Whistler Exhibition, hung in this way, the Paris Memorial Show hung any way,—virtually the same pictures —certainly nearly all the most important—were shown in both. Of the first Jacques Blanche said the London Exhibition gave the impression that Whistler was a great artist who occasionally made a mistake, while the Paris show made him look a very insignificant person who once in a while did a fine thing. It was all due to the hanging and lighting, and bad hanging and lighting can kill any artist's work.

Another method of concentration is to cover each door with a double hanging of the colour of the dado—it cuts off false lights and prevents people staring into other rooms.

Under no circumstances should screens or cases be allowed in a gallery—they ruin it.

As to the hanging, the fewest works should be hung and they should be so disposed as to be seen to the best advantage. In the case of prints and drawings, the intelligent director—or committee of artists—who should never be painters only—should invite the artist, if it is an invited exhibition, to send a definite number of works, they having first—as they usually do not—worked out the amount of line space at their disposal for each artist. The number of works hung should always be an even one, as in a gallery arranged as I have pointed out: if the number of exhibits by each artist is an even one, they can be hung in two lines or grouped, or made into groups; and still more easily can this be done if the artist has the brains to make his frames uniform. Whistler only had one sized frame for all his prints—the mounts of each alone differed. I have two, one for large lithographs, the other for etchings, and all the etchings are framed as uprights. These details—never considered—are of the utmost importance, not only to artists for the better showing of their works, but the hangers for ease in hanging them— in finding places for them—and to curators not supported by state funds. So far as I know no Japanese-European expert has ever pointed out that there are standard sizes in Japanese prints—about the only merit in the majority of them. Again and again I have known good works to be thrown out and inferior ones hung, because the good ones were unequally framed and no group of them could be made. The design of each artist's frames should be uniform and the colour the same in all his exhibits. The mounts may differ in colour, but this should be as little as possible. Or the artist may be given a definite space to fill, he being told the length of the line space and the height his works may extend to. Between each artist's group there should be a break—say the works of a group are an inch apart, there should be at least three inches between that group and the next. It is unfair and unjust to an artist to be asked to send only one or two prints to an exhibition, as is the general rule—the fixed rule in Salons and the

Academies. It is unjust to the artist and unfair to his reputation. The etcher or engraver, if his work is worth showing at all, should have as much space allotted him as the oil painter, and the gallery in which his works are hung should adjoin that of the paintings—not be in a basement or upstairs, as is too often the case. By drawing and engraving to-day the greatest artists are expressing themselves in a way which will last. But in most shows they are treated as inferiors by men who are incapable of producing either drawings or engravings of merit. In fact I believe in hanging prints with paintings as they are hung in a private house.

The arrangement of a print show presents many difficulties, the works having been sent in, judged, and all that possibly can be, rejected, always, however, remembering the group. The hanging committee, which, as I have said, should also be the selecting committee, should arrange them on the floor in front of the space it is proposed they should occupy. It will then usually be found that they will have to be changed several times before they are right—or will look right on the walls, and even after they are up they most likely have to be rearranged. Meanwhile the workmen can be putting in the screw eyes on the backs of frames, on which they are to hang. The time that is wasted otherwise is enormous. Having the two definite lines top and bottom to go by, the hangers should take the height of the tallest frame, and put everything else up to the same height in the room. This is scarcely ever done, but either a middle line or, easiest of all, the bottom line is chosen, and the works straggle in a most offensive and undecorative manner all round the room. By my scheme there is a uniform decorative line made round the entire room. I have never seen anything so badly arranged as was the Leipzig Exhibition, the first great show of black and white. Every one had something in one of the fifty rooms, and in most there were more than fifty artists. Had one hundred—if they could have been found—distinguished artists been asked to contribute the exhibition would not only have been more interesting but more important.

Between certain groups of prints, water colours and pastels should be hung—in groups also; this gives variety, and increases the spectator's interest, while the effect of a gallery is brightened. Small sculpture may also be introduced between the groups. And I am in favour of and have hung galleries containing works in all mediums—including oils. Why should one not make a public gallery as delightful as a private room? Only the stupidity and jealousy of painters and sculptors prevents it. In each group too the greatest care in arrangement and balance should be exercised. Over and over one has seen a charming young lady—in a framed print—gazing longingly, not at a handsome young man in a near frame but into a corner, while he turns his back on her. Common sense, one would have thought, would have made the hangers reverse things— they probably left the hanging to the workmen, or were too busy discussing futurism or football or the workmen their union to attend to business. A tenth of an inch up or down in one print will knock a whole wall out. And no chalked or plumbed or spirit-levelled same-height-stick game will make a fine wall. The artist hanger's eye alone will do it.

In those antiquated monstrosities, Academies and Salons (no, this is not envy) a rule is usually in force that only gold frames may be used. Let the artist use the frames he likes, so long as they are of the same size and design. If one wishes to see how horribly and artlessly water colours and prints can be hung by using uniformly coloured frames—and by frames without uniformity—go to the Old Water Colour and the Painter Etchers Societies' Exhibitions in London, or the Salons in Paris, and there are shows of the same sort in America.

To see prints well hung once one could go to the International Society in London. Alas, no longer. The best recent hanging I have seen was in the Austrian and German Pavilions in the Roman 1910 International Exhibition. The Panama Pacific Exposition San Francisco—save my room—was a nightmare; even the painters hung theirs anew when they saw it.

I have lately seen in practical use in the Camera Club of London, the simplest and best system of hanging yet invented.

The print is laid face downward on the floor and two double ended steel pins are driven into it, with an open ended punch; the print is then offered up—the background may be of any material, but wood is best—and when it is level and of the required height a slight blow with the hand on the face of the frame over the pin drives it completely and securely and immediately into the wall—the pin going in the full length. To remove the print it is only necessary to pull it straight away from the wall. This is by far the simplest and securest method of hanging I have ever seen. One man hung unaided in a recent exhibition of the Senefelder Club fifty frames—fixing the pins and everything in a morning. The pins are used in looms, and are only made by Messrs. Hattay Brothers of Dundee, Scotland. They are called Hattay Pins.

The system of building or arrangement, decoration and hanging of galleries I have described is simple, cheap, and rapid; it however requires brains and courage and knowledge to practise. When it is successfully done the result is fascinating, decorative, restful. And the result is a work of art, for there is no evidence of the means by which it was produced.

The print curator of the Metropolitan Museum has completely lost his temper over this book—maybe it is because his new print gallery walls are concrete—or some sort of stuff into which no nails can be driven and he instead of covering them with wood as I suggest has drilled holes in them and put up a rail to hang his prints from; his stupidity equals the architects—and the same firm did the same thing at the American Academy of Arts and Letters—but standardized idiocy is the aim of most architects in these matters today—and the directors of galleries too know no better and accept the bungling given them.

THE fashion or fad of cataloguing an etcher's work has of late years increased and multiplied enormously; it is as catching as the hunt for decorations, and is indulged in by the same kind of people. The artist is probably not decorated but his cataloguer is, but as Monet once said, "the only decorated people are those who are not decorated."

A catalogue properly made is an invaluable record of an artist's work, provided his work is worth recording and cataloguing. But starting in a modest and reliable fashion by recording facts for the use of dealers, students, collectors, and curators, of late it has become a medium for hacks and compilers to display their ignorance of what they are writing about, and for dealers to lean on; especially are the introductions to some of these complicated compilations amazing.

The idea originated with Rovinsky's catalogue of Rembrandt, and has reached its climax in the Grolier Club's portfolios. The result of this catalogue mania is that every little etcher has a big catalogue made by a compiler, illustrated with all, if possible, the etcher's productions. These being manufactured in limited editions are quickly acquired and sometimes the catalogue brings a higher price than the etchings which are described in it. Such is fame or fate. The language in which the descriptions are written is usually unintelligible, worthless, as a description. Nothing is so difficult as to describe prints simply, but the average catalogue maker thinks more of himself and his language than of his subject.

The following are all from catalogues of Whistler's works, taken at random.

194. *Nocturne Shipping.*
Several ships in middle distance and toward the horizon.

195. *Old Women.*
Gossips before their doors in Venice.

196. *Alderney Street.*
Looking partly along and across Alderney Street in Pimlico.

Fancy the puzzled collector or infuriated dealer trying to identify his proofs from such inconsequent rubbish. Yet these manufacturers of significant rubbish are beaten by the following:

10. *Return of the Fishing Boats.*
A stretch of water with a number of fishing boats in the distance. Wonderful quality of surface on the water. In the foreground some men are standing on the shore waiting for the boats. Butterfly monogram in lower right-hand corner.

26. *At Sea.*
A long deck of ship passengers leaning over rail looking intently at the sea. Wonderful effect expressed in a few lines. Butterfly monogram upper right corner.

34. *Street, Corsica.*
A busy scene, many figures coming and going along a rather broad street. Buildings of some height and consequence on either side of the street, view in distance. Butterfly monogram in left corner.

In the first whether the subjects are signed or not is not stated; in neither is the size given.

Anyone who could identify any of the works from such descriptions would be a genius, anyone who would write such rubbish is incredible. Yet one catalogue was issued by a dealer, the other by a collector, one was written by a critic, the other by a curator. This is the sort of trash the amateur is fed on.

Even the best catalogues are only useful for reference. As Whistler said, "It is the business of the cataloguer to describe not to comment." On the other hand if the artist made his own catalogue, he might make it as interesting as the works described; however, everything is done for the poor, but unfortunately necessary, artist; before long some mechanical toy will make etchings just as well as he can—at least the world will think so, a world which prefers canned music and movies to the real things.

The cataloguer states that his business is merely to catalogue, but everybody knows the most interesting and reliable catalogues are those which describe, explain, elucidate, and the man to make the catalogue of an artist's work is the artist himself assisted by a clerk and a foot rule.

As I have pointed out, states are often all wrong, dry point generally all wrong, half inked early proofs described as late pulls and so on and so on. This is the way of cataloguers who are mainly most superior persons. Too superior ever to be conscious how inferior they are. In fact, to sum up. Howard Mansfield's description of a cataloguer may be quoted: "The value of a catalogue should be in the fulness and accuracy of its facts, and not in the personal opinions of the compiler, which if thought worthy of expression should be expressed elsewhere and not forced on print lovers seeking information, who are apt to have opinions of their own." And these "opinions" of Mr. Mansfield contain errors as well as truths. There is no reason why a catalogue should not be as interesting as a biography, as concise as a dictionary, so authoritative as to be final. Still Mr. Mansfield's catalogue of Whistler's etchings, published by the Caxton Club of Chicago, is far the best yet issued, for he describes completely and concisely every plate and state he could find.

A S I said in the Preface to this edition, the most important happening to me is the starting of my school of Etching and Lithography at the Art Students' League, New York. I have always believed with Whistler that any one can be taught to draw and to paint—by a master painter—not by a modern teacher—but God alone can make him an artist, and with William Morris that all students should be taught a craft—if only to make a living for themselves. But these, the hard roads for the plodding, are the last things that are taught in America.

Everything here is standardized in art, academies, schools, professors, exhibitions, cubism, expressionism, dynamic symmetry, short cuts for the incompetent, are all sterilized and hypnotized artlessness—and whether a student imitates a cubistic compiler, or snow storm manufacturer—each sort is produced with its own kind of stencil. Also the students are supposed to be taught drawing; they are taught in most schools, from the materials they use to the drawings made with them, to do just as the teacher does. The teaching of drawing at the League under Bridgman and DuMond is, however, very good and very different.

Now it will be said that imitation of the master's methods was the method of the old masters. It was not. The pupils were the master's assistants trained by him to work as he worked and to help him; when they had mastered their craft, and had something to say for themselves, they left him properly trained and, setting up a shop of their own, said what they wanted to say in their own way. If they had nothing to say for themselves they went on helping the master till he had no further use for them, or he or they disappeared. To-day the pupils in most cases do not work with masters or not as assistants, they do not aid the master, he may come round once a week and criticise their work and tell them where they are wrong, he does not show them how to get right, how to do practical work. The master is too often an out-of-work unsuccessful artist with no ideas of his own, no practice of his own, no ability of his own, who only pretends to teach what he cannot practice and only does it because he cannot make a living otherwise. The students follow him for years till at last it dawns upon them that he is leading them nowhere, and then most of them, cursing him and art, quit a profession they usually were unfitted for in the beginning, or, if they might have done something, find themselves lost in a desert with occasional lounges to loaf in, libraries to steal from, lectures to attend, but especially balls, the end of most art schools—and still students, unless they kill themselves by marriage. This last has almost ruined my classes. They all think that once they have a small smattering of drawing and a glimmer of oil paint—they are made. They hate all other forms of art save a little sculpture—though they hope for a fortune from commercial art, posters and comics—America's ideals of art. Their designs prove they were brought up on the comics—they are pure vulgarians. Look at the human types to-day—we are approaching the comics. We hate the arts and crafts, not only the students but the masters. This was proved this year when the National Academy of Design, by a secret vote of which the membership was not informed, excluded all engravings and drawings from their exhibition. Architecture is no longer shown in the Academy exhibitions. Thus two classes of their members were unrepresented on the oil painted walls—while water colours have no footing at all in the National Academy of Design. The excuse made was, there were so few engraver members, that it was not fair to exclude the hundreds of oil painters for the engraver's benefit—when as a matter of fact—and the Academy authorities knew it—they were not excluding the members, whom by the constitution they could not exclude, but the artist engravers of America—to hang the unsalable works of unsuccessful oil painters—such is American art and American business and American publicity to-day. A proof also, that the painter hates prints. All this happened in the Fine Arts Building in which both the Academy and the Art Students' League are housed and is worth remembering as a proof that not only does the American public hate art, but the American artist does too.

As to practical school work, there has been something of interest done though how well it has been done—or if anything really has been accomplished—it is too soon to say; that is, in the teaching of etching and by me.

Two years ago I was asked to take charge of the Etching Class at the Art Students' League of New York which had been in operation for many years, but only, like that at the National Academy of Design, as a side show, and run in a half-hearted manner. I was glad, for though I had been lecturing at the Academy—as at the Slade School, London—for several years, I found it impossible to arouse here any interest in the students, mostly foreigners out for cash, or to forget their native art—when I gave them lantern slides; or Americans out for short cuts, fresh from correspondence schools and colleges, ignorant of everything, highly educated in the last new things on the town, though of actual education they had none. But the offer from the League gave me a chance to see if I could practise what I had been preaching for years, that the Graphic Arts could be taught. I accepted the post but found that the school room was bare—and the school authorities blank—on the subject. I went to Europe at once and saw first the excellently arranged school conducted by Sir Frank Short at the Royal College of Art, in London, far the best equipped in England, and the London County Council Central School. And I then went to the Leipzig School again and found it under the same management in the engraving and etching departments, doing even more—and more interesting work than before. Then to Berlin with the intention of seeing Prof. Emil Orlik's school in the Arts and Crafts Academy, but it was closed. However, Prof. Orlik passed the winter of 1923–1924 here and we have, in and out of my school, talked and practised many things and he has been an inspiration to my students even to the whole League. There are no other important schools in Europe. I came back and succeeded in getting, beside the one old copper plate press the school owned, two others and three lithograph presses and many other aids and supports, putting in proper and practical fittings. I must thank the New York group of lithographers and especially their leading spirit, P. R. Heywood, of Heywood, Strasser & Voight, Messrs. Ketterlinus & Co. and Mr. Gorr of the Model Specialty Co. for valuable help.

I started after a good deal of preliminary heralding. Some twenty or thirty prospective pupils submitted work, for I refused to take that of those who had not been through an art school, and I selected about twelve. I admit I was disappointed—but my eyes were opened. I thought my "international," I had been told, position, would draw crowds and the League did too, and were even more disappointed than I. For as soon as the students found that etching meant work, that I meant they should work, and that they could not learn to do it all and know it all in a month by seeing it all, more fell by the wayside. One young lady told me that she not only expected to learn etching in that time, but to teach as well. They were not only disappointed but shocked, and a lot left. They had come to me from all over the country, one from Sir Frank Short's class in London. I am sure he must have been as glad to get rid of this pupil as I was when he disappeared. There were disabled soldiers on government pensions, another was a famous international sculptor, and I was not sorry when he had enough, and there were many threats from other real artists that they would join, but luckily they changed their minds. This year the "real artists," even an Academic American and two serious German students are in the class. But the greater number were old League students. The rest arrived from Portland, Maine, to Portland, Oregon, from New Orleans to New York. This sounds like a large crowd, but though there were many during the year, not all stayed any length of time or did anything of any value, but the best did remain. It is the few who count with me—if not in most schools where numbers and fees are the aim.

I had plenty of ideas and beliefs as to how I should run this class, but no experience with American pupils, and I started with two propositions. First: If you have nothing to say yourself, go somewhere else and say it. Second: Dont imitate me. I supposed that they had something to say for themselves and that they came to me to learn how to say it. I was safe I thought in laying down these propositions, for all these students showed work which they said proved that they had been years in art schools and now only wanted a chance to express themselves by learning the technique of etching. I explained the methods, but when I referred to Haden or Hamerton, Lalanne, or Meryon, I was greeted mostly by a blank stare. Zorn's snap shot prices they knew—and Whistler they thought out of date, and Rembrandt was a fetish, but actually I found that in this God-gifted Middle West uplifted land, many of them had never heard the name of Dürer. It is incredible, but a fact. But they knew Cézanne and Renoir. I also had proved to me that what most of them wanted, but not all,—they mostly disappeared—was to make big money quick out of etching. However, I went ahead in my own way, it may be some others' way also, it is the way in Leipzig, on the supposition that the pupils, having been in art schools before they came to me, could draw. That is, if they could draw I could teach them technique, the last thing they think of learning, for their idea was just to express themselves— especially those who had nothing to express which is the outcome of the New Art.

I showed them how to ground plates as I have told in this book, but to show the method is better, and then suggested that if there was anything any one of them wished to say on the plate to do it, and in their own way, after I had pointed out to them, as I have in the chapter *Of Drawing on the Plate*, not how it should, but how it must be done, and this *must* was the most difficult thing to get into their heads, that certain things must be done in certain ways and not in the easiest way or their way. I am always willing to consider and adopt any other person's methods, student's or professor's, if they are better than mine, and in this way and by experimenting I learned much, and some of them did too. I taught them, by making them work it out, everything I knew about etching and most of them were willing to work. I endlessly preached to them that it was practice they wanted, once I had showed them the technical methods, and many did as I told them. I was not teaching drawing—but a craft. In return for this, they found at the end of the first year that their work was not like that of untrained students, but of trained craftsmen, and in a show we gave this was acknowledged by the few so-called critics who noticed it, and some of my pupils found work to do.

I discovered many things: That some of these young Americans have no knowledge of or use for cleanliness, time, order, work, though he has a bath tub and creases in his pants and she has bobbed hair. There were waste paper cans, but everything went on the floor—nothing was cleaned up in the beginning, nothing put away—nothing done decently. Now they have learned a lot about cleaning up and a little of technique, but will they do anything? That does not depend on me—but on themselves. I can teach them and have taught them the way to etch, will they make it of use to themselves? Another point is their conceit. The least encouragement, the least success, and the American's head is turned. Any American's head, in any walk in life. He ceases to experiment, to try to make progress, this is the case with the whole country to-day. He either does nothing at all but admire himself or turn out endless replicas of himself, and he knows it all too—and no one can teach him anything. Will such a state of things produce good craftsmen or artists? It has not. I do not believe it will. I do not know if it is worth while to go on. As to what the best students think of the class and as I have said there are some interesting ones in the class, it is interesting to learn. The following article was written without my knowledge and published in *The American Printer*. If it proves anything, it shows what some of the pupils think and those like Miss Reinthaler, do think.

" Joseph Pennell's name is internationally known. To most people it represents a distinct personality in the realm of art and letters, it stands for a great artist and fearless critic. To me it means even more, for Joseph Pennell is my teacher, and there is no eye more searching than that of a pupil, no greater opportunity of learning to know a man from an angle even his best friends may never have glimpsed, than during those hours spent in the close association of teacher and student. In this instance I should say 'student and pupil,' for Mr. Pennell is and always will be a student with an avid desire for knowledge. He is always learning, and if anyone would have the right to say 'I know all there is to be known about etching and lithography,' it is Joseph Pennell. But no, he works with his class as a co-student, is as much excited about a discovery, a new way of doing things, an experiment, as we are, and maybe more so than most of us. He is filled with the spirit of adventure, and is the least conceited, least opinionated, the most open-minded man I have ever met. That is one of the things that contribute to

his greatness as a teacher.   Never does he put forward his own way of doing things.
Rembrandt and Whistler are his two authorities in etching.   Our class-room or 'shop'
is hung with enlarged photographs of the works of both of these artists, so that we may
constantly be confronted by the best, and only the best is good enough for him.   Nothing
slipshod nor superficial is tolerated.

"No matter how amateurish and clumsy our work, Mr. Pennell divines by some sixth
sense what we are trying to say, and helps us find our own way of saying it.   You will
see no 'imitation Pennells' in our class exhibition.   You will be surprised at the variety
of work and expression.   Portraits, landscapes, caricatures, fantastic, imaginative and
realistic compositions, lettering and ornament, expressed in many forms of graphic art.
I have wandered around art schools enough to realize what this means, everybody who
has will appreciate it.   It means good teaching, of which, alack, there is only too little.
People now-a-days are in such a hurry, a hurry to create 'works of art that will sell.'
They copy what they admire, know not why they admire it, or if it is even worthy of
admiration, and are more interested in tricky technique and weird colour schemes, in what
they term 'originality' and 'expression,' than they are in what they have to express,
or if it is worth while expressing at all.   They lack thoroughness because they don't
know how to study.   Study takes time.   One cannot sell study.   After a year and a half
our class is beginning to realize this, but we are learning to study.

"In teaching us graphic art, Mr. Pennell is thorough.   He admitted only a comparatively small number of pupils into his class, men and women from all parts of the country, and carefully examined the portfolio of work each applicant submitted before making
his choice.   The sixth sense I spoke of came into play here again.   From tempera designs,
oil paintings, pastels and water colours he, with diagnostic eye, determined what branch
of graphic art, if any, the applicant would be fitted for.

"Our first lesson was a lantern slide lecture on the various forms of graphic art, a
brief history of each, and each method taken separately.   Cross sections, diagrams, and
the why, wherefore and how of each step.   Etching was taken first because the greater
percentage of the class was interested in it.   One day was spent in grounding plates.
The next in learning to bite, the third in printing and so on, systematically through the
various processes.   Then came lithography.   That being in a way a lost art seemed to
me much more thrilling.   There is nothing like the joy of discovery and experiment.
We would come excitedly to Mr. Pennell with our 'discovery.'   The fact that unknow-
ingly we had stumbled upon something that was an accepted principle before we were
born could never rob us of the thrill, nor the knowledge we gained in thinking it out.

"There were trips to Museums with our teacher, heated debates, violent discussions
as to how this artist 'got this effect' or 'how he probably did that,' that continued on
the street cars and sidewalks long after the Museum had closed.   There was a splendid
spirit of coöperation in the class, and fortunately a saving sense of humour.   We had
some successful accidents and made many messes.   Now the messes are a little less frequent.   We have learned a great deal.   We can now make drawings which without the
intervention of any middleman can be printed.

ETCHERS AND ETCHING

" Mr. Pennell is teaching us etching and lithography as crafts and trades, and with fine ideals trying to start a department of Graphic Arts in an American school, 'The Art Students' League of New York,' that will come up in standard to the teaching of these subjects in the schools of France, Great Britain, and Germany, where pupils get practical, technical information, and can go right from school into the industry as craftsmen, or into the art world as sincere artists who instead of allowing their prints to be pulled, or transfers made by professionals because they can not do so themselves, send forth their work solely the product of their own hands, talent, labour and skill."

MARCH 23, 1924.   HELEN T. REINTHALER.

Miss Reinthaler is not only still in the class but she is working for herself—going to Europe to study methods in the schools this summer and returning to work again in the class in the fall as monitor,* and she is not the only one, as Mr. Locke another pupil, now an assistant instructor, is spending the summer in the Ohio Mechanics Institute and in lithographic shops in Cincinnati. Others have obtained work, show in exhibitions and with dealers. This is the sort of teaching I like—and that America wants —but gets nowhere else.

* She has made up her mind to get married instead, and two other of my best young lady pupils have gone the same way in the last year.

FINALLY TO ETCHERS

B E not led away by isms or ists. Be yourselves, if you have anything in you, having studied with intelligence the work of the great workmen of the past; say what you have got to say, in your way, only your way and your work must be based on theirs. Do not copy them, but carry on their work, the traditions they carried on, remembering they were known and hated, most of them, in their day, because they did their work better than their fellows; because they worked their lives out learning how to work. To-day is the day of small things, of small men and large women; the more incompetent, clumsy, stupid you are the more pull you will have, the more you imitate, prig, and steal from your contemporaries, always denying that you ever saw their work, the more you will be bowed down to, praised up, and collected—if you have the proper business ability. The artist is always ignored, till his work which he has done as well as he could by the sweat of his brow and the anguish of his soul, is unobtainable, because, if an etcher, he pulled only a few prints, or, in a fury at the imbecility of his contemporaries, destroyed his plates. Do not confound cleverness with technical mastery. Whistler and Rembrandt were the greatest technicians who ever lived; Meryon and Haden were mostly the stodgiest duffers; their followers are the appreciated of the artless, because they are so easy to imitate. Whistler and Rembrandt left no followers; they cannot be followed—that is, imitated—in their greatness; but you may gain ideas and help from them, and if you have genius surpass them just as Whistler surpassed Rembrandt. If God did not give you this, you may be a very successful person, without being an etcher at all.

Do not hark back to the catalogued mistakes and messes of the Middle Ages; if you make something like these back numbers, you will be acclaimed by the critics of to-day and ignored by the artists of to-morrow and may be forgotten by all but those who have collected you in the present—and reviled by them when they try to sell their collections.

Be yourself, carry on tradition, doing the best work you can, and if you have anything in you, you will come off sometime.

If you do not make etchings because you love to—fear to—have to—you are not, and never will be, an etcher.

INDEX

INDEX

INDEX

INDEX

INDEX

INDEX

INDEX

INDEX